Southern Literary Studies
FRED HOBSON, EDITOR

IMAGINING OUR TIME

Recollections and Reflections on American Writing

Lewis P. Simpson

LOUISIANA STATE UNIVERSITY PRESS
BATON ROUGE

Published by Louisiana State University Press
Copyright © 2007 by Louisiana State University Press
All rights reserved
Manufactured in the United States of America

FIRST PRINTING

DESIGNER: *Amanda McDonald Scallan*
TYPEFACE: *Whitman*
PRINTER AND BINDER: *Edwards Brothers, Inc.*

Library of Congress Cataloging-in-Publication Data
Simpson, Lewis P.
  Imagining our time : recollections and reflections on American writing / Lewis P. Simpson.
    p. cm. — (Southern literary studies)
  Includes index.
    ISBN-13: 978-0-8071-3202-9 (cloth : alk. paper)
    ISBN-10: 0-8071-3202-0 (cloth : alk. paper)
  1. American literature--History and criticism. 2. National characteristics, American, in literature. I. Title. II. Series.
PS121.S544 2006
810.9'358—dc22

                            2006013848

The paper in this book meets the guidelines for permanence and durability of the Committee on Production Guidelines for Book Longevity of the Council on Library Resources. ∞

Ideas are what the gods once were.
—LIONEL TRILLING, "The Meaning of a Literary Idea"

The cannons of Kronburg speak in the story of Holger Danske. Nothing has remained of the story but the cannons. When the ships pass by, the cannons say "boom."

That is somewhere far away in the north, where the world has gone farthest, with nothing beyond. Ships will pass there, and nobody asks whence they are coming and where they are going. Where they pass without a sound, there is nothing; no human being; only the cannons; and they say "boom" with solemn sadness, at the end of the world.
—ERIC VOEGELIN, "Anamnetic Experiments," in *Anamnesis*

CONTENTS

INTRODUCTION, BY FRED HOBSON ix

Eric Voegelin and the Story of the Clerks 1

The Betrayal of the Clerks in American Context: Benjamin Franklin and Thomas Jefferson 40

Days of Faith: Malcolm Cowley and the Legend of the Fellow Travelers 53

The Poet and the Father: Robert Penn Warren and the Redemption of Thomas Jefferson 81

Lionel Trilling and Allen Tate: The Agency of Terror 110

Diana Trilling: A Poetic of Cultural Politics 128

A Charleston Jew and the Shaping Form of Memory: Louis D. Rubin, Jr. 153

The Last Agrarian: Andrew Lytle 165

Eudora Welty: The Outside of the Inside 172

Walker Percy and the Closure of History in the Self; or, The Loneliness at the End of a World 187

ACKNOWLEDGMENTS 251

INDEX 253

INTRODUCTION
by Fred Hobson

What strikes me first about this collection of essays is that Lewis P. Simpson, long one of our finest literary and intellectual historians, did not, even in his eighties, miss a beat. Until just before his death at age eighty-eight, in April 2005, he continued to be an insightful and elegant essayist, and *Imagining Our Time*—on writers ranging from the political scientist–philosopher Eric Voegelin to critics Malcolm Cowley, Lionel and Diana Trilling, and Louis Rubin to novelists Robert Penn Warren, Eudora Welty, and Walker Percy—covers a great deal of twentieth-century thought and writing. In fact, when I consider the first two essays—which deal with the intellectual and his or her relation to the state and to the larger world, and which take Simpson and the reader as far back as St. Paul, Augustine, and Petrarch—I would have to say that this collection ranges far beyond twentieth-century American letters. Lewis Simpson's amazingly wide learning informs all these pieces, and his trademark essay form, which usually consists of beginning with a personal anecdote or recollection and then moving into a discussion of ideas, is highly effective. As I read these essays another thing struck me—that is, the extent to which Lewis Simpson himself has been a significant part of American literary history over the past half century. He was personally acquainted with nearly all the subjects of these essays—particularly with Warren, Welty, Percy, Rubin, Allen Tate, and Andrew Lytle—and thus he brings himself into the essays (though all the while trying to deflect attention from himself) in a manner that is most engaging.

I suggested that most of these essays were products of Lewis Simpson's ninth decade. Indeed, nearly all were either published in his eighties or, if previously published, were extensively reworked during his last decade. Such productivity is characteristic of the professional life Simpson led after retiring from teaching duties and the editorship of the *Southern Review* in 1986; including this collection, three of his six major books were published after he was seventy. *Mind and the American Civil War: A Meditation on Lost Causes* appeared when he was seventy-three, the masterful essay collection *The Fable of the Southern Writer* when he was seventy-eight.

Nearly all of his books consisted of essays, thematically related, and it is in the essay form, as James Olney has written, that Simpson operated most effectively. The quality that seems to me most to distinguish his essays, those contained here as well as earlier ones, other than their intellectual breadth, is their author's narrative sense; although Lewis Simpson deals with ideas, he is, in fact, a storyteller, weaving a tale, turning intellectual and literary history into a riveting drama, introducing a subject, then digressing, proceeding at a leisurely pace, often keeping the reader in suspense before he returns to his original thought. The titles and subtitles of many of his essays suggest as much: in this volume, "Eric Voegelin and the Story of the Clerks" and "Malcolm Cowley and the Legend of the Fellow Travelers," earlier "The Fable of the Agrarians" and "A Fable of Black and White." Stories, legends, fables: in such manner did Lewis Simpson depict the history of ideas. As is the case with Robert Penn Warren—a writer he greatly admired and with whom he shared much in common—his is the allegorizing mind. And it is hard to imagine any southern historian or critic of the twentieth century, save perhaps W. J. Cash, C. Vann Woodward, and Warren himself, who was so given to the memorable phrase (the North's "garden of the covenant," the South's "garden of the chattel," "the Great Literary Secession," "a postsouthern America") as Lewis Simpson.

One sees his approach, in this collection, in his first essay on Voegelin, an essay on a subject—the role of the intellectual in Western history—that might not seem at first to lend itself to high drama. But with Simpson we are immediately engaged. He begins with a personal recollection: as a new instructor at Louisiana State University in 1948, he first encountered Voegelin, in a manner of speaking, when he requested a library book, long overdue, that—he noticed later on the library card—had been held by Voegelin. He knew something of Voegelin, a refugee from Hitler's Germany: "Campus rumor had it that [he] was engaged in writing a multivolume work of monumental Germanic obscurity in which he would presume to explain the meaning of history." The library book Voegelin had long held and Simpson had requested was Julien Benda's *La trahison des clercs* (The Treason of the Intellectuals) (1927), a polemic in which Benda accused his fellow twentieth-century European intellectuals of becoming "the servants of political power and greed," in particular, servants of "the modern nation state." Simpson never actually found that Voegelin, in his work, referred to Benda and his book, but the fact that Voegelin shared critical concerns with Benda—that Voegelin in his own work was constructing an "implied tale of the clerks" (in medieval times, "men of learning")—leads him, in this essay, into a consideration of several of Voegelin's works, including sections of Voegelin's five-volume *Order and History*: the "clerk's character in the Voegelinian drama—and the melodrama—is more often a dark figure of the semi-villain or villain than of the hero." In the process of telling, Simpson weaves his own tale of the clerks from St. Paul ("the first clerk") forward, and in doing so traces a movement of Western intellectuals from "a world in which they were a cohesive part of a church-state structure to a world in which they would conceive of themselves as belonging primarily to a realm of secular letters and learning"—i.e., "the Republic of Letters . . . the universal homeland of the modern Western mind."

In his second essay Simpson brings his argument to this side of the Atlantic and considers, as his title has it, "The Betrayal of the Clerks in American Context." Although he first discusses Benjamin Franklin—"the printer as man of letters"—and the early-nineteenth-century Federalist literati, he seems most interested in Thomas Jefferson as one who, though a child of the Enlightenment, was still inclined to subordinate "to the political order" his own "professed dedication to unbounded freedom of the mind." Simpson cites in particular Jefferson's vision for the University of Virginia, and the requirements he set forth for its sole professor of law, one uncorrupted by "toryism," a native Virginian who would teach "the true principles of republicanism" as Jefferson himself saw them. This second essay, though complete in itself and previously published essentially as it stands, is nonetheless the only one in the volume that Simpson had planned to expand, and his plans for the expansion, to bring his discussion up to Henry James, were intriguing indeed. In a note accompanying the essay, he wrote: "The discussion will suggest that James changed his citizenship during the First World War from American to British because, paradoxically, he felt he would remain an American only by becoming an Englishman." Such a statement offers a characteristic Simpson intellectual puzzle, one whose solution we can only surmise.

Both the Voegelin essay and the treatment of the "clerks" in "American context" concern what Simpson calls "the Republic of Letters"—that "realm additional to those of church and state, and independent of both," which "originated in the eleventh and twelfth centuries"—and, in fact, nearly all the other essays in this volume (as much of his previous work), in some manner, share that concern. Essays on Malcolm Cowley, Lionel Trilling, and Diana Trilling treat literary and cultural politics, particularly politics of the left in the 1930s, although they (particularly the Lionel Trilling essay, in which Allen Tate plays a part) go beyond that subject as well. The first several pages of the essay on Cowley (and "the legend of the fellow travelers") is a model of Simpson's method of beginning with the particular—the personal—and moving out to the general. Cowley's is a story of cultural politics but it is also a tale of the Great Depression, of the hard times of the 1930s and Cowley's empathy with the dispossessed, and Simpson begins with his own story of the Depression, hard times, and the dispossessed—an engaging tale of his uncle who ran a "soup-and-gospel mission" in Fort Worth, Texas.

Simpson begins his essay on Robert Penn Warren and Thomas Jefferson ("The Poet and the Father") with another personal reminiscence—that of a 1970s taxi ride through the streets of Washington on a foggy early morning, in which he passes the Washington Monument and Lincoln Memorial, "both wreathed in mist," and then sees, breaking through the fog, the Jefferson Memorial, coming "into view with startling clarity," with the figure of Jefferson "invested with an ineffable aura of loneliness." Such a vision leads Simpson to consider Jefferson as a figure in the American pantheon, neither as beloved as Lincoln nor as altogether revered as Washington. For Warren, however, Jefferson was a figure of fascination, with whom he had long had a "brooding involvement," an involvement that is seen most clearly in the two versions of Warren's long poem *Brother to Dragons*—a poem that concerns the especially brutal murder of a slave in 1811 on the Kentucky frontier, a slaying of which Jefferson's two nephews were guilty but on which (so far as Warren knows) Jefferson himself never remarked. Such a silence fascinates Warren, who includes Jefferson himself as a figure in the poem and who transforms the events of 1811 into "a myth about a Thomas Jefferson who finally recognizes the evil of his overweening pride in the intellectual capacity of man to direct his own destiny." And in his "involvement with the story of Jefferson," Warren "is telling the story of his own quest as a twentieth-century American poet for a redeeming vision of the meaning of history."

Warren was indeed involved with Jefferson on some level, and it also seems to me that Simpson, in his own writing, had an involvement, though hardly a "brooding" one, with Warren himself. He was, of course, personally acquainted with Warren—who himself had taught at LSU much earlier and had been one of the founders and editors of the original *Southern Review*—but the identification went far beyond that. Of all the American literary figures about whom he wrote—and he wrote about Warren several times—it seems to me that Simpson had greater interests in common with Warren than with any other, indeed possessed a point of view similar to Warren's in many respects. There was in Simpson the same fascination with history and with time, more specifically with what Warren would call man's responsibility in time. Lewis Simpson was not principally what is generally called a creative writer (although one might argue for that designation in the case of his cultural commentary), but he did write a limited amount of poetry and in 1995 published a small volume of well-crafted verse, *The Circus in the Cemetery*. In that collection I find more than one poem that reminds me, thematically, of Warren, but one, "Thomas Hole," particularly so. Based on Simpson's recollections of his Texas boyhood, the poem begins with five boys whiling away a summer afternoon at a swimming hole—named Thomas Hole for a man who had drowned there—knowing they will have to return to their homes when the town clock strikes five. The speaker, having himself once climbed up to the clock tower (as Simpson himself—he lets us know elsewhere—had as a boy), is particularly aware of "the awful jerk of time / toward the moment on the great bell." Turning contemplative, the speaker considers the case of Cobb Thomas—"rusty iron wheel / roped to his neck"—and a creator that "made us to live in world and time." The speaker, as a youth, had been "baptized in Thomas Hole," but "Only to rise again into Time." Concluding with a sentiment reminiscent of Warren—not only at the end of *All the King's Men* but also in his poetry—the speaker adds: "What we do in Time with Time / is history . . . ."

Lewis Simpson does not, in his essay on *Brother to Dragons*, call attention to what he must have recognized as his own kinship with Warren, but he does acknowledge, in another of the essays collected here, a certain affinity with another of his subjects, Walker Percy. The two men knew each other for some twenty years; they had a "literary friendship," one built partly on an editor-author relationship, but, Simpson adds, "it was somehow more than that." What Simpson has in mind is that he and Percy were almost exact contemporaries, born seven weeks apart in 1916, and thus shared a certain generational sensibility. Both were southerners, the descendants of strong figures who had identified closely with the Confederacy, both had been in college in the mid-1930s, and both had been introduced to European high culture at the same time, in their late teens.

Simpson begins his lengthy Percy essay—so lengthy that it could be a small book in itself—by reflecting on the pain he had felt at Percy's death in 1990 and the difficulty, six months later, of performing "the symbolic task of transferring the Walker Percy file from the active section of the *Southern Review* correspondence files to the drawer bearing the stark label 'Deceased.'" A few days later Simpson took the letters out again, reread them, reflected on his own similarities to Percy and, then, on Percy's unique "quest," the long journey of a man, trained in medicine, who gave up science to determine what *man* is in a way that science could not determine. The metaphor of a journey is one often applied to Percy's life; he was a "wayfarer," a "pilgrim," in search of ultimate truth, part—though not all—of which he found in Roman Catholicism. In his journey, he became philosopher, theorist of language, and—not until age forty-five—published novelist. Believing himself to be living in "the final stage of the dissolution of the world of Christendom," he became engaged "in writing the drama of the ending of what he called 'the old modern world.'" In his essay Simpson considers Percy's attempts in his various novels, particularly his middle and later ones, to arrive at some version of truth. But he finds that Percy's most important book in this quest may be not a novel at all but rather his nonfiction (or, rather, "nonfictional fictional") "treatise on the pathology of self-consciousness," *Lost in the Cosmos* (1983). In what Percy subtitled "The Last Self-Help Book," the author, "without explicit recognition of what he is doing, also in effect transforms his older vision of the artist-writer as wayfarer, or pilgrim, into a vision of the artist-writer as a savior figure."

Percy's career, Simpson writes early in his essay, "represented a lengthy, highly self-conscious, lonely quest for a transforming vision of the meaning of his vocation to writing." It is to the *vocation* of writing that Simpson returns often in this essay, as indeed he does in many of the other essays in this collection. His essay on Lionel Trilling is about the question of vocation, specifically "the pathos of [Trilling's] struggle to define his vocation": Trilling agonized over the direction he should take—"art" or "reason," the life of the creative writer or the life of the scholar and critic—and at more than one moment he believed he had chosen the wrong path. "I defeated myself long ago," he wrote late in his career, "when I rejected the way of chutzpah and michagas [which, as Trilling saw it, was the way of the creative artist] in favor of reason and diffidence." Similarly, what else but vocation is at the center of Simpson's essay on Cowley: "In his self-conscious enactment of the role of man of letters Cowley became the moral historian, even in a sense the moral conscience, of his generation." And even at the center of his essay on his friend Louis Rubin: here Simpson considers Rubin's memoirs— including his boat-building book, *Small Craft Advisory,* and his account of a love affair with newspapers, *An Honorable Estate*—and what else, in various and sometimes unlikely ways, are these books about but a strong commitment to an activity, the birth of vocation even if that subject was unclear to the author at the time? What else are Simpson's numerous explorations of the "Republic of Letters," his tale of the "clerks" and their calling, but a study of vocation? And what else, finally, is Simpson's own story? In his first year of graduate school at the University of Texas—as Otis Wheeler relates in a moving essay on Lewis Simpson in the Spring 2006 *Southern Review*—Simpson remarked in a letter to his parents, "I have three great loves in my life: one is for my family and its welfare; one is for Mimi [whom he later married]; and the other is for literature, art and the world of the mind and spirit."

Lewis Simpson knew in his early twenties the object of his commitment—his *vocation*—and it is a commitment he kept, a vocation he served honorably and gloriously, for well over half a century.

IMAGINING OUR TIME

ERIC VOEGELIN AND THE STORY OF THE CLERKS

In the official academic sense Eric Voegelin was a political scientist, but this label is hardly an adequate description of his vocation. It is appropriate to refer to him as a philosopher of history or perhaps more simply and grandly as a philosopher; or it may be, if we accept the arresting argument advanced by Marion Montgomery, as a prophetic philosopher.[1] Compelled by the recognition of his sense of dramatic structure and the sweep of his imagination, I often think of Voegelin as, in the generic meaning of the term, a poet, the author of an epic summation of the spiritual history of modernity. Seeking to define his vocation more precisely, however, I will refer to Voegelin in the following discussion as a clerk.

In doing so I appeal to the meaning of this term that has long since become archaic in the English language, having lost its "generic meaning," one "not necessarily associated with banks and insurance offices." In medieval times *clerk* (in late Latin *clericus*) referred to "a man of learning," who, like all men of learning in that age, belonged to the realm of the Church. The ecclesiastics, as Herbert Read says, were "intellectuals who devoted their lives to unworldly causes, the cultivation of the mind and spirit." We think of course of a representative clerk we are all familiar with, Chaucer's semi-emaciated clerk of Oxenford in the *Canterbury Tales*. His clothes were shabby and his horse lean as a rake, but he possessed a treasure: "Twenty bookes, clad in blak or reed, / Of Aristotle and his philosophie," and he was happy in his vocation, "a philosophre" who would both gladly learn and teach.[2]

Although I have not run across a reference to Chaucer in Voegelin, it seems plausible to suppose that in his voluminous reading he had made at least a passing acquaintance with the Canterbury Pilgrims, and, as all scholars must, had experienced some sense of identification with the gently satirical portrait of the clerk of Oxenford. But the personal recollection of a small event in my first years at LSU brings to mind more certain and more significant evidence of Voegelin's awareness of the figure of the clerk.

I had arrived in Baton Rouge in the fall of 1948, a fresh Ph.D. from the University of Texas at Austin, who had partially fulfilled the requirements for an interdisciplinary degree in American literature and American history by writing a long and somewhat unwieldy dissertation on the period in New England between the end of the American Revolution and the end of the second war with England in 1815. In this study I was particularly interested in exploring the way in which the Boston and Cambridge of this period had anticipated the development of the literary and intellectual community that would foster the flowering of American letters in the three decades before the Civil War. Pursuing this interest, I became aware of how the sensibility of literary order that guided the men of letters of this time and place was dependent on a complex of symbols, these ranging from such common terms as *book, printer, publisher, author, man of letters* and such conventional institutional terms as *academy* and *university*, to a metaphorical term that appeared so often as to be commonplace yet seemed to be freighted with meaning, the "republic of letters."

It was not until later, to be sure, not until I had finished the dissertation, that I discovered an English contemporary of the Boston-Cambridge literati, Samuel Taylor Coleridge, had employed the term "clerisy" in *Church and State* (1830) to describe the idealized association of secular and ecclesiastical intellectuals and writers he envisions there as the proper cultural authority of England. Resulting from an interest in the symbolism of literary order that had persisted after I had completed my dissertation project, I found Coleridge's use of the term *clerisy* a strikingly appropriate description of the members of the Boston-Cambridge literary community I had been studying, and I felt led to develop more thoroughly the European context of this community. In a catch-as-catch-can process of research, while teaching a fifteen-hour load of basic composition courses, I happened in the spring semester of the 1948–1949 school year upon the title of a polemic that had engendered a bitter debate in Europe in the twenties and thirties of the century just ended, Julien Benda's *La trahison des clercs*. The catalog of the LSU library showed that we had no English translation of the book; so, in spite of a less than perfect reading knowledge of French, I sought in the stacks for the Paris edition. Failing to find this, and learning at the library desk that it was out to a faculty member on a long overdue charge, I requested that it be recalled. It was promptly returned and I soon had it in hand. Since in that long ago uncomputerized time, the LSU Library followed the practice of writing the names of faculty members who borrowed books on a card affixed to the back of each volume, I learned that the name of the delinquent borrower of *La trahison des clercs* was Professor Eric Voegelin.

At the time I knew Voegelin only by his campus reputation as a distinguished member of the political science faculty who had arrived in the United States as a refugee from Hitler and had subsequently become an American citizen. I had been told that he was not Jewish. My first personal impression of him confirmed this. When one day at the Faculty Club he was pointed out to me as he strode imperiously through the lounge smoking a formidable cigar, I branded him as Prussian.

Campus rumor had it that Voegelin was engaged in writing a multivolume work of monumental Germanic obscurity in which he would presume to explain the meaning of history. Obviously I did not know Voegelin's work well enough to realize why he had an interest in Benda's book. Actually I do not precisely know until this day. For one thing, I never asked him. Although I later had some personal acquaintance with Voegelin, this was destined always to be at a respectful distance. For another thing, although his writings amply document his knowledge of Proust, Valéry, Sartre, Camus, and other twentieth-century French writers, so far as I can ascertain Voegelin never mentions Benda. But I have no doubt that he read *La trahison des clercs* at the time it first appeared in 1927 or shortly thereafter. In any event this is a work that, like Oswald Spengler's *Der Untergang des Abendlandes*, illuminates not only the historical context of Voegelin's earlier professional career but the thought and emotion that prompted his quest—in the midst of the intense intellectual and spiritual crisis that pervaded the high culture of Europe in the years between what then was called the "Great War" and the second great war of the twentieth century—to establish history as the symbolic form governing the order of human souls.

A subject of vast and endless discussion, the character of this crisis may be suggested by listening briefly to the voices of two of Voegelin's older contemporaries, one from Paris, the other from Vienna, the two great centers of European high culture: Paul Valéry and Hermann Broch. They asked essentially the same question: to what extent are the men of mind (whether they be creators of poems, novels, and plays, or authors of learned critiques of man and society) responsible not only for defining and expositing the nature of the all-embracing cultural crisis but for its existence in the first place?

In one part of his graphic meditation on the "The Crisis of Mind" (1919) Valéry fancifully transforms Shakespeare's doomed Prince of Denmark into a visionary representative of the doom of his own time.

> Standing now, on an immense sort of terrace of Elsinore that stretches from Basel to Cologne, bordered by the sands of Nieuport, the marshes of the Somme, the limestone of Champagne, the granites of Alsace . . . our Hamlet is watching millions of ghosts.
>
> But he is an intellectual Hamlet, meditating on the life and death of truths; for ghosts, he has all the subjects of our controversies; for remorse, all the titles of our fame. He is bowed under the weight of all the discoveries and varieties of knowledge, incapable of resuming this endless activity; he broods on the tedium of rehearsing the past and the folly of always trying to innovate. He staggers between two abysses—for two dangers never cease threatening the world: order and disorder.
>
> Every skull he picks up is an illustrious skull. *Whose was it?* This one was *Lionardo*. He invented the flying man, but the flying man has not exactly served his inventor's purpose. We know that, mounted on his great swan (*il grande uccello sopra del dosso del suo magnio cecero*) he has other tasks in our day than fetching snow from the mountain peaks during the hot season to scatter it on the streets of towns. And that other skull was *Leibnitz*, who dreamed of universal peace. And this one was *Kant . . . and Kant begat Hegel, and Hegel begat Marx, and Marx begat . . .*
>
> Hamlet hardly knows what to make of so many skulls. But suppose he forgets them! Will he still be himself? . . . His terribly lucid mind contemplates the passage from war to peace: darker, more dangerous than the passage from peace to war; all peoples are troubled by it. . . . *Peace is perhaps that state of things in which the natural hostility between men is manifested in creation, rather than in destruction as in war.* Peace is a time of creative rivalry and the battle of production; but am I not tired of producing? . . . Have I not exhausted my desire for radical experiment, indulged too much in cunning compounds? . . . Should I not perhaps lay aside my hard duties and transcendent ambitions? . . . Perhaps follow the trend and do like Polonius who is now director of a great newspaper; like Laertes, who is something in aviation; like Rosencrantz, who is doing God knows what under a Russian name?

"Farewell, ghosts! The world no longer needs you—or me. By giving the name of progress to its own tendency to a fatal precision, the world is seeking to add to the benefits of life the advantages of death. A certain confusion still reigns; but in a little while all will be made clear, and we shall witness at last the miracle of an animal society, the perfect and ultimate anthill."[3]

Valéry's portrayal of the surrender by the post–World War I European mind of its poetic and philosophical capacities to its adverse desire to become the agency of the positivistic ideology of progress forecasts a world in which it would be discovered that war is peace (the world of Mussolini, Hitler, and Stalin). What Valéry projected from the Paris of 1919 with a terrible clarity—a vision of mind betraying its own power to envision the life of spiritual reality by a vision of the perfect life to be realized by ideological schemes—would be more amply and profoundly projected by the Central European imagination, particularly by certain minds associated with the Vienna of the late empire and, later, of the period between the world wars. This Vienna was, George Steiner has said, "the chosen and ironic ground" of minds characterized by an arresting but "powerless lucidity." One of most notable of these minds was that of Hermann Broch, who in his novel *The Sleepwalkers* (1932) depicts "the dissolution of the European value system" that once, "delimited by a common faith," had constituted a cultural totality but in its degeneration has left a cultural vacuum, in which various types of somnambulists move about attempting to fulfill delusionary dreams they mistake for reality. Some of the sleepwalkers are ruled by hedonistic impulses; others, those in the deepest trance, are ruled by an inflexible attraction to a vision of society that resembles Valéry's image of a "perfect and ultimate anthill." The character called the "hero" in Broch's story, Eduard von Bertrand, resembles the Hamlet in Valéry's "The Crisis of the Mind." Gifted with the power of transcendent perception, he is acutely aware of the disorder that marks the modern cultural situation, and of the threat that the response to it will be the imposition of inflexible order, but he is powerless to imagine, let alone erect, a new value system.

The sophisticated symbolic depiction of the modern "clerks" by Valéry and Broch—a Hamlet brooding on the skulls of the germinal intellectuals of the European high culture, an Eduard von Bertrand looking on the end of the culture of mind as a death-in-life society of sleepwalkers—avoids confrontation with the question of the clerks either for their own personal condition or that of the world they have made. We are left with the question asked about Broch, "When is clairvoyance also responsibility?"[4]

In 1927 Julien Benda deeply disturbed his fellow men of letters by presenting an indictment against them not only alleging a general corruption of their motives but specifying the source of the corruption and naming many of the offenders. The aftermath of the appearance of *La trahison des clercs* was a furor in Paris unequalled since Emile Zola had intervened in the Dreyfus case with "J'accuse." Benda's polemic was not simply another document in the perennial French debate about whether the writer should be engaged or disengaged with respect to politics. *La trahison des clercs* declared the existence of a crisis in the whole concept of the vocation of the life of the mind as this had been known until the twentieth century but was now threatened by the surrender of its eminent representatives, the clerks, to passions contrary to their vocation, the most noble being a passion for the modern nation state. Succumbing to this passion, the clerks have identified themselves with the "laymen," or "all that portion of the human species . . . whose whole function consists essentially in the pursuit of material interests," thereby denying their descent from a "series of philosophers, men of religion, men of literature, artists, men of learning" who for two thousand years stood "in direct opposition to the realism" of the lay multitudes. Speaking specifically of the political passions of the "lay multitudes," Benda argues that the clerks had once opposed these "in two ways."

> They were either entirely indifferent to these passions, and, like Leonardo da Vinci, Malebranche, Goethe, set an example of attachment to the purely disinterested activity of the mind and created a belief in the supreme value of this form of existence; or, gazing as moralists upon the conflict of human egotisms, like Erasmus, Kant, Renan, they preached in the name of humanity or justice, the adoption of an abstract principle superior to and directly opposed to these passions. Although these "clerks" founded the modern state to the extent that it dominates individual egotisms, their activity undoubtedly was chiefly theoretical, and they were unable to prevent the laymen from filling all history with the noise of their hatreds and their slaughters; *but the "clerks" did prevent the laymen from setting up their actions as a religion, they did prevent them from thinking themselves great men as they carried out these activities.* It may be said that, thanks to the "clerks,"

humanity did evil for two thousand years, but honoured good. This contradiction was an honour to the human species, and formed the rift whereby civilization slipped into the world.[5]

When "at the end of the nineteenth century," the clerks began to identify themselves with the laymen and "*play the game of political passions,*" they created nothing less, Benda contends, than an "upheaval in the moral behavior of humanity." Admitting that at times some of them were inclined to be "'clerks' of the forum," Benda extends his list of great clerks to include Dante, Petrarch, Thomas Aquinas, Roger Bacon, Galilei, Rabelais, Montaigne, Descartes, Racine, Pascal, Leibniz, Kepler, Huygens, Newton, Voltaire, Buffon, and Montesquieu. He also includes Rousseau, Maistre, Chateaubriand, Lamartine, and Michelet, for although they felt the passions of the forum, they "did so with a generalizing feeling, a disdain for immediate results, which in fact makes the word 'passions' incorrect."

But this cannot be said of "Mommsen, Treitschke, Ostwald, Brunetière, Barrès, Lemaître, Péguy, Maurras, d'Annunzio, Kipling," in whom we find "the tendency to action, the thirst for immediate results, the exclusive preoccupation with the desired end, the scorn for argument, the excess, the hatred, the fixed ideas." Clerks like these look with disdain on Plato's archaic demand that "the philosopher should be bound in chains in order to compel him to take an interest in the State." Yet they do not disbelieve that the clerk has a transcendent calling: ironically they conceive that the clerk has "as his function the pursuit of eternal things" while at the same time "he becomes greater by concerning himself with the State," thus imbuing political passions with "the tremendous influence of his sensibility" and the "persuasive power" of his thought, with, in short, his "moral prestige." Cloaked in the guise of his presumed vocation to the nonmaterial and the transcendent, employing the pen rather than the sword, clerks become in actuality "the spiritual militia of the material" and enemies of the universal. The "priests of the new mind," as Ernest Renan called them, become the servants of national pride and its extension in imperial conquest; or, in more basic terms, the servants of political power and greed.

But, according to Benda, the ultimate treason of the clerks is realized not in their commitment to the imperial nation state but in what this commitment is a symbol of, a dedication to "an imperialism of the species."

> Above classes and nations there does exist a desire of the species to

become the master of things, and, when a human being flies from one end of the world to the other in a few hours, the whole human race quivers with pride and adores itself as distinct from all the rest of creation. At bottom, this imperialism of the species is preached by all the great directors of the modern conscience. It is Man, and not the nation or the class, whom Nietzsche, Sorel, Bergson extol in his genius for making himself master of the world. It is humanity, and not any one section of it, whom Auguste Comte exhorts to plunge into consciousness of itself and to make itself the object of its adoration. Sometimes one may feel that such an impulse will grow ever stronger, and that in this way inter-human wars will come to an end. In this humanity would attain "universal fraternity." But, far from being the abolition of the national spirit with its appetites and arrogance, this would simply be its supreme form, the nation being called Man and the enemy God. Thereafter, humanity would be unified in one immense army, one immense factory, would be aware only of heroisms, disciplines, inventions, would denounce all free and disinterested activity, would long cease to situate the good outside the real world, would have no God but itself and its desires, and would achieve great things; by which I mean that it would attain to a really grandiose control over the matter surrounding it, to a really joyous consciousness of its power and grandeur. And History will smile to think that this is the species for which Socrates and Jesus Christ died.

In sum, in *La trahison des clercs* Benda discovers the ultimate treachery of the human mind not in the alliance of its highly self-conscious agents—men of letters, intellectuals, philosophers, scientists, historians, poets, and visual artists—with the modern nationalistic ethos, but in their desire altogether to reject their capacity for "disinterested activity" in the interest of becoming the omnipotent power in the world.[6]

In *La fin de l'éternel*, published a year after *La trahison des clercs*, Benda makes his discovery more explicit:

Whether we think of the "Being" of the Eleatics, of the "Good Superior to Being" of Plato, of the "thought of the thought" of Aristotle, or of the "Soul of the World" of the Alexandrians, of the spaceless and timeless God of Christian theology, of the Substance of Descartes or of Spinoza, even of the Noumenon of Kant or the Universal idea of Hegel—all the systems of metaphysics which have until now influenced mankind have conceived the ideal as *different in essence* from the real. All have defined the divine by negation of the attributes which condition phenomenal existence; all have made God an *absolute,* the word thus implying a *rupture of continuity* between what it designates and the world of sensible and changing things. Doubtless all or nearly all have afterwards wished that this Absolute, by a condescension of its nature (a condescension which several of them, however, find unintelligible, even while asserting it) comes to form the phenomenal world; all have wanted the divine, by a dilution of its essence, to end by forming the human; but none has ever admitted *that the human by elevation of itself could end by constituting the divine;* none has ever admitted that concrete existence, by a sublimation of its nature, and *without renouncing this nature,* could end by constituting the Absolute.[7]

The "apotheosis of the real," as Benda says elsewhere in *La fin de l'éternel,* embraces the divinizing of the human. But the consequence of the divinization of the human, which is to say, of the humanizing of the divine, is to be discerned primarily not in the loss of the sense of the infinite but in the loss of the tension between the ideal realm of universal moral values (the realm of the true clerks) and the "barbarous" realm of the laymen. Always precariously maintained, this tension, which makes civilization possible, requires, Benda says, that the "morality of the clerks" influence "but not be influenced by the morality of the laymen." Brought "under the influence of the clerks, the laymen modify their code, but recover themselves afterwards when in danger of being softened to an extreme degree." If the clerks, instead of "clerizing" the laymen, become themselves "laicized," they will thereupon as "false clerks" "organize the world" according to "terrestrial laws" and "allow all ideal and disinterested values to be despised by men."[8]

In sum, like Valéry and Broch—like Proust, Kafka, Mann, Joyce, T. E. Hulme, or T. S. Eliot—Benda was in the formal sense neither philosopher nor historian, and still less sociologist of knowledge. Nor was he an "intellectual." More than his contemporaries, he explicitly recognized his role to be that of the "man of letters" and as such to represent the survival of the heritage of the clerk as embodied in the modern man of letters. The term *man of letters,* it is well to remember, like the term *clerk* in its original signification, referred to a man who possessed a *lettered* mind, a mind capable of exercising the skills of reading and writing, in contrast to the majority of men who did not have these skills. Concerned, like Valéry, about the cultural status of mind, Benda was intensely aware of the moral authority and consequent responsibility incumbent upon the lettered mind in the twentieth century because of its privileged character. Represented by, embodied in, individual clerks, the lettered mind as it emerged in the early modern age, that is, in the fifteenth and sixteenth centuries, sought to make its own realm. As the secularization of the clerks proceeded in the following two centuries and they were transformed into men of letters, the secular descendants of the clerks conceived of themselves as forming a historical order, a "republic of letters," distinct from, and in the ideal independent of, the realms of church and state. Essentially a secularization of the ideal of order represented by the universal *republica Christiana*, the Republic of Letters, a modern secular-spiritual order, still possessing even now something of the aura of transcendent moral and spiritual authority that had been associated with the Republic of Christ, was for four centuries or more a major symbol of the realm of the mind in the West. Concerned about the cultural status of mind, Benda was, like Valéry, intensely aware of the responsibility of mind for its own character. In his representation of mind, it is not, as it may appear to be, formed by any given historical situation, but, embodied in individual clerks, has come in the modern age to constitute its own symbolic realm. Existing apart from church and state, this realm—the realm of the clerks, of men of letters, of the Republic of Letters—is a prime symbol of order in Western history. When Julien Benda in *La trahison des clercs* and *La fin de l'éternel* pronounced that men of letters, seduced by nationalistic passions, had become traitors to this, their own order, and that their treason was responsible for the riven European cultural situation, he hit a central nerve in the sensibility of a world that as never before had come to equate mind and civilization.

Assuming that Voegelin was familiar with *La trahison des clercs*, that he likely also knew *La fin de l'éternel*, I am not sure how to account for his apparent failure to comment somewhere on Benda's at times rather precise anticipation of the dominant motive in *Order and History*. I refer to the way in which Voegelin, himself a member of the clerkly order, conducts his own internal investigation, comprehensive and often passionate, into the betrayal of this order.

One explanation of Voegelin's seeming disregard of Benda may be his rejection of any aspiration to cast himself in the image Benda sought eagerly to emulate, that of the "good European." His refusal of aspiration may probably be attributed to the two years (1924–1926) Voegelin spent as a visiting scholar at Columbia University, Harvard University, and the University of Wisconsin on a Laura Spellman Rockefeller Memorial Fellowship. In the invaluable "Autobiographical Memoir" taped for Professor Ellis Sandoz in 1973, Voegelin points to the "great break" in his "intellectual development" that occurred when, through extensive reading in the American university libraries and attending the lectures and making the personal acquaintance of American teachers and thinkers, he was introduced to the Anglo-American tradition of the Scottish Common Sense philosophy. He points also to the "strong influence" on him of his encounter for the first time of the Spanish-American philosopher George Santayana. Voegelin was never to meet Santayana, who had left America in 1912. But when, following the suggestion of Irwin Edman of Columbia, he began reading Santayana, he experienced a "revelation . . . comparable to the revelation I received at the same time through commonsense philosophy." In Santayana the young Viennese scholar found "a man with a vast background of philosophical knowledge, sensitive to the problem of the spirit without accepting a dogma, and not interested at all in neo-Kantian methodology."[9] The most immediate intellectual consequence of his initial American period was Voegelin's first book, a study of the "form of the American mind" published in 1928 under the title *Ueber die Form des Amerikanischen Geistes*. But this book Voegelin says in his memoir does not do justice to the importance to his life of his first two years in America.

> The great event was the fact of being thrown into a world for which the great methodological debates of the neo-Kantian type, which I considered the most important thing intellectually, were of no importance. Instead, there was the background of the great political foundation of 1776 and 1789, and of the unfolding of the founding act through a political and legal culture, primarily represented by the lawyers' guild and the Supreme Court. There was the strong background of Christianity and Classical culture which was so signally fading out, if not missing, in the methodological debates in which I had grown up as a student. In brief, here was a world in which this other world that I had grown up in was intellectually, morally, and spiritually irrelevant. That there should be such a plurality of worlds had a devastating effect on me. The experience broke for good, at least I hope it did, my provincialism of a central European or generally Euro-

pean kind without letting me fall into American provincialism. I gained an understanding through these years of the plurality of human possibilities realized in various civilizations, as an immediate experience, an *expérience vécue*, which hitherto had been accessible to me only through the comparative study of civilizations, as I found them in Max Weber, in Spengler, and later in Toynbee. The immediate effect was that upon my return to Europe certain phenomena which were of the greatest importance in the intellectual and ideological context of Central Europe, as for instance the work of Heidegger, whose famous *Sein und Zeit* I read in 1928, no longer had any effect on me. It just ran off, because I had been immunized against this whole context of philosophizing through my time in America and especially in Wisconsin [where Voegelin knew John R. Commons, the author of *Human Nature and Human Property*, whom he saw as a "Lincolnesque figure," a real heartland American]. The priorities and relations of importance between various theories had been fundamentally changed, and as far as I can see for the better too.[10]

Wrenched out of the world in which the "mind" of the "good European" clerk was supposed to function in an ideal vacuum of disinterestedness, Voegelin discovered in America the efficacy of a principle he had heard enunciated by the historian Eduard Meyer in Berlin a year or two before his American sojourn: a "historical situation" is to be understood "through the self-understanding of the persons involved." At this time Voegelin became convinced, Sandoz observes, that a "thinker himself best knows what he is doing." In a passage in his memoir Voegelin explicitly declares the basic significance of self-interpretation in his own thought: "The reality of experience is self-interpretive . . . through symbols; and the symbols are the key to understanding the experience expressed. . . . [This is the] principle that lies at the basis of all my later work."[11]

Guided by this principle, Voegelin not only assumes what Benda says directly, namely that the clerk is a crucial figure in modern culture, but envisions the clerk in the mingled aspects of philosopher, poet, and historian—in the role of the man of letters as the primary interpreter of history; but Voegelin, through the intensity of his insistence on the integrality of interpreter and interpretation, increases the burden the clerk must bear. According to Voegelin's conception, the individual clerk becomes nothing less than the carrier of the "advancing process" of the experiential, or existential, differentiation that is the "substance of history." To play on the words of Gerhart Niemeyer, Voegelin emphasizes that history is the clerk's consciousness and the clerk's consciousness is history.[12] If, at the risk of distorting the Voegelinian vision, though I think not unduly so, we substitute the term *drama* for *process*, and speak of the "drama of differentiation," we may with considerable appropriateness refer to the clerk as appearing in both Benda and Voegelin in the guise of both hero and villain. But in contrast to the clerk's character in the drama—or at times the melodrama—of the modern clerks as envisioned by Benda, in which we have at least a few heroes as well as villains, the clerk's character in the Voegelinian drama—and the melodrama—is more often a dark figure of the semi-villain or villain than of the hero.

The most pertinent texts in Voegelin's story of the clerks are *From Enlightenment to Revolution*, *The New Science of Politics*, and *The Ecumenic Age*, the fourth volume of *Order and History*. The first volumes of *Order and History*—*Israel and Revelation*, *The World of the Polis*, and *Plato and Aristotle*—suggest the indispensable antecedents of the story in the Hebraic and classical cultures. Obviously I cannot discuss all of the elements of the "tale of the clerk" as it emerges in Voegelin's intricate study of history. I shall attempt to indicate certain major aspects of the story told by him.

Voegelin's first and most direct telling of the tale is in *From Enlightenment to Revolution*. Not published until 1975, a year after the appearance of the fourth volume of *Order and History*, this work, according to its editor, is but a "portion of an unpublished history of political ideas" written "in the nineteen forties and early fifties." William C. Havard recalls that this work was well along when Voegelin came to Louisiana State University in 1942. As he conducted his course at LSU in the history of political ideas, Havard adds, Voegelin both continuously added to the study and just as continuously revised it. But after writing several thousand pages, he abandoned it. It was not that it failed to fulfill the intention he had begun with. He had decided that the intention was too narrow in scope. For one in search of the fundamental entity of history, Voegelin had decided, will find it not in the idea or ideas that seem to govern a given society but in the *experiential knowledge* of it. This knowledge is available through an evaluation of the historical experience of the complex symbols concrete societies have employed, or presently employ, to represent themselves in history. This means that the primary field of investigation for the historian of ideas is the history of myths, and connections of myth, philosophy, and revelation. What is required therefore is a "retheoretization" of history in the interest of developing a systematic theory of history.[13] Voegelin announced his intention to fulfill this awesome requirement in the Walgreen Lectures at the University of Chicago in 1951. Five years after the publication of his series of lectures by the University of Chicago Press (1952), the Louisiana State University Press brought out the first three volumes of *Order and History*.

When he began what he envisioned as a massive "inquiry into the order of man, society, and history," Voegelin projected the accomplishment of *Order and History* in six volumes. The three volumes published in 1956–1957 were to be completed by three to be entitled "Empire and Christianity," "The Protestant Centuries," and "The Crisis of Western Civilization." Although there would be some interweaving of the subject matter in the six volumes of the whole, *Order and History* would progress in a linear fashion from the depiction of the "imperial organizations of the Near East, and their existence in the form of cosmological myth," to a study of Hebraic "existence in historical form," to an analysis of "the polis and its myth, and the development of philosophy as the symbolic form of order," to a discussion of "multicivilizational empires" following Alexander and the rise of Christianity, to the development of the "modern nation states" based on "Gnosticism as the symbolic form of order." Yet even as he published the initial volumes of *Order and History*, Voegelin was, as we know, growing more and more dissatisfied with the linear time scheme. As a consequence the final three volumes of the work did not appear as promised in 1958. Fifteen years later the publication of *Order and History* was resumed with a fourth volume called *The Ecumenic Age*. This volume—a profound meditation on the problem of the "form which a philosophy of history has to assume in the present historical situation," which defies placement in "a story of meaningful events . . . arranged on a time line"—is also by implication a deep meditation on the way in which a modern clerk acquires a kind of tragic significance as an interpreter of history.[14]

But to understand this, I think, we have to have some familiarity with Voegelin's *From Enlightenment to Revolution*. Although his dissatisfaction with the limitations of the history-of-ideas approach to the problem of meaning in history led him to abandon this work, in it Voegelin displays a broader and more penetrating comprehension of the meaning of an "idea" than have many intellectual historians. "The historian of ideas," he said, "has to do more than to report the doctrines advanced by a thinker or to give an account of a few great systems."

> He has to explore the growth of sentiments which crystallize into ideas, and he has to show the relation between ideas and the matrix of senti-

ments in which they are rooted. The idea has to be studied, not as a concept, but as a symbol which draws its life from sentiments; the idea grows and dies with the sentiments which engender its formulation and, with the great thinkers, its integration into a system of thought approximating the asymptote of rationality. Only insofar as the idea is understood as the approximately rational expression of the life of sentiments can we understand it as a historical entity. For the interpretation of ideas in this process of historical growth, the minor thinkers sometimes may be more important than the great ones in whose systems the motivation of ideas through sentiment is covered by the exigencies of immanent logical consistency.[15]

Pursuing in *From Enlightenment to Revolution* the connection between the ideas not only of the most prominent authors of the Enlightenment but of a host of minor ones, Voegelin is initially interested in seeking to identify points where we may see ideas "begin to separate as symbols from the matrix of sentiments," for at such points the motives that animate the creation of the ideas become visible. His search begins with a depiction of the clash of sentiments engendered in the age when the "elimination of Church and Empire as public powers" had become decisive; and minds, in their acute "consciousness that . . . an epoch had come to an end," began to apprehend the necessity of a "gigantic effort of interpretation in order to recover for the existence of man in society and history a meaning which he could substitute for the lost meaning of Christian existence." In the first chapter of *From Enlightenment to Revolution* Voegelin makes a highly effective illustration of how this effort marks an epochal ending in the consciousness of existence in the West. Drawing a contrast between Bossuet's *Discours sur l'histoire universelle* and Voltaire's *Essai sur les moeurs*, he points out that when the first was published in 1661, the patristic model was still the only model available for a universal history. Not until Voltaire's essay appeared in 1753 did it become evident that the "center of universality" had "shifted from the sacred to the profane level." As the awareness of this shift spread, Christianity ceased to be accepted by historians as a complete revelation—a total interpretation—of history and became simply one event in history. As a consequence the distinction between sacred and profane history disappeared, for "profane history is profane only as long as sacred history is accepted as the absolute frame of reference." When this frame is no longer taken for granted, sacred and profane history "merge on the level of secularized history." On this level "history, including the Christian religious phenomena, is conceived as an innerworldly chain of human events, while at the same time, there is retained the Christian belief in a universal meaningful order of human history." Although it has effectively degenerated from spiritual concept to sentiment, the ideal of universality is so appealing it demands to be embodied in any secular reconstruction of history. Voegelin cites Voltaire as a case in point. He "did not see himself as the spiritual substance by which history advances" and thus was "not a revolutionary spiritual founder." Rather he "remained in suspense before the revolution," making plain the Christian analogues that would be followed in the secularistic reconstruction of history.

> The *esprit humain* and its changes have become the object of general history. The transcendental pneuma of Christ is replaced by the intramundane spirit of man, and the change of heart by the change of opinion. The *corpus mysticum Christi* has given way to the *corpus mysticum humanitatis*. The meaning of history on this intramundane level is constructed as an analogue to the Christian meaning of history so closely that we can trace the parallelism step by step. In any construction of a meaningful universal history, in the first place the object that shows a meaningful structure has to be constituted as a whole. In the Christian system, the whole is constituted through the idea of creation and the descent of mankind from Adam; in the secularistic construction, the whole is evoked as a totality of empirical knowledge. The ideal of empirical completeness ... becomes the secularistic analogue of the divine creation of mankind if it is coupled with a new construction of historical meaning.[16]

Voltaire's suggestion of a new construction of historical meaning, Voegelin observes, had in a sense been foreshadowed by Joachim of Flora, a thirteenth-century monk who had envisioned the development of an independent realm of monks. This realm would be one separate from the realms of church and state, in effect a Third Realm, which, according to Voegelin's interpretation of Joachim's intention, would "perfect the autonomous Christian personality." When Voltaire "speaks of the extinction, renaissance and progress of the human spirit," he may be interpreted as offering a parallel to Joachim's trinitarian concept, in which "the extinction corresponds to the Fall" of the human spirit, the renaissance to its "Redemption," and "the progress to a Third Realm" to its "spiritual perfection." So we have the conventional trinitarian pattern of historical interpretation: the

Middle Ages (extinction), the Renaissance (toleration), the eighteenth century (progress). In the age of progress the secular spirit of the autonomous intellectual replaces Joachim's conception of the spirit of the autonomous Christian personality. Or to adapt the argument to the idea that Voegelin is the teller of the tale of the clerk, the medieval clerk undergoes a transfiguration and emerges as the modern clerk.

But actually Voegelin's telling of the story of the clerk is not quite so neat. He finds in Voltaire only a partial embodiment of the modern clerk. Although the "range and quality" of Voltaire's dazzling performance as a man of letters "can never quite anesthetize the awareness" of his ultimate lack of spiritual substance, he must be praised for his "spirit of tolerance, his common sense, his indignation at scholastic obscurantism, and at bigotry, his hatred of oppression and persecution, his advocacy of freedom of speech and thought."

> Voltaire's strength lies in this twilight zone of procedural values which are peculiar to a man who has lost the old faith sufficiently to see its shortcomings as an outsider and to attack them without compunction, and who has not enough substance of new faith to create its laws as the master but enough to fight with skill and courage for its establishment. This intermediate position . . . is a realm not of the spirit, but between the spirits, where man can live for a moment in the illusion that he can, by discarding the old spirit, free himself of the evil which inevitably arises from the life of the spirit in the world, and that the new one will create a world without evil. . . . The child-of-the-world's dream of a terrestrial paradise of compassion and humanity is only a shadow of the heavenly city, but still it is a shadow cast by the eternal light.[17]

That Voltaire lived in the shadow of the eternal light, that he had an authentic compassion for men who were "trampled underfoot" by forces of postmedieval history "beyond their understanding" redeems him to an appreciable extent from his championship of the notion that "every unsound utterance has to be considered an opinion" and from his making "irresponsibility of thought . . . synonymous with freedom of thought"—from, in short, his participation in the descent on the world of the "darkness of enlightened reason."[18] Voegelin's critical explication of the eighteenth-century clerks other than Voltaire is in general devoted to their unmitigated involvement in the fall of freedom of thought into this "darkness."

Tracing this fall from Helvétius, D'Alembert, and Turgot into such nineteenth-century figures as Comte, Bentham, Hegel, Bakunin, Engels, and Marx, Voegelin sees the progressive fading of the Voltairean tension between transcendence and immanence—between the heavenly city ("a paradise of compassion") and the earthly city—progressively disappearing; this happens as the genuine passion of a great clerk for compassion to victims of historical disorder moves toward the moment when the modern clerk (in the guise of the intellectual) would become a "closed intramundane person," a "world-immanent self," possessed of the delusion that the mind has the power to interpret history, organize it into an ideological system, and control it. The prophecy of the coming of such a figure, Voegelin says, may be found in Voltaire's minor contemporary Helvétius, who, "with comparative unawareness of its implications," advanced a theory of the passions that—defying the Pascalian (the Christian) conviction that the "true life" is one lived "without passion in openness to the Grace of God"—holds that the "life of passion" is man's fate and "all that one can do is to provide a social situation in which the results of passionate action are virtuous." Since such a result must essentially be untrue to the nature of reality, Helvétius puts a kind of omnipotent "analyst-legislator" in control of the social situation.

> The legislator has the function of entangling man in the veil of *maya* in such a manner that the fabric shows a surface iridescence of virtue. Man is left in the life of appearance but, by means which remind us of Hegel's *List der Vernunft*, the appearance is overlaid by a further appearance of virtue. As the spider in the web of appearances sits the managing legislator—the intramundane counterforce to God—guiding the spectacle of the struggle which has so much success with the audience because everybody recognizes in it his own struggle. This truly Satanic vision reveals the extent of the catastrophe of the Western spirit even in the eighteenth century. Helvétius . . . simply was dead to the possibility of a Christian existence.[19]

The first specific formulation of the catastrophe of the Western spirit, Voegelin argues, occurred when the "new" religious spirit intimated by Helvétius, the spirit of one who dedicated himself to the skillful management of the passions of individuals in the interest of social "virtue," was embraced by Comte. An astute philosopher of history, Comte assumes a "more sinister quality" when we consider that he aspired to be "a spiritual dictator of mankind." Denying that Comte "the positivist and founder of the science [he called] sociology" is to be distinguished from the Comte who founded the Religion of Humanity in, as John Stuart Mill said, the "melancholy decadence of a great intellect," Voegelin regards the earlier character of Comte as having had an underlying consistency with that of Comte as an "intramundane eschatologist." With Marx, Lenin, and Hitler, he belongs wholly to "the series of men who would save mankind by divinizing their particular existence and imposing its law as the new order of society." He is the first expression of the "satanic Apocalypse of Man" that is the "signature" of the crisis of Western civilization.[20]

Marx is not, as we might logically expect him to be, the climactic figure in the story of the clerks as Voegelin tells this in *From Enlightenment to Revolution*. The treatment of Marx is the resolution of, let us say, a story line or plot that reaches its apex in the analysis of Comte as the source of the Marxian "spiritual disease," whether this be defined as the "self-divinization and self-salvation of man," or the substitution of the "*logos* of human consciousness" for the "transcendental *logos*." Like Comte, Marx "was a Paraclete in the best medieval, sectarian style, a man in whom the *logos* has become incarnate and through whose action in the world mankind at large would become the vessel of the *logos*." What on the Marxian surface appear to be "symptoms of antiphilosophism and logopobia" are to be "etiologically . . . understood" as the Marxian differentiation of "Gnostic socialism" and the "revolt of immanent consciousness against the spiritual order of the world."[21]

Turning to the bearing of *The New Science of Politics* on the analysis of this revolt, we find that Voegelin focuses on the role of the individual clerk in the "retheoretization" of history less intensely than in *From Enlightenment to Revolution*. Elaborating on the significance of the Third Realm of a perfected community of monks envisioned by Joachim of Flora, he reveals more fully, if largely by implication, not only the symbolic structure of the autonomous Gnostic political state as this began to evolve early in the postmedieval world but the structure of a secular-spiritual order that began to be differentiated by the clerks: a polity of mind—or a republic of letters and learning—separate from both the church and the state. Offering a deeper analysis of Joachim of Flora at the same time that he pursues his chief subject in *The New Science of Politics*—namely, the way in which empirical political societies seek not only to be embodiments of existential truth but incarnations of transcendental truth—Voegelin further expands the tale of the clerks in an exploration of the relation of the Third Realm to Greek symbols, especially the symbol of the polis.

In the case of the polis, Voegelin is concerned with a symbol in a polytheistic world that still bore the strong impress of a cosmological or compact culture. In a tension between their inherited acceptance of Athens as the representation of "cosmological truth" and the existential experience of Athens as the representation of the truth that the individual human being is the "measure of society because God is the measure of his soul," we have the ultimate meaning of Plato and Aristotle. The Greek tragic poets had represented the truth known to the Athens of Marathon in a "public" or "state" cult of the representative suffering of the tragic hero, whose fate as the victim of a struggle to uphold the ethos of Athens against a "demonically disordered world" arouses "the shudder of his own fate in the soul of the spectator." But Plato and Aristotle had to face the problem of the representation of truth in a post-Marathon Athens.

> When Aristophanes complained that the tragedy died from philosophy, he had at least an inkling of what actually took place, that is, of the *translatio* of truth from the people of Athens to Socrates. The tragedy died because the citizens of Athens no longer were representable by the suffering heroes. And the *drama*, the action in the Aeschylean sense, found now its hero in the new representative of truth, in its Suffering Servant Socrates—if we may use the symbol of Deutero-Isaiah. The tragedy as literary genus was followed by the Socratic dialogue. Nor was the new theoretical truth ineffective in the social sense. Athens, to be sure, could be no longer its representative; but Plato and Aristotle themselves created the new type of society that could become the carrier of their truth, that is, the philosophical schools. The schools outlived the political catastrophe of the polis and became formative influences of the first order, not in Hellenistic and Roman society only, but through the ages in Islamic and Western civilizations.[22]

Asserting that in *The Republic* Plato created a "Polis of the Idea," a "paradigmatic" social order in which the "philosophical type of man" is the chief figure—saying, moreover, that Plato and Aristotle themselves consciously conceived of a transfiguration of the polis into a new, autonomous spiritual-intellectual realm, a "holy city" of the philosophers—Voegelin seems to bring into question the logic of his vision of the nature of the Greek compact order. The self-conscious creation of a "holy city" could happen only in a society that had become more distinctly divided into temporal and spiritual orders than would appear to have been possible in the polis, a compact society guided by a cyclical vision of history. The possibility of such a division began to appear, Edmund Zeller says, only when the Hellenistic philosophers of the early and middle Stoa and the Roman philosophers of the later Stoa developed the creed of cosmopolitanism as a replacement for a declining faith in the compact state. The assimilation of the cosmopolitan creed by a rising Christianity is of large importance.[23] Yet save for a glance at the ironic subversion of Stoic cosmopolitanism in Cicero's idea that the "perfect order of philosophers" had been realized in the *imperium Romanum*, Voegelin largely passes over the Stoics in the *New Science of Politics*, thus allowing his conception of the transfiguration of the polis to stand unmodified.

Voegelin's reference to Cicero in this connection is, however, consonant with the implied modification of his idea of Platonic-Aristotelian "cosmopolitanism" in his description of the effort, as in Eusebius, to connect the *Pax Romana* with the "mysteries of the Kingdom of God" during the early stages of the Christianization of Rome. This effort occurred, Voegelin says, before St. Augustine put an end to "political theology" in orthodox (or Trinitarian) Christianity and "radically redivinized" the sphere of political power. As a result the "double representation of man in society through church and empire appeared for the first time in history" and—with the church conceived as the primary and the empire as the secondary realm in history—lasted throughout the Middle Ages.[24]

Observing that the problem of the "re-divinization" of society emerged in early modern times when the temporal order began to seek power over the church, Voegelin holds that the quest would become successful because of a profound modification of the Augustinian version of history. Augustine had taught there is "one Christian society . . . articulated into its spiritual and temporal orders." The temporal order "accepted the *conditio humana* without chiliastic fancies, while it heightened natural existence by the representation of spiritual destiny through the church." But, Voegelin says, the "eschatological expectation of the Parousia that would bring the kingdom of God" envisioned by the first generation of Christians as the truth of history had only been suppressed, not conquered, by Augustine's "tour de force of interpretation" in the *Civitas Dei*. The millennial expectation emerged again and again in the course of the Middle Ages, but it did not afford the basis for a redivinization of society until it emerged once again in the "person and work" of Joachim at the end of the twelfth century.

As I earlier indicated, Voegelin considers Joachim to have been a self-conscious rebel against the Augustinian conception of history. Applying the "symbol of the Trinity to the course of history," Joachim invented a "trinitarian eschatology." Dividing history into three ages of "progressive fulfillment"—the age of the Father, of the Son, and of the Spirit—he set forth the "aggregate of symbols which govern the self-interpretation of history to this day." The first symbol, that of the three ages of history, is remarkably comprehensive in its anticipation of modern symbols of history ranging from the conception of Turgot and Comte that history is a sequence of theological, metaphysical, and scientific periods; to Hegel's "dialectic of the three stages of history and self-reflective spiritual fulfillment"; to Marx's vision of history as moving from the time of "primitive communism," to the age of "class society," and from thence to fulfillment in the communist classless society; or, in "a special case," in the "National Socialist symbol of the Third Realm." The second symbol Voegelin detects in Joachim is that a paraclectic leader, who, figured forth in the *homines spirituales* of late medieval times, finally appears as the superman of modern times. The third and fourth symbols Voegelin sees in Joachim appear to be closely related to the first and second. The third, the "Gnostic prophet or, in the later stages of secularization, the Gnostic intellectual," was realized in the first instance in Joachim himself, the forerunner of the intellectual as "an appurtenance of modern civilization." The fourth symbol of history in Joachim is that of the "brotherhood of autonomous persons." As a perfected realm of the human spirit, this may become a model for any kind of intellectual or literary movement seeking authority for its existence outside the realm of the church. The last two symbols are clearly of the first importance in the translation of the clerks into a self-interpreted independent polity of humanists.[25]

The implied story of the clerks in Voegelin becomes far more complex in *The Ecumenic Age*, in which the linear concept of history is replaced by a spatial-temporal concept derived from the Platonic vision of the "In-Between" structure of human existence. Between the time of the writing of the third volume of *Order and History* and the writing of the fourth, Voegelin discovered the "constant in history" to be found not in its development in a time line but in its evolvement in the "constancy of a process that leaves a trail of equivalent symbols in time and space."

> Existence has the structure of the In-Between of the Platonic *metaxy*, and if anything is constant in the history of mankind it is the language of tension

between life and death, immortality and mortality, perfection and imperfection, time and timelessness, between order and disorder, truth and untruth, sense and senselessness of existence; between *amor Dei* and *armor sui, l'âme ouverte* and *l'âme close;* between the moods of joy and despair; and between alienation in its double meaning of alienation from the world and alienation from God. If we split these pairs of symbols, and hypostatize the poles of the tension as independent entities, we destroy the reality of existence as it has been experienced by the creators of the tensional symbolisms; we lose consciousness and intellect; we deform our humanity and reduce ourselves to a state of despair or activist conformity to the "age," of drug addiction and television watching, of suffering from the absurdity of existence or indulgence in any divertissement (in Pascal's sense) that promises a substitute as a "value" for reality lost. In the language of Heraclitus and Plato: Dream life usurps the place of wake life.[26]

In appealing to the Platonic vision of the *metaxy,* Voegelin makes a magisterial philosophical maneuver that allows him to argue that the Greek philosopher and the Christian saint created visions responding to a "theophany," or an epiphany of God. But, as he must acknowledge, these are opposing visions. In St. Paul—whose "mythopoetic genius" is "not controlled by the critical consciousness of a Plato"—the stress has decisively shifted from the "divinely noetic order incarnate in the world to the divinely pneumatic salvation from its disorder, from the paradox of reality to the abolition of the paradox, from the experience of the directional movement [of the "differentiating consciousness" within the *metaxy*] to its consummation." Consequently, Voegelin says—and I largely pass over an analysis too complicated to be summarized here—St. Paul regarded his vision of the transfigured Christ as an eschatological symbol, the conclusive sign that the Second Coming was imminent; that "the meaning of history was now known, and the end was near." A response to the social, intellectual, and spiritual ferment that boiled up toward the end of the Middle Ages, the resurgence of the millennial vision—which defied the Augustinian interpretation of post-transfiguration history as an indefinite period of waiting—was powerful enough to make "transfiguration" a "historical constant." The "turbulence in history" caused by the rare "theophanic event" was replaced as time went on by a series of disturbing "egophanic events" marking the emergence of a succession of "new Christs," including Comte, Hegel,

Nietzsche, and Marx. They are the fruit of the initial deformation of the "movement of transfiguration in history" by a late-twelfth-century clerk like Joachim, who, having created a "pattern of new expectations," was followed by a fourteenth-century clerk like Petrarch, the first embodiment of the "humanist intellectual." Petrarch conceived of the centuries that began with the birth of Christ as the "dark ages" and announced a new age illuminated by a renewal of the light of Greco-Roman paganism. As Voegelin indicates elsewhere, Hitler announced a new age illuminated by the light of Germanic paganism.

Following the implied tale of the clerks in the *Ecumenic Age*, we find that Voegelin suggests it properly begins in Paul's misinterpretation of history. Although his failure was corrected, or rectified so to speak, by Augustine, Paul's misconception of history as having a beginning and an ending was too compelling to be suppressed, and the "Pauline time of the tale" has remained "a millennial constant resisting dissolution by analysis." Assuming the license of poetic irony, we may say, the story of the modern clerks begins with the apostle Paul, the first clerk. Unlike the clerks of the high medieval church, who lived in the Augustine vision of history, Paul anticipated the typical psychic condition of the modern clerk: an acute need—prompted by the consciousness of displacement in history—to discover the meaning of existence in history. Paul's vision of the resurrected responded to his overwhelming desire to confer meaning on history by interpreting "the transfiguring incarnation of Christ" as "the beginning of the end," a proof of the imminence of the Parousia.[27] Pointing to the inclination over the centuries to embrace the Pauline expectation of the immediacy of the Second Coming, Voegelin observes:

> The experiential cause of the difficulties is the Paradox of Reality, or the Exodus within Reality, as I have called it. Reality is experienced as moving beyond its own structure toward a state of transfiguration. In Paul's language reality is in transition from the Anaximandrian state of *genesis* and *phthora* (perishing) to the state of *aphtharsia* (imperishability). At this point the troublesome complications begin, for the insights as well as the symbols found for their expression are inseparable from the theophanic events in which they read the luminosity of consciousness. The insights belong, in the Anaximandrian case, to the field of pneumatic revelation. They occur in the Metaxy, i.e. in the concrete psyche of concrete human beings in their encounters with the divine presence. There are no Greek

insights into the structure of reality apart from those of the philosophers in whose psyches the noetic theophany occurred; nor are there Israelite, Jewish, and Christian insights into the dynamics of transfiguration apart from the prophets, apostles, and above all Jesus, in whose psyches the pneumatic revelations occurred. The noetic and pneumatic luminosity of consciousness is not an "object" on which somebody stumbles by accident, but a concrete historical event in the Ecumenic Age; and its carriers are the human beings who by virtue of their function as carriers become the historical types of "philosophers" and "prophets." Moreover, the event is experienced as an intelligible advance beyond the more compact experiences and symbolizations of reality in the form of the myth whose principal carriers in the civilizations of an ancient Near East were the royal unifiers of the cosmological empires and the priesthoods who developed the imperial symbolism. Structure and transfiguration do not begin when they become conscious through the theophanic events of the Ecumenic Age; they are experienced as the problems of reality both before and after their differentiation. Transfiguring incarnation, in particular, does not begin with Christ, as Paul assumed, but becomes conscious through Christ and Paul's vision as the eschatological *telos* of the transfiguring process that goes on in history before and after Christ and constitutes its meaning.[28]

The truth of history—and this seems to be the overwhelmingly ironic climax to Voegelin's quest for order in history—was not available to the man who encountered the presence of the resurrected Christ on the road to Damascus. Had he known the thinking of Plato and Aristotle, it might have been. Paul might have been able to differentiate between the "hard core of truth" and his own "metastatic expectations"; for he would have been aware of the "noetic theophany" and the contrasting "pneumatic theophany" as being dual aspects of the "movement of transfiguration" within the *metaxy* and been able therefore to evaluate the quality of his vision. But then he would not have been Paul, the persecutor of Christians, who, transformed into the Apostle of Christ, became the forebear of the succession of post-Augustinian clerks in Western civilization down to the present day.

Having heretofore presented the clerks essentially as Gnostic deformers of the order in history as decreed by Christian revelation, in *The Ecumenic Age* Voegelin brings into dramatic opposition the Platonic and Pauline visions of the structure of history. Presumably, unlike Paul, having had the advantage of reading Plato and Aristotle and thus of becoming acquainted with the fundamental truth about the constitution of being, the post-Augustinian clerks have betrayed the truth—that is, the duality of the "movement of transfiguration" within the *metaxy*—by willing themselves to ignore it.

Ascribing the treason of the clerks, not like Benda to the nationalistic ethos, but to their subscription to the Pauline vision of history, Voegelin in effect places such an emphasis on the source of the vision in an individual consciousness that he seems to question his own theoretical principle that the valid historical entity is society. In his essay "The Concrete Consciousness" in *Anamnesis* he states that the "concrete consciousness of concrete man is the only consciousness given in our experience." The specific minds of individuals create societies through casting "social fields of consciousness." Only in this sense can one refer to the "self-interpretation of a given society."[29]

Voegelin's conviction of the integral connection between history and the individual consciousness has considerable significance for the story of the clerks. For one thing, it results in a marked distortion of the character of the modern clerk—a distortion that is also evident, though not in quite the same way, in *La trahison des clercs*. I refer to the misrepresentation deriving from the inclination of both Benda and Voegelin to identify their sense of vocation with a community of mind and spirit shared, at least in a general way, by the Attic, Hellenic, and Roman philosophers and poets, and the Christian and post-Christian clerks. When Benda appeals to Socrates and Jesus as the supreme clerks, he indulges a fanciful humanist cosmopolitanism to the fullest. Voegelin clearly resists any such indulgence. In his crucial discrimination between the classical discovery of philosophy as the symbol of existence and the Hebraic-Christian discovery of history as the symbol of existence, he would indeed appear to offer it strong resistance. Even so, in spite of his massive historical research and his complex imagination of history, Voegelin seems never to have explicitly recognized that Joachim's symbol of a "Third Age of the Spirit" (in which men of a monastic type will live in a realm beyond church and empire) and Petrarch's symbol of a third age of the secularized clerk (in which, freed from the ecclesiastical dominion, the clerk will live in an autonomous realm of humanists) are complementary symbols, signifying not simply the post-Augustinian development of the autonomous secular clerk but the appearance in history of an altogether novel realm of men of letters and learning—or of mind—the modern polity of the clerks. To understand the complex drama of Voegelin's life—a life so completely of mind and spirit—we need to take into account the fundamental tension he experienced toward this polity. Representing a corporate life in which he was inextricably involved, it yet is a dominion that he, no less than Julien Benda, attempted both to refute and transcend as a realm that has become treasonable to itself.

Bearing a certain analogical relation to the Greek and Roman concept of the *res publica*, the polity of the clerks is more basically analogous to the *corpus mysticum Christi*, or the *res publica Christi*. An immanent *corpus mysticum humanitas*, or *res publica litterarum*, it originated in an exodus of clerks from a world in which they were a cohesive part of a church-state structure to a world in which they would conceive of themselves as belonging primarily to a realm of secular letters and learning independent of church and state. A symbolic dominion, but concretely embodied in various literary and intellectual institutions and agencies, including the university (its embodiment in the modern university being one of the major distinctions of this institution from the medieval university), the Republic of Letters, although it has been suppressed at times by church or state or both, has been the universal homeland of the modern Western mind. It has been the scene not only of the great critique of man and God, and of nature and society, that marks the five-hundred-year period of the modern age but of the often ruthless critique of this critique, as, for instance, by such modern clerks as Benda and Voegelin. In the ideal a realm of independent discourse, operating without the constraints of political or ecclesiastical authority, the polity of the modern mind is the dominion of freedom recognized by Pierre Bayle in 1684, when, having fled to Amsterdam from France to escape the persecution of the Huguenots, he founded *Nouvelles de la république des lettres*. In his periodical Bayle proclaimed that all men should "lay aside the terms" that divide them "into different factions, and consider only the head upon which they are joined together, which is the nature of enlightened Man in the Republic of Letters." Expanding his argument in his ambitious and influential *Dictionnaire historique et critique*, Bayle argued that men united in the literary polity is the "only permanent example of pure and original democracy." In this polity each man is sovereign yet subject to the ruthless criticism of each of its citizens. Yet, Bayle suggests, dissension in the Republic of Letters fosters rather than inhibits the bonded society Voltaire saw as having been gradually established in the age of Louis XIV, a great "fellowship" of free minds, "spread everywhere."[30]

The idea of the essentially corporate nature of the Republic of Letters was more clearly anticipated by Petrarch (whom Voegelin treats almost incidentally) than by Joachim. To be sure, in a "Europe still subject to ecclesiastical and feudal authority," one scholar has said, Petrarch "founded a new power, outside Church and outside State—altogether moral, altogether modern—the Republic of Letters." While he did this through the impact of his total career, Petrarch announced what he was doing in one specific act, designing and staging his coronation as self-appointed poet laureate in the Senate House on the Capitoline Hill in Rome on Easter Sunday, 1341. In this famous ceremony, after a Roman senator had placed the crown of laurel on his head, Petrarch delivered an oration on a text taken not from the Bible but from Virgil's *Georgics*, thereby suggesting, as one who held minor orders in the Church, that the act of coronation was indicative not merely of the spiritual nature of his vocation to classical (or "profane" or secular) literature but in taking place on Easter Sunday was a symbol of the resurrection of "profane" letters. But this was not all. Leaving the Capitoline Hill, Petrarch went across the Tiber to St. Peter's, where he placed his laurel crown on the altar.[31]

Superficially considered, laying his crown on the altar completed a pledge of allegiance by Petrarch the poet and man of letters to state and church. But his actual intention in performing the bizarre drama of self-coronation was to invest secular letters with spiritual authority, and thus establish a dimension of power that had never before existed, an order resting on the spiritual, the assimilating force of a new Logos, the secular-spiritual Logos of humanism. The new Logos had been revealed to him with such clarity and force that he conceived himself to be the incarnation of a new kind of authority.

Institutionalized as a secular-spiritual polity of the literary and learned, this new authority would be referred to by Carlyle as a "church"—a church which subscribed to the Protestant doctrine of the priesthood of all believers. Yet Carlyle's image of the Republic of Letters represents a distinctly self-conscious reaction by a nineteenth-century humanist to the imposition of limits on literary meaning. Benda's reference in the twentieth century to the clerks as "priests of the mind" reflects the Petrarchan sensibility, as does, for instance, with an elevated intensity, Hemingway's dictum: "A writer should be of as great probity and honesty as a priest of God."[32] Yet in historical context the Hemingway sensibility represents the almost complete fracturing of a unified humanist sensibility. It had not occurred to the eighteenth-century mind to distinguish between "literature" and "learning." The Baconian dictum "Knowledge is power" was still broadly connotative. Samuel Johnson defined literature succinctly as "learning: skill in letters" and made no distinction between the terms *literature* and *science*.

But under the pressure of the explosion of knowledge created by the great critique, it became increasingly obvious in the nineteenth century that humanists and scientists no longer shared a common language. The meaning of the Republic of Letters—of the Third Realm—became subject to definition by humanists on the one hand and by scientists on the other. Even in the later twentieth century it was still possible for the humanist to appeal to the spirit of eighteenth-century cosmopolitanism, as W. H. Auden did in 1967, when he accepted a literary award "in the name of my fellow citizens in the Republic of Letters, that holy society which knows no national boundaries, possesses no military hardware, and where the only political duty on all of us at all times is to love the Word and defend it against its enemies."[33] The tone of this latter-day celebration of the *studium* transfigured as the *sacerdotium* differs markedly from that of the description of the scientific realm Hannah Arendt offered in 1958 in her treatise on *The Human Condition*. Having made her well-known case for the realization of the "Archimedean point" as the crux of modernity—this point having been reached when, after Galileo had divorced appearance and reality forever with his telescope, Descartes based knowledge on doubt—Arendt says:

> The human mind changed in a matter of years or decades as radically as the human world in a matter of centuries; and while this change naturally remained restricted to the few who belonged to that strangest of all modern societies, the society of scientists and the republic of letters (the only society which has survived all changes of conviction and conflict and without ever forgetting to "honor the man whose beliefs it no longer shares") this society anticipated . . . by sheer force of trained and controlled imagination, the radical changes of mind of all modern men which became politically demonstrable reality only in our time.

Referring to the "society of scientists and the republic of letters," Arendt tacitly acknowledges the present-day disjunction of men of letters and men of science yet speaks of the two groups as nonetheless comprising a larger society of "trained and controlled minds." An eminently "trained and controlled mind" herself, Arendt was a participant in the latter-day self-interpretation of the Third Realm. Although she had deep reservations about the ultimate consequences of the epochal alteration of consciousness in the modern age, Arendt in effect accepted the validity of the experience by the clerks of a profound change in the structure of consciousness that began with their exodus from the medieval *studium*. The journey out of the *studium*—which existed not only in an integral relation with the *imperium* and the *sacerdotium* but in a close connection with a relatively "compact" or "organic" culture, the medieval culture of hierarchy and icon—developed a mode of secular inquiry and reflection that, whether devoted to examination of classical and biblical texts or natural phenomena, exhibited the will of the human mind to interpret analytically all that previously referred to myth and revelation. Ultimately, through its will to analytic interpretation, the human mind would transfer God and man, nature and society, and even mind itself, into mind. The radical subjectivity of this process—which implies that from the end of the Middle Ages on history in its most fundamental aspect is the movement of existence into mind—makes it impossible for the human mind to deal with itself save on its own terms of self-interpretation.

"Without his mythologies," as Allen Tate said, "man becomes an interpretant." As he said this Tate was attempting—as T. S. Eliot did, more logically, in his symbolic interpretation of the Middle Ages—to employ the "Old" or pre–Civil War South as a symbol of premodern society governed by myth. Ironically the very irony of the attempt is the subject of one of Tate's most successful poems, "Ode to the Confederate Dead," which records his discovery that the world cannot be remythologized; that the modern man of letters cannot escape from his enclosure in his self-interpretation of his condition as a modern clerk: even when he assumes the role of the man of letters as poet, he can only be an interpreter of history. Such self-knowledge, Tate says in the preface to *The Man of Letters in the Modern World*, is analogous to the self-discovery of his situation in classical tragedy.[34] Prompted by the pressure of his desire to relieve the burden of this perception, Tate envisioned a reversion to the pre-exodus status of the clerk and became a convert to the version of the Christian myth as it is embodied in Roman Catholicism. He even made an attempt, not notably successful, to accept not only the circumscriptions the doctrines of the faith impose on personal and social behavior but those it places on literary expression.[35]

The tension Voegelin experienced in his relationship to the polity of the clerks is more complex and less easily fathomable than it is in the instance of either Arendt or Tate. Tate's case may provide the more illuminating comparison. Although Voegelin's story hardly affords a precise parallel to Tate's, it is apposite to it inasmuch as the political scientist–philosopher Voegelin shared a primary motive with many contemporary poet-critics, novelists, and dramatists. The motive of all these poets (to use the term in its generic sense) was imaged in Eliot's *The Waste Land:* a quest for the ground of being, which took the form of an attempted recovery of an experiential knowledge of the ground, this being understood as the harmony of God, the self (the soul), and history. Pursuing their effort, twentieth-century poets have developed what one recent student of twentieth-century letters has called a "modernist poetics of history." Rejecting linear concepts of history, seeking to align history with the arts rather than with the sciences, stressing the integral connection between the individual experience and the consciousness of history, the modernist poetics of history encourages the rendition of the past in spatiotemporal terms or in a "palimpsest," in which there is displayed a "present woven" from the complexities of the "remembrance of things past," a "past that exists only as it lives in the texture of the present."[36] In the modernist poetics of history, it is clear, the poet in the role of the interpreter of history is not a detached observer—not even, say, Stephen Dedalus whom Joyce ironically depicts at the end of *Portrait of the Artist* as aspiring to be God. As Stephen learns in his reappearance in *Ulysses,* nothing is more impossible than to alienate oneself—the actor in history—from the "nightmare of history." For the actor as poet cannot know, as Stephen at first falsely conceives he can, the *essence* of the drama of history in which he is acting. He cannot know the essence of history any more than, as Voegelin says in "Eternal Being in Time" (an essay in the collection entitled *Anamnesis*), the actor as philosopher can know it.

> For the drama of history is not yet completed and thus not given as a thing about the essence of which one could state propositions; and the philosopher does not look at this nonthing as an observer but, in philosophizing, turns into an actor in the drama about which he wants to make statements. The model of a subject of knowledge confronting his object is not applicable to a knowledge in which the act of knowing is part of the process that is to be known. This reflection compels us to recognize, beyond the

concepts of thing and essence, a reality of being that comprises both philosophy and history.[37]

If we substitute the terms *poetry*, *poet*, and *poetic* for *philosophy*, *philosopher*, and *philosophical* in the above passage, we realize, I think, the rich complexity of the appositive relationship of Voegelin and his poetic contemporaries. This would be especially so if we made a substitution of terms throughout "Eternal Being in Time." In lieu of attempting that, let me suggest the substitution of Voegelin's summary in his essay of the "four relations" which express "the reality of being that comprises both philosophy and history":

(1) Philosophy as a phenomenon of history
(2) Philosophy as a constituent of history
(3) History as a constituent of philosophy
(4) History as a field of phenomena for philosophical investigation.[38]

Effecting a substitution of terms, we have:

(1) Poetry as a phenomenon of history
(2) Poetry as a constituent of history
(3) History as a constituent of poetry
(4) History as a field of phenomena for poetic investigation.

Going one step further we have as the four relations which express "the reality of being" as this is comprised of poetry, philosophy, and history:

(1) Poetry and philosophy as phenomena of history
(2) Poetry and philosophy as constituents of history
(3) History as a constituent of poetry and philosophy
(4) History as field of phenomena for poetic and philosophical investigation.

Voegelin, one may hazard to suggest, would not have objected to such a paradigmatic relationship of poetry, philosophy, and history as symbolic components of the reality of being. The essay on "Eternal Being in Time" is a series of philosophical statements by an actor-author about his experience in a quest not simply, through the translation of the "logos of history" into the "logos of philosophy," to define a "philosophy of history" but, through a translation of the logos of philosophy into the logos of poetry, to reach the ultimate goal of his quest, the "realization of the logos of eternal being in time." But such a translation is finally beyond the reach of expression in philosophical statements. One of the most striking instances in which Voegelin endeavors to sum up the meaning of his commitment to the quest for a philosophy of history occurs in his reference in "Eternal Being in Time" to a passage about the Exodus of the Chosen People in Augustine's *Enarrationes in Psalmos*.

> Incipit exire qui incipit amare
> Exeunt enim multi latenter,
> et exeuntium pedes sunt cordis affectus:
> exeunt autem de Babylonia.

> He begins to leave who begins to love.
> Many the leaving who know it not,
> for the feet of those leaving are affections of the heart:
> and yet, they are leaving Babylon.[39]

It is not any philosophical statement that can be made about it, Voegelin indicates, but the luminosity afforded by the emotional intensity of the Augustinian text that makes possible our understanding of the actual historical event of the Exodus of the Israelites as a symbol of the numerous "processes" in history of "exodus, exile, and return"; and beyond that, as a "figuration of the tension between time and eternity," which stems from the "love of eternal being."

In such a moment in Voegelin, sensing that he is interpreting the logos of history as much through the logos of poetry as through the logos of philosophy, we clearly realize that his affinity with a poetics of history underlies his philosophical response to the ideological deformations of history he spent his life revealing and combatting. We realize further, I think, that in his affinity with modern poet-clerks as actors in history Voegelin shared with many of them the experience not only of a tragic exile from a native homeland but a tragic alienation from the dominion of the clerks, an intellectual and spiritual homeland that had been largely taken over by the "new Christs." More complex, sustained, dramatic, and passionate than

Benda's, Voegelin's version of the betrayal of the clerks is central to the modernist poetics of history, placing him not only in the company of such clerks as Spengler and Toynbee, but also, perhaps preeminently, in the company of Yeats, Henry James, Proust, Joyce, Eliot, Mann, Broch, Tate, Auden, Hemingway, Faulkner, and Camus. Perhaps most poignantly in the company of Camus, with whom, although we might not expect it, he felt a strong sense of identity.

> Apart from the mystery of participation that is hidden between God and man, where in the dimension of history of consciousness can we find the hidden reality? And where can we find, together with the reality, the men with whom we can live and die in the community of knowledge? Let us ask concretely: From where did Albert Camus get the strength that sustained him for decades in the tension of his meditation and enabled him to look through the perversion of rebellion and to overcome it? For Camus it came from the myth. "We shall choose Ithaca, the faithful land, frugal and audacious thought, lucid action, and the generosity of the man who understands." The "madness" of the time is no home for man; he must choose the home in which he, living, will again create a home in time. Camus chooses the myth: "The world where I feel most at ease: the Greek myth." The course of his meditation is the course of his life in which he comes to be "the man who understands." Yet what bends at the end is the beginning. The "understanding man," who gains insights, is the "knowing man" of Parmenides who permits himself to be led to the truth. In the *Carnets* one finds the plan of his work in three phases: I. The Myth of Sisyphus (the absurd). II. The Myth of Prometheus (rebellion). III. The Myth of Nemesis. From the very first the work was deliberately designed with a view to a meditation in the medium of the myth. In the degree in which his quest through knowledge is illumined, the mood of existence changes. "Now there rises the strange joy which helps us to live and to die, and which we shall henceforth refuse to send back until later." The rebellion aims at the presence of life in the tension to the divine ground; it manifests itself in the ideological apocalypse of the futuristic utopias; when the futuristic alienation from the presence subsides, the joy of the here and now of existence can stir again.[40]

Like the poets, Voegelin's subject is an exploration of the way in which, for the individual, consciousness is history and history is consciousness—or, to put this more starkly, Voegelin's subject is an exploration of the way in which the individual is isolated in history and history is isolated in the individual. While it would, gravely perhaps, distort the significance of his career as a whole, I have at times thought the biographer of one of the last great European clerks might employ as epigraphic notations the records of two "anamnetic experiments"—or "experiments in memory"—the historian and philosopher once conducted on himself. One is the memory of "The Cloud Castle":

> The Cloud Castle always remained in the clouds, as it should. I knew nothing about it. The Cloud Peak [Wolkenstein] is one of the seven mountains. On it there is the Wolkenburg [Cloud Castle] and in it there dwells the Knight of the Wolkenburg. There was a legend about this knight. I have forgotten it and do not know whether it ever was important to me. The only thing important was that he "dwelt" up there.
>
> The great attractiveness of the Cloud Peak was its inaccessibility. There were quarries at the mountain, and the ascent was not permitted. The castle itself could not be seen from below—if it existed at all. I, at any rate, did not doubt its existence.
>
> The fuzziness of the details possibly accounted for the fact that the Cloud Castle and its knight were firmly ensconced in my soul. The place was dark and moist, surrounded by rags of clouds; the knight, a vague, sad, lost figure, traveling much on mysterious business, always returning in order to "dwell there" for a while.

The other "anamnetic experiment" I will refer to here is entitled "The Cannons of Kronburg."

> The cannons of Kronburg speak in the story of Holger Danske. Nothing has remained of the story but the cannons. When the ships pass by, the cannons say "boom."
>
> That is somewhere far away in the north, where the world has gone farthest, with nothing beyond. Ships will pass there, and nobody asks whence they are coming and where they are going. Where they pass without a

sound, there is nothing; no human being; only the cannons; and they say "boom" with solemn sadness, at the end of the world.[41]

These two "experiments" in memory—out of the nineteen recorded in *Anamnesis*, each based on recollections of an experience recalled from the first ten years of his childhood—imposed themselves so forcefully on his memory that he felt compelled to set them down, even though, unlike the other recollections he has recorded, they erupted in his memory unsummoned by "present problems" and were not readily understandable. In the instance of "The Cannons of Kronburg" Voegelin believed that he did come to understand it after he had written it down. He does not, however, indicate what his understanding was. Voegelin evidently never recovered the reason why he was compelled to recall the castle in the clouds and the figure of the wandering knight. But both of these memories of legends he encountered in his childhood are clearly symbols of an austere loneliness of spirit. Kafkaesque in quality, they graphically suggest the pervasive tone of estrangement that marks the work of the symbolists, the creators of the modernist poetics of history. I think of a particular moment in Voegelin's vast examination of symbols of order in *Order and History*. In his great meditation on how a world ended and another began in the second volume of this work, *The World of the Polis*, he deals with the experiences of poets and thinkers who, in a still dominantly cosmological order, apprehended the experience of differentiation in their souls, and so became strangers in their society. The further the revelation of "a transcendent truth valid for all mankind" opens to them, "the more intense becomes the solitude of the mediators" of that truth.[42]

Voegelin cites the elegy on Sophia in which Xenophanes observed that only warriors and athletes are celebrated by the polis but "Senseless indeed is custom in such matters; / it is not right / to judge strength higher than holy wisdom," when "better than the strength / Of men or horses is our wisdom!" Yet Xenophanes did not feel that the emphasis he placed on wisdom as superior to physical prowess separated him from the populace. Wisdom, the poet thought, was developing as "our wisdom," and was, like the value of physical strength would be, shared as a common possession of the polis. Later Socrates would appeal in his apology to the same illusion. But by then the "Xenophantic revolt against the unrighteous judgments of custom" had "sharpened to the deadly rejection of the mediator by his people," and his "isolation"—which he himself had not recognized, or chosen not to recognize—had "become fatal."[43]

Referring to the symbolic significance of Socrates as an inaugural mediator of, or articulator of, the experience of the differentiation of wisdom and the truth of the soul, Voegelin was perforce self-consciously aware of his identity with Socrates as a mediator of, and articulator of, the centuries of struggle since the Greek philosopher's time to preserve the Greek experience of differentiation of the soul through philosophy. In the course of his own mediatorial struggle there is reason to believe that Voegelin became more attached to the Greek than the Hebraic-Christian experience of differentiation. But he could know the Greek world only through his self-conscious participation as an actor in the drama of the secular-spiritual polity of clerks that came into historical existence as a differentiation of symbols at the end of the Christian world. The Kafkaesque knight and the Kafkaesque cannon speaking at the end of the world are symbols of a sensibility of alienation that was beginning to be comprehensible to the Shakespeare who created Hamlet and the John Donne who wrote "Anatomy of the World" ("'Tis all in pieces, all coherence gone; / All just supply, and all relation") but was a world unknown to the Plato who dramatized the life of Socrates. It was a world expressing a sensibility of alienation not simply from a society of archaic values that—as in the case of the ancient polis—had not yet realized its own demise, but from the realm, unique in history, that for five hundred years had been making and remaking the world in its own image. This world is a realm from which it is far more difficult to imagine an exodus than it was for the Israelites to conceive of an exodus from a society of conquerors. Paul Valéry had a vision of the difficulty in an address to "men of mind" in 1939—the year Hitler invaded Poland, one year after Voegelin had barely escaped from the Gestapo.

> The creation and organized existence of intellectual life have, at present, the most complex and yet the clearest and closest relation to life itself, to the whole of human life. No one, however, has explained the real point about us men, and our peculiarity which is mind. Mind is a certain power in us that has involved us in an extraordinary adventure; our species has diverged from all the original and normal conditions of life. We have made the world like the mind—and we want to live in this mind's world. The mind wants to live in what it has made.[44]

In identifying and exploring the differentiation between what the human mind has made—"this mind's world"—and what God has made as the central drama of modernity, Voegelin is both the teller in and the teller of the story of his age, both actor and author, and altogether a consummate representative of the story of the modern clerks—a story that in the deepest sense may be said to symbolize a grand negotiation between the past and present of Western civilization.

NOTES

1. Marion Montgomery, "Eric Voegelin as Prophetic Philosopher," *Southern Review*, n.s. 24 (January 1988): 115–33. Also see Stephen A. McKnight, *Sacralizing the Spiritual: The Renaissance Origins of Modernity* (Baton Rouge: Louisiana State University Press, 1989). McKnight's concept of "sacralization" is highly illuminating, especially with respect to the development of what I refer to in the course of the present remarks as the "secular-spiritual polity of letters and learning." See also McKnight, "Voegelin's New Science of History," in *Eric Voegelin's Significance for the Modern Mind*, ed. Ellis Sandoz (Baton Rouge: Louisiana State University Press, 1991), 46–70.

2. Herbert M. Read, "Julien Benda and the New Humanism," introduction to Julien Benda, *The Betrayal of the Intellectuals*, trans. Richard Aldington (Boston: Beacon Press, 1955). Benda's work was first published in Paris in 1927 as *La trahison des clercs*.

3. Valéry, "The Crisis of the Mind," in *The Outlook for Intelligence*, trans. Denise Folliot and Jackson Mathews (New York: Harper Torchbooks, 1963), 28–30. The punctuation of the quoted passage follows that of the Folliot and Mathews translation.

4. George Steiner, "Dream City," *New Yorker* 59 (January 28, 1985), a review essay of Broch's *Hugo von Hofmannsthal and His Time: The European Imagination, 1860–1920*, trans. and ed. Michael P. Steinberg (Chicago: University of Chicago Press, 1984).

5. Benda, *Betrayal of the Intellectuals*, 29–31.

6. Ibid., 31–33, 57, 129–30, 162–63.

7. Benda, *La fin de l'éternel* (Paris: Gallimard, 1928). Quoted in Read, "Benda and the New Humanism," in *Betrayal of the Intellectuals*, xxiv–xxv.

8. Ibid., xxv–xxvi.

9. Ellis Sandoz, *The Voegelinian Revolution: A Biographical Introduction* (Baton Rouge: Louisiana State University Press, 1981), 21–22.

10. Ibid..

11. Ibid., 22–23.

12. "Preface" to Voegelin, *Anamnesis*, trans. and ed. Gerhart Niemeyer (Notre Dame: University of Notre Dame Press, 1978), xxii.

13. "Editor's Preface" to Voegelin, *From Enlightenment to Revolution* (Durham, N.C.: Duke University Press, 1975), viii; see William C. Havard, "The Changing Patterns of Voegelin's Conception of History and Consciousness," *Southern Review*, n.s. 7 (January 1971): 49–67.

14. *Order and History*, vol. 4, *The Ecumenic Age* (Baton Rouge: Louisiana State University Press, 1987), 1, 57.

15. *From Enlightenment to Revolution*, 68.

16. Ibid., 7, 31, 10.

17. Ibid., 11, 32–33.

18. Ibid., 32, 34.

19. Ibid., 32–33, 59.

20. Ibid., 136–37, 159.

21. Ibid., 276.

22. Voegelin, *The New Science of Politics* (Chicago: University of Chicago Press, 1952), 74–75; see also 70, 73.

23. See Eduard Zeller, *Outlines of the History of Greek Philosophy* (New York: Meridian Books, 1955), 225 et passim.

24. Voegelin, *The New Science of Politics*, 100–106.

25. Ibid., 110–13.

26. Quoted in Hallowell, "Editor's Preface," *From Enlightenment to Revolution*, viii.

27. Quoted ibid., viii.

28. *The Ecumenic Age*, 269–70.

29. Voegelin, *Anamnesis*, trans. and ed. Gerhart Niemeyer (Notre Dame: Notre Dame University Press, 1978), 201.

30. See Lewis P. Simpson, "Federalism and the Crisis of Literary Order," *American Literature* 32 (November 1960): 255–57; also, see Simpson, *The Brazen Face of History* (Baton Rouge: Louisiana State University Press, 1980), 4–8.

31. See Alvin B. Kernan, *The Imaginary Library* (Princeton: Princeton University Press, 1982), 37–41.

32. Quoted in Malcolm Cowley, *And I Worked at the Writer's Trade* (New York: Viking Press, 1978), 264.

33. Quoted in Lewis P. Simpson, *The Man of Letters in New England and the South* (Baton Rouge: Louisiana State University Press, 1973), 229.

34. See Lewis P. Simpson, "The Critics Who Made Us: Allen Tate," *Sewanee Review* 94 (Summer 1986): 471–75.

35. See Simpson, "The Critics Who Made Us."

36. James Logenbach, *Modernist Poetics of History* (Princeton, N.J.: Princeton University Press, 1987), 27–28.

37. *Anamnesis*, 116.

38. Ibid., 117–18.

39. Ibid., 140.

40. Ibid., 189–90.

41. Ibid., 41–42, 50.

42. Ibid., 37; *Order and History*, vol. 2, *The World of the Polis* (Baton Rouge: Louisiana State University Press, 1957), 202.

43. *The World of the Polis*, 185, 202.

44. "Freedom of the Mind," *The Outlook for Intelligence*, 208–9.

THE BETRAYAL OF THE CLERKS
IN AMERICAN CONTEXT
Benjamin Franklin and Thomas Jefferson

Sometime after my retirement from the classroom a few years ago I was asked for an interview about my career. Flattered by the request, I half seriously indulged the fancy that I had reached the time when I might assume the role of a detached academic sage talking about American literary life as I had known it for half a century, albeit in a small way, not only through an editorial association of thirty-five years with the second series of the *Southern Review* but for a considerably longer time than that in my experiences as undergraduate and graduate student, would-be teacher, literary historian, and cultural critic in the academic field of American studies. But when I saw what I had said in print, I discovered that not only had my response to the interviewer been less than magisterial, it had taken a somewhat strident turn when he had asked, "Do you think it will ever be possible for another magazine to have the impact the original *Southern Review* had in its short life (1935–1942)? If so, what conditions might make this possible?" Let me quote from my reply:

> Frankly, no I don't think it possible; I can't imagine any future time when the possibility might exist. The historical circumstances cannot possibly rise again in the so-called postmodern age. This is a silly term. Modern means here and now, and you can't be post-now. But you can be anything if you assume that words don't mean anything, have nothing but ideological referents; and that has been the tendency of the past twenty years or so, certainly in the hothouse of American academe, and unfortunately language and literature have come to have almost the whole of their self-conscious existence in this rather fetid hothouse. Only in the most marginal sense is there a literary life left—the life that Hemingway and Faulkner knew, a life once lived in the printing houses, cafes, salons, and clubs of Paris and London and Rome and Berlin, and in a more limited fashion in Boston and New York, and even in little cities like Nashville, Tennessee,

and even in country towns like Oxford, Mississippi. This was the life I have attempted to describe in *The Brazen Face of History* and elsewhere, the life of the Republic of Letters. This was the secular yet spiritual community of minds that emerged with the ending of the medieval cast of mind. Out of it, I have argued, came the Declaration of Independence, the U.S. Constitution—also the Confederate Constitution. Out of the Republic of Letters, in other words, came the American Republic, which was an idea, not an ideology, though the difference between ideology and idea is hard to define, and idea is easily transformed into ideology.

Only one thing seems clear in this fumbling comment: the foolishness of any thought I had about making myself out to be a withdrawn interpreter of history. I could not pretend that I had escaped the disturbing sense of having spent half a century on American university campuses while much of the time feeling lost on familiar grounds. The source of this sense, one I think I share with any American academic humanist of my generation, is uncertain, even elusive. In a general way, however, it would seem to be our anxiety about the displacement—to be sure, the virtual disappearance in the twentieth century—of faith in the university as the embodiment of a transcendent realm of humanistic letters and learning. Although our anxiety about the loss of this faith prompts us to hold numerous conferences on the crisis of the university in America, when we look into its history in America, we may well conclude that our anxiety is an expression of nostalgia for a faith that was displaced by historical circumstances even at the beginning of the nation.

The concept of the realm of letters, a realm additional to those of church and state and independent of both—a "republic of letters"—originated in the eleventh and twelfth centuries with the beginning of the differentiation of the university as a realm apart from the realm that had created it, the ecclesiastical realm, the *res publica Christiana*. An aspect of the historical process in Western civilization Hegel described as the "secularization of the spiritual," the rise of the university was at first marked by the increasing inclination of "masters" in the medieval universities—i.e., "clerks" like Abelard, the most famous example—to recover the significance of the classic authors of a pagan antiquity. Drawing increasing numbers of students to study under them at the sites of learning in Paris, Bologna, Oxford, and elsewhere, masters and students provided for the rise of the medieval universities when, for their mutual protection and other benefits, they organized themselves as corporations. But as the humanistic movement became more definitive during the fourteenth and fifteenth centuries, it resulted in the formation of a novel order in history: a moral dominion, so to speak, of secularized clerks. In an age when the terms *letters* and *literature* referred to "knowledge in general" (as they did down to the time of Samuel Johnson's dictionary and beyond) the clerks became known as "men of letters," or, in the eighteenth century, by the French alternative "philosophes." Either term was comprehensive, embracing philosophers, scientists, poets, novelists, essayists, etc. By the seventeenth and eighteenth centuries the realm of men of letters was asserting its presence in history in myriad ways: in academies like the French Academy, the British Royal Academy, and the American Philosophical Society; in the literary and intellectual life associated with clubs, salons, coffee-houses, book stores, and printing shops; in the ever growing number of books and periodicals; and not least in the massive correspondence among men of letters. Bonded in "a fellowship of intellect, spread everywhere and everywhere independent," Voltaire declared in the mid-eighteenth century, the Republic of Letters had become a "great society of free minds."

Wherever they lived—in St. Petersburg, Leipzig, Paris, London, Edinburgh, Philadelphia, Boston, New York—the members of this society were dedicated, in the name of mind's capacity for rational inquiry, to a great critique not only to the state of our knowledge of God, man, and nature but to the question of how we acquire knowledge, to, that is, a critique of mind itself. This critique had one moment of fulfillment in the American Revolution and the subsequent invention by the American philosophes—Benjamin Franklin, Thomas Jefferson, John Adams, Alexander Hamilton, and others—of the Republic of the United States—the moment, so to speak, when out of the great critique came the Great Experiment. The great critique had another, and more violent, moment of fulfillment in the outbreak of the French Revolution, and the subsequent Reign of Terror, followed by the crowning of Napoleon as the emperor of France.

The relationship between the Republic of Letters and the "Great Experiment," as the new American republic was called, is illuminated, I think, when we recognize the formative centering of the life of the mind in our late colonial and early national epochs in two American philosophes: Benjamin Franklin and Thomas Jefferson.

Franklin is indissolubly associated with Philadelphia. But it is important to recall that he began his career as a man of letters in 1722 in Boston with the anonymous publication of *Dogood Papers* in the *New England Courant,* a weekly of news and opinion edited by his older brother James, to whom he had been apprenticed at the age of seven. When the seventeen-year-old Ben quarreled with James in 1823 and ran away to Philadelphia to seek his fortune, he left his literary mark on the place he was leaving in the satirical sketches that compose the *Dogood Papers.* In one sketch the fictitious author, Silence Dogood, the self-educated daughter of a country preacher who assumes the guise of a feminine Mr. Spectator, describes an allegorical dream vision in which Learning, attended by figures representing the Latin, Greek, and Hebrew languages, is seated on her "magnificent Throne" in the Temple of Learning writing the *New England Courant.* In the broad sense the message Silence conveys in her vision is a prophecy of what Franklin's massive career would represent, the freeing of letters and learning, not only in New England but generally, from the authority of the university tradition. Franklin gives a still more radical twist to his satire by imagining the observer of this triumph to be a self-made woman of letters, a type of what a later age would call a "feminist."

Had he had the privilege of attending Harvard, Franklin would probably have taken an attitude toward the university different from that he assumed in his early fable of learning. The basic motive of his youthful satire on Harvard may have been personal: his resentment of his exclusion by social status from, as one contemporary described it, the Boston-Cambridge "intercommunity of the learned." As it was, the largely self-educated Franklin, one of the greatest minds of the Enlightenment, began his education and his career simultaneously in a printing shop and always considered his vocation to be that of printer. But he was not a self-made man who discounted the value of formal education. He had spoofed the elitism of Harvard, not the value of a university education, and thirty years later, after his career in printing and other enterprises had rewarded him so well that he could afford to devote himself altogether to public service, he established the Academy of Pennsylvania in 1749, and in 1779 supported its transformation into the University of Pennsylvania. But Franklin had first turned his attention to the founding in 1742 of the American Philosophical Society. According to his perspective, the connection between the man of letters and the university was secondary to the role societies of men of letters had played in the rise of the great secular polity of letters celebrated by Voltaire. Meanwhile, Franklin was a participant in the rise of letters as a profession and in publishing as a business, activities conceived as essentially independent of both the university and associations such as the American Philosophical Society.

Self-consciously enacting the role of printer as man of letters, Franklin was aware that printing had become the most important activity in the Western world; but he was also aware that it marked the historical moment when the printer's art, having become sufficiently advanced to make the uniformity and repeatability of the printed word seem virtually analogous to a natural process, had transformed the image of the scripted word into the image of the printed word. With this transformation, Franklin was further aware that the basic distinction between literacy and illiteracy—between the man of letters and the man of no letters—was being replaced by a more subtle distinction between the man who has a vocation to letters and the man who, whether he has abundant or limited skills in reading and writing, simply employs his abilities as a necessity for getting along in the print society.

The mere ability to use letters being no longer a reliable guide to the difference between civilization and barbarism, a serious vocation to letters demanded from the man of letters a commitment to protect the literary republic from those who employed the knowledge of letters for the vulgar, and essentially immoral, purpose of merely getting on in the world. The quality of literacy, as in Pope's *The Dunciad*, became a central issue in the politics of the Third Realm. As literacy increased with the expansion of printing and as the quest for power through the use of the printed word became ever more important in modern history, the relationship between the politics of the political state and a politics of the literary order became ever more complex. Although it would not be defined explicitly until after the French Revolution, this relation centered in an analogy between what was conceived on the one hand to be the decorum of a "republic" and the disorder of a "democracy" on the other.

Franklin, who died just as the revolution in France was getting fully under way, never drew such an analogy. But as the new nation began its life as a federal republic in the decade following Franklin's death in 1790, a fear that the American Revolution might be transformed from a republican revolution into a democratic revolution seized American men of letters like the "American Addison," Joseph Dennie, a native Bostonian and graduate of Harvard, and arch Federalist, who in 1801 had transplanted himself in Philadelphia, where he founded a weekly periodical called *The Portfolio* and devoted himself to opposing the threat of the democratization of letters.

But the Federalist case against this threat was formulated less explicitly by Dennie than by the group of Boston-Cambridge men of letters, nearly all young, nearly all graduates of Harvard, who from 1803 to 1811 jointly edited the *Monthly Anthology and Boston Review.* In their effort to grasp the literary and intellectual situation in the new nation the Anthologists drew on a singular resource, a deeply felt regard for the nature and meaning of literacy as this had been expressed in Harvard's representation of the realm of letters and learning for a period now approaching two centuries.

Harvard's founding in 1636 had been an act motivated not only by the Puritan theocracy's determination to perpetuate in New England a learned ministry that in England, according to Michael Walzer, had acquired the status of an "intelligentsia," a "clerical third estate." Emphasizing values quite different from the burgher values of "sobriety, caution, and thrift," which have been misrepresented as the core of Puritan values, the seventeenth-century Puritan intelligentsia, Walzer points out, were moral activists imbued with the sense of "ascetic discipline" and "high-mindedness" that not only produced the great Puritan preachers but the great lay disciple John Milton, who, out of his concern that the "commonwealth" of letters, as he called it, not be "damnified" by the laws of the Puritan Commonwealth, wrote in *Areopagitica* a classic assertion of the moral authority of the polity of letters over a quest for power that at the extreme sought to reunify state, church, and letters as one seamless authority.

By the time of the Anthologists the issue of the separation of church and state in New England had largely become redundant, but the issue of the connection between the political state and the literary polity had become a consuming one. In their concern with this problem the Anthologists drew a direct analogy between politics and literature. In a Phi Beta Kappa Address delivered at Harvard in 1802 and later published in the *Monthly Anthology,* the Reverend Theodore Dehon asked, "Shall we be pardoned the expression if we . . . observe that through the innovating spirit of the times the republick of letters may have its dignity and prosperity endangered by sliding inadvertently into a democracy?" Responding to his own rhetorical question, Dehon pronounced that it "is with literature as with government. Neither is the subject of perpetual experiment. The principles of both are fixed. They spring from sources and have relations, which are unchangeable and eternal." In another Harvard Phi Beta Kappa Address published in the *Monthly Anthology* the most brilliant member of the Anthology circle, the Reverend Joseph Stevens Buckminster, appealed to a more complex analogy between politics and letters. Effective opposition to the democratization of letters in the new nation, he said, must recognize the paradoxical nature of the literary republic. In truth it is not antidemocratic, it is the "only permanent example" of a "pure and original democracy." But it is a democracy that exists only in its own self-defined boundaries.

> In this state under the protection of truth and reason, whose authority alone is acknowledged, wars may be carried on with the utmost innocence, though not always with impunity; for here every man is sovereign, and every man is also under the jurisdiction of every other. The laws of *civil society* have in no degree abridged the independence of the state of nature as to error and ignorance. No man can be excluded from the social compact because of his inalienable right to be a fool; and, on the other side, every man retains the right of the sword and may exercise it without a commission.

Buckminster's depiction of the polity of letters as a dominion in which those who champion "truth and reason" are perpetually engaged in warfare with those who, exercising their "inalienable right" to be fools, champion the dark forces of "error and ignorance" was inspired less by his adherence to Federalist politics as such than by his realization that, in a nation that had originated as a verbal invention, the relation between the politics of the literary order and the politics of the state was without historical precedent. The realm of letters and the realm of the state, the one being necessary to the other and vice versa, have been joined in something like a symbiotic relationship. Consequently, the perpetuation of the political state will involve generation after generation in a crisis of verbal interpretation, and men of letters will be responsible for the character of this interpretation. Moreover, in a nation not so much written as printed into history—a nation in which literacy seems destined to become universal and in which the power of interpretation no longer resides in the small group of men who possess letters in contrast to the majority of men who have no letters—the characters of interpretation will depend as never before on the *quality* of the literacy possessed by the interpreters.

In this situation the Federalist literati might well ask what hope there could be for letters and learning in a nation that had as its chief official a man of letters who not only supported the French Revolutionists but was capable of proclaiming, at least in one of his more extreme pronouncements, that a bloody revolution should occur each generation in order to "water" the "tree of liberty" with "the blood of martyrs." Ironically, however, in making Jefferson out to be a virtual Jacobin, New Englanders ignored the fact that, even if the term *democracy* was not a sacred word to him, he no more desired to see the Republic of Letters "slide" into a democracy of letters than they did. Although Jefferson had no college degree and was not quite a university man in the way the New Englander with a Harvard degree was, like his Boston-Cambridge enemies he assumed that the relationship between the realm of letters and the American republic basically subsisted not in the connection between the Franklinian academy and the state but between the university and the state. This assumption was owing in good part to the youthful Jefferson's association, while a student at the College of William and Mary for two years (prior to reading for the law with George Wythe), with a Scotsman of independent views, William Small. In contrast to the other members of the faculty, undistinguished Anglican clerics committed to maintaining the official connection between the Church of England and Virginia, Small, according to Jefferson, was a scholar "profound in most of the useful branches of science, with a happy talent of communication, correct and gentlemanly manners, and an enlarged and liberal mind." As one of his biographers says, Small made Jefferson into a lifelong disciple of the Enlightenment; and it may not be an exaggeration to say that the long years Jefferson spent devising plans for a state-supported university and persuading the Virginia legislature to fund it were a tribute to his brief sojourn at William and Mary under the tutelage of William Small.

"Mr. Jefferson's university" was not the first state university in the new nation. The University of North Carolina had been established by legislative act in 1776, but, viewed at its inception as primarily an instrument of the Federalist cause, it became hostage to the politics of the state for a hundred years or more. The University of Virginia affords the first historical instance in any country in which the university was deliberately and purposefully conceived as an agency of the realm of the secular state, yet as a realm of letters and learning was presumed to be independent of the state. Responding to the need to provide for the continuity of freedom in Virginia and the nation as a whole through the operation of the "free rights to the unbounded exercise of reason and opinion," the University of Virginia, as Jefferson initially envisioned it, would not only become a "bulwark of the mind in the western hemisphere" but would institutionalize a new kind of relationship between the state and the Third Realm. But this new relationship, it must be noted, would not be predicated on intellectual egalitarianism. According to Jefferson's plan, as the apex of a selective educational system that would provide all Virginia youths (white males, that is) with a basic education, the university would admit only those youths who had proven themselves to be members of the only aristocracy, the "natural aristocracy" of intellect. Upon graduation from the university, these young men would be entrusted with the welfare both of the political state and the Republic of Letters, and with the relationship between these realms.

Witnessing the first great crisis about the nature of the Federal Union over the question of whether the new state of Missouri should be admitted as a slave state or a free state, Jefferson had distinct intimations that the perilous and endless effort to answer the multiple questions about freedom and equality through legislative and judicial interpretations of the wording of the Constitution would defy the efforts of even the best-educated citizens.

Seeking to avert the catastrophe that would come with the collapse of these efforts, trying always to make the rational mind the model of society, Jefferson, led to some indeterminate extent by his understanding of the way in which the new nation had been invented through the power of secular letters, asserted the paradoxical centrality of the university, an *imperium in imperio* created and fostered by the imperium as the source of the educated citizenry necessary to nurture its conception of itself as a free political entity. But Jefferson did not contemplate that in nurturing freedom the state within the state would be allowed to endanger the state's existence. In 1820 he wrote a letter to a member of the Virginia Assembly pleading that funds for beginning the university be provided as soon as possible, for the institution was needed to fulfill the "holy charge" of "inculcating young minds with the principles of Virginia." He was, he said, especially concerned about the way in which Virginians were spending thousands of dollars to send their sons to Harvard and elsewhere, "there to imbibe opinions and principles in discord with those of their own country."

There is an interesting ambivalence in Jefferson's reference to "their country." Is it to Virginia, the South, or the whole nation? In any event, Jefferson's inclination to subordinate his professed dedication to unbounded freedom of the mind to the political order was not limited to the year of the Missouri crisis. It is graphically present in the anxious letters Jefferson exchanged with James Madison during the next five years about the courses of instruction to be offered by the University of Virginia and the recruitment of its faculty. While in general these letters show that both subscribed to the policy of making the university a place where no one should be "afraid to follow truth wherever it may lead, nor to tolerate error so long as reason is left free to combat it," they also reveal a consistent qualification of the pursuit of truth. Jefferson and Madison were especially fearful of allowing unguarded freedom of thought in the case of the branch of the university in which the relation between literature and politics was the most intimate, the law school.

In an eloquent argument to the Board of Visitors about the appropriateness of inviting eminent Europeans to assume professorships at the University of Virginia, Jefferson had said that "with scientists and men of letters, the globe itself is one great commonwealth, in which no geographical divisions are acknowledged; but all compose one fraternity of fellow citizens." But looking at the list of those who were at one time or another considered to be possibilities for the law professorship, we find that, in contrast to the cosmopolitan breadth of the names that came up in connection with other appointments, the list of candidates for this professorship is distinctly "geographical," all of the real possibilities being Virginians. As a matter of fact, Jefferson and Madison never intended to be anything but parochial in the selection of the law professor. Basing his conception of "orthodoxy" in a teacher of law on whether or not he exhibits a devotion to the principle of freedom exemplified by what Madison referred to as the "Virginia Creed," Jefferson had said at the beginning of the search for the faculty of the university that "our professor of law must be a native," and he meant of Virginia. He stipulated this because he believed that "nearly all" the young men who had recently entered "the nursery of our Congress" (i.e., the nursery of the legal profession) in recent years had been corrupted by the reliance on the "toryism" of the universally used law text, Blackstone's *Commentaries*. It was up to the University of Virginia to address the shortcoming of a legal education that had led youths to "suppose themselves . . . to be whigs, because they no longer know what whiggism or republicanism means." The teaching of the true character of "republicanism" will ensure that "in a dozen or twenty years a majority of our own legislature, and many disciples will have carried its doctrines home with them to their states, and will have leavened thus the whole mass."

Since the imparting of "true" political doctrines would be of prime importance to the formation of the "character of our state, and the U.S.," Jefferson asserted that he and Madison not only had the "duty to lay down the principles which are to be taught" in the law school but to prescribe the legal texts to be consulted by the students. To this end he made a mandatory list of the texts to be used. It included items ranging from the writings of Locke and Sidney to the Declaration of Independence to *The Federalist* to "the Virginia Document of 1799" (the resolution passed by the Virginia Assembly during the administration of John Adams denouncing the Alien and Sedition Acts).

Madison was not so adamant as Jefferson in seeking the assurance of "political purity," or as it might be put today, "political correctness," in the teaching of law. He suggested that instead of being regarded as prescriptive the works on Jefferson's list be considered simply the "best guides" for the law students. But Madison and Jefferson alike were adamant in their agreement that, in Madison's words, "the most effectual safeguard against heretical intrusions into the School of Politics" will "be an Able and Orthodox Professor, whose course of instruction will be an example to his successors"—so adamant, in fact, that when the University of Virginia opened its doors for the first time on March 7, 1825, the law professorship was still vacant. It would be another year before the faculty of the fledgling university was completed with the "safe" appointment of one of the less distinguished candidates to the law professorship. Yet Jefferson and Madison undoubtedly saw this appointment as marking the completion of a faculty roster that was a true representation of the Republic of Letters.

Two decades after Jefferson's death, his prediction that in "a dozen or twenty years" the teaching of the true principles of republicanism at the University of Virginia would "leaven" opinion, not only in Virginia but also in other states, came to ironic fulfillment. Citizens of the southern states decided that to preserve the "truth" of the union of American states—to continue to foster, as Jefferson had said, "our habit of thinking of our country as one and indivisible"—it had become mandatory to insist that the American Republic is based on the paradoxical principle that the preservation of the institution of chattel slavery is necessary to the preservation of freedom. Since the citizens of the northern half of "the one and indivisible nation" did not agree, southerners invented a southern nation, a southern civil religion, and a southern literary polity. In its representation of the southern nation the University of Virginia, committed to defending, and if possible extending, its "politically correct" version of liberty, fulfilled Jefferson's trust that "our Seminary" would keep alive what he called the "Vestal flame" of freedom and Madison called "the sacred fire" of freedom.

As he designed and attended to the construction of the academical village that is still cherished as the historical center of what would become known as "the Grounds of Mr. Jefferson's University," Jefferson, failing to recognize that he was even then using the institution he envisioned as an agency of the cosmopolitan Republic of Letters as in effect a political agency of the state, was lost on his own grounds. If we today recognize the irony of Jefferson's situation, it is because we are aware that the association between the university and the political state has drastically changed in character. The period in modern history when the subscription of intellectuals to faith in the idealism of the Republic of Letters was sufficient to maintain a generative tension between the existential political republic and the symbolic Republic of Letters now seems to have been remarkably brief. Writing in the dark aftermath of the First World War, the French critic Julien Benda argued vividly in his once notorious *La trahison des clercs* that the decline of faith in the cosmopolitan polity of mind and letters was owing to "the treason" the "clerks" (or the intellectuals) committed when they not only accepted but glorified the nationalization of the literary polity.

Yet the influence of nationalism may be reckoned as secondary to another, if closely related, phenomenon in the decline of the symbolic power of the Republic of Letters in the nineteenth and twentieth centuries, namely, the progressive loss of the identity of the Third Realm that has occurred in the struggle to effect a radical democratization of letters and learning. The central issue with respect to the character of the American university, we may well conclude, was defined in the beginning of the nation—no more so by the conservative Federalist literati than by Jefferson and the "liberal literati"—as the opposition between the idea of a "republic of letters" and the idea of an egalitarian "democracy of letters." For a century and a half after the founding of the nation the dynamics of the opposition between these concepts of the literary and intellectual realm—an opposition involving the most fundamental conflict in American culture, freedom versus equality—constituted a meaningful quarrel in American culture. The quarrel sustained a sense of connection with the literary origin of the nation in the revolutionary inquiry, not only into knowledge but into consciousness itself, that had been undertaken with progressive diligence by the secular realm of letters and learning. With the decline of the Third Realm as the major symbol of modernity, the university in America has lost its sense of identity as a representation of faith in the ideal dominion of letters and learning as this was known to Franklin, Jefferson, and the other makers of the American Republic. And, as a consequence, the American university campus has lost its capacity to serve as the scene of the moral and intellectual, the humanistic process of political self-interpretation necessary to the functioning of a nation invented by the Republic of Letters.

There is even yet a tendency to assume—perhaps this assumption is the chief motive of the National Endowment for the Humanities—that we can restore the status of the humanities in America through somehow recovering the generative tension in American cultural history between a "republic of letters" and "democracy of letters." But in our historical moment, when the utilization of the scientific knowledge and techniques developed by university scientists is deemed by Washington to be essential not only to the enhancement of national power but to the very preservation of the nation, it is difficult to imagine how such a recovery could occur. The only truly meaningful connection that presently exists between the university and Washington is necessarily the one that exists between the relation of the university to a major educational agency of the government, the National Science Foundation.

DAYS OF FAITH
Malcolm Cowley and the Legend of the Fellow Travelers

In the 1930s one of my uncles on my mother's side of the family ran a soup-and-gospel mission in a dilapidated district of Fort Worth, Texas. A member of a farming family that had moved to the city, he had become a successful new-car salesman in the 1920s and was well on his way toward middle-class affluence, when he suddenly gave up the trading life for a call to the Christian ministry. Following a period of schooling he was ordained by the Methodist Church; but moved by increasingly strong fundamentalist leanings, within two or three years he rebelled against the "modernist" tendencies of urban Methodism, resigned as the assistant pastor of a well-established Methodist congregation in Fort Worth, and went to Chicago to attend the Moody Bible Institute and serve as a preacher in the missions of the Southside slums. By now he conceived his ministry to be nonsectarian and completely independent. A year or two later, alienated not only from his former denominational affiliation but from the very concept of such affiliation, he returned to Fort Worth, where, aided by a charismatic personality, he soon attracted a following and founded what he called simply and grandly The Church.

The visible manifestation of The Church was a modest structure in a middle-class area of the city, where my uncle presided over a faithful congregation he had converted to his vision of salvation. At the same time he felt compelled to continue his ministry to the poor, and as the Great Depression of the 1930s worsened and the jobless and the dispossessed took increasingly to the road, he established a mission in an unused warehouse the owner was willing to give to the glory of the Lord until times got better. Here hundreds of nameless men, white and black—the building was divided into separate quarters for the races—were provided thin soup made with over-age vegetables (courtesy of local grocers), week-old bread (courtesy of local bakers), a temporary place to sleep, and all the spiritual sustenance my uncle could force down them.

My uncle, I remember, always had a few disciples in training. One of them I recall in particular. A young man, slight of build with sallow complexion and anxious pale blue eyes, he was the live-in director of the mission. My recollection of him centers on a scene one cold December afternoon—it must have been in 1933—when I happened to be at the mission having sought out my uncle, not for religious reasons (by this time I was too torn between doubt and faith to be easily susceptible to my uncle's kind of commitment) but to fulfill some family errand. That afternoon the disciple was worried about the black guests, who had begun to hold religious sessions on their own, during which they stomped on the floor with enough force to shake the building. This brought impolite protests from the white guests. When asked about what should be done, my uncle's response was prompt: individuals could pray at will, but there was to be no singing or organized religious expression except as directed by the mission (and no foot-stomping ever). The disciple still looked worried. He himself had obviously already issued such a directive to no avail. There was a long silence. The disciple seemed to have become transfixed. I followed his gaze through a dirty plate-glass window toward a bank of gray clouds moving swiftly across the drab skyline before a chilling Texas norther. Suddenly, with a flat yet terrible intensity, he broke the silence: "My, I wish the Lord would come today!" After a little, my uncle said "Amen," and the disciple went back to the kitchen.

I might add another, slightly exotic, element to that faraway moment of apocalyptic longing. Although I cannot be certain, on that cold afternoon fifty years ago I may have been wearing an elegant, double-breasted black wool overcoat that had belonged to a deceased Chicago gangster. It had come to me earlier that year, or maybe the year before, as a hand-me-down gift from my uncle; it had come to him as a gift from the dead gangster's girlfriend, who, having somehow heard of my uncle, had asked him to conduct her lover's funeral after his body had been discovered dumped in an alley somewhere on the Southside. He had performed the funeral office on a bitter midwinter day, the services being attended only by two living persons besides himself, the girlfriend and a sinister-looking guy who, my uncle surmised, might well have been the assassin come to see his work confirmed. As they left the graveside, the bereaved girlfriend had asked my uncle to visit her at a fashionable address on Lakeshore Drive. When he arrived a day or so later, she told him that on the night her lover was murdered she had seen a vision of Christ on the Cross and now believed that she had entered into a redeemed life. He prayed with her, and when he rose to leave, she asked him to remain long enough to take whatever he might want from a closet full of expensive male apparel. Shivering through a second Chicago winter in a flimsy outer coat, he overcame mixed revulsion and pride and picked out one item, the warmest coat in the closet. It was the kind you once saw gangsters wearing in 1930s movies, a dressy black overcoat with a handkerchief pocket. It was a bit tight, but he made do with it. After he gave it to me I wore it when Texas northers hit, until I managed to acquire a less costly but more modish trench coat. I don't remember for sure what happened to the gangster's coat. I think my mother gave it away. Occasionally I fancy I see it in an old gangster film.

I bring up this inconsequential recollection because it came back to me when I read *The Dream of the Golden Mountains: Remembering the 1930s,* Malcolm Cowley's account of American writers in the early years of the Great Depression. This is not to say that I recalled the story of the gangster's funeral because Cowley tells any stories about gangsters in his account of the thirties. Gangsterism had no appreciable impact on the life he knew in that time. Everyone, he recalls, walked city streets—in his case mostly the streets of New York—which were far safer than they are today. Nor does Cowley recollect that preachers or priests, save in the instance of the fascist-minded Father Coughlin of Detroit, played conspicuous roles in the history of 1930s. The impression in *The Golden Mountains* that a vital political alliance between religion and the jobless in America did not exist is, I think, correct. My uncle's disciple (if I may intrude one further personal memory) left the mission to fill the pulpit of a small congregation in a workers' district. When he began to appear in bib overalls on Sunday mornings the effect was so novel that the local newspaper ran a picture of him in the pulpit attired in proletarian garb. To my uncle, his disciple's behavior probably seemed both heretical and socially dangerous. By this time he had begun to question the doctrinal soundness of sponsoring a mission for the dispossessed, and in another year or so gave up feeding the poor save with spiritual food. Assuming a nonsocial, wholly antinomian position, he preached only the apocalyptic message of "Christ and Him crucified," the imminence of the Second Coming, and the bitterness and rapture attending the Last Judgment. Taking to the radio, he created a modest evangelical empire in Texas and Oklahoma. As for the disciple, the newspaper photograph is my last recollection of him; but I would imagine that he soon gave up the overalls, returned to the conventional business suit of the evangelical Protestant minister, and devoted himself also to proclaiming the one imperative of salvation: Believe in Christ and Him crucified for the redemption of our sins.

My memory of my personal experience of the thirties, including the recollection of my uncle and his disciple, coalesces with Cowley's remembrance of the Great Depression as an age in which a number of American writers experienced the allure of conversion to an apocalyptic political faith that promised the rebirth of American society out of the body of the death that it had become. It was in the very world of the Chicago gangsters and Moody missionaries in which my uncle had preached that Richard Wright first attended a meeting of the John Reed Club and was introduced to *Left Front*, the club magazine. Responding to a passionate plea in one of the articles he read to redeem (in Wright's words) "the experiences of the disinherited," Wright began his literary career by writing a series of social-protest poems for Communist periodicals. But, as Cowley says, the conversion of Wright to Communism, followed by his admission to membership in the Party, did not represent the typical conversion experience undergone by American writers. A black migrant from Mississippi, Wright arrived at the door of the John Reed Club as one who had never known anything but the poverty-stricken, repressed world of southern blacks. According to Cowley, far more often the literary converts to Communism were middle-class Americans, who "felt a personal need to bury the corrupt past and be reborn into a new life." American writers "had been too idle, so it seemed to them, and perhaps too fortunate."

> Poor as most of them were, they had profited indirectly from the bond-salesman's racket. They had let themselves be bribed into acquiescence by publishers' contracts and penthouse parties and weekends on the north shore of Long Island. Even when they had escaped to Europe, they had been corrupted by the mood of the times, and now, back in New York, they dreamed of changing everything in the world and in their hearts. They wanted to bury the corrupt past and be reborn into a new life. After all, that is one of the oldest dreams, expressed in the rituals of great religions.[1]

Seeking "a faith that would supply certain elements heretofore lacking in their private and professional lives," American writers discovered that the Marxian vision of history offered the solution not only to the political and economic problems of the time but to its "moral and personal" problems. Yet, even though caught up in the dream of transforming not only themselves but the world, they generally did not seek membership in the Communist Party. Nor did the Party encourage them to seek it. Regarding their commitment to the faith as unreliable, the Party believed a more valuable, and safer, role for American writers to play in promoting the cause of world socialist revolution would be that of active sympathizers or, in a name that was invented for the purpose, "fellow travelers." The full significance of Cowley's version of the story of the fellow travelers in *The Golden Mountains* emerges when we understand it as a continuation of the story of his life and of his generation that he had begun in his very first book, a volume of poems entitled *Blue Juanita* (1929). When he gave me the augmented edition of this book, *Blue Juanita: Collected Poems* (1968), he inscribed on the fly leaf: "This record of a Life." Perhaps, as Hans Bak suggests, in imitation of Whitman and Baudelaire, Cowley intended to write the inner history of his life and of his generation in a series of poems that in effect would be a single poem. Although no doubt in a more limited way than he had originally hoped, he fulfilled his intention in 1985 when he added the poems he had written since 1968 to a final collection he entitled *Blue Juanita: A Life*.

Yet although Cowley referred to himself as critic and poet, and at times as literary historian, his vocation is more accurately described, as Hans Bak further suggests, by the inclusive term "man of letters."[2] In his self-conscious enactment of the role of man of letters Cowley became the moral historian, even in a sense the moral conscience, of his generation. But he played his role in twentieth-century American letters largely in the carefully crafted prose of his innumerable essays and reviews and his seven books. The books date from 1934, when he published his best-known work, *Exile's Return: A Narrative of Ideas*. The 1951 edition of this work—with a new subtitle, *A Literary Odyssey of the 1920s*; a considerably revised text; and a significant retrospective "Epilogue"—has its own identity and may in effect be considered another rendering of the story told in the first *Exile's Return*. There followed two collections of essays, both edited by Henry Dan Piper with the collaboration of the author: *Think Back on Us: A Contemporary Chronicle of the 1930s* (1967), a collection of essays from the *New Republic* during the years of Cowley's association with its literary department; and *A Many-Windowed House: On American Writers and American Writing* (1970), a collection of essays from various sources of original publication other than the *New Republic*.

As *A Many-Windowed House* convincingly demonstrates, Cowley wrote important essays on subjects besides writers and writing in the twenties and thirties, but the central motive in his writing reveals itself as his constant sense of the need to interpret and reinterpret what he regarded as the most crucial years of his own life and the life of his generation. The second version of *Exile's Return*—in which Cowley sees the writers of the twenties as "interwoven into a larger pattern of exile and return from exile, of alienation and reintegration," larger even than he had grasped in the first version of *Exile's*—anticipates the purpose of what he planned as the culminating and final work of his career: a comprehensive rendering of the story of the twenties and thirties, in which he would not only delineate the character of American writers and writing in the twenties and thirties but would define the historical relation between these decades.[3]

The initial volume of this undertaking, *A Second Flowering: The Life and Times of the Lost Generation* (1973), redefines the generation of the 1920s as one that in its alienation from its homeland paradoxically "found" itself, and in finding itself created a literary renaissance in American letters comparable to the literary flowering in the age of Emerson, Hawthorne, Melville, and Whitman. A third collection of essays, originally published in various places, in 1978, *And I Worked at the Writer's Trade: Chapters of Literary History, 1918–1978*, may be read as something like a supplement both to *A Second Flowering* and to *The Dream of the Golden Mountains*. Published in 1982, this volume recounts the story of what happened in the first half of the Great Depression decade, when the American writers known as "fellow travelers" sought to envision the salvation of America through faith in communism, in particular, Russian Communism. Cowley intended to follow *The Dream of the Golden Mountains* with a sequel, in which he would trace the decline of the revolutionary faith in the later thirties amid the bitter controversies that arose among the fellow travelers. But although he published two or three essays that were intended to be chapters of this work, it remained uncompleted when Cowley died nine years later at the age of eighty-seven. The reason why may perhaps be partly explained by the problems of advancing age. But the basic reason may well have been that, as he indicated to me at the time he completed *The Golden Mountains*, it was going to be much more difficult to write an account of the years when a dwindling number of fellow travelers were trying to hold on to what was left of their faith in the Marxist vision in the face of its utter degradation by Stalinist Russia.

Although it is never put quite this way in *The Golden Mountains*, an underlying motive in the attraction the Communist cause held for Cowley and others like him was an assumed equation between the inherited vision of America as a world-redemptive nation and the vision of Russian Communism as the redemption of world history. This equation is implicit in Cowley's emphasis on various images of aspiration and hope the fellow travelers subscribed to. The most prominent and vitalizing of these in the early thirties was the heady vision of American workers and American writers joined in a "revolutionary brotherhood" that, becoming worldwide, would in a foreseeable future ensure the well-being of all humanity. Cowley recalls that his initial involvement in the "movement" occurred in April 1931, when he attended a meeting of a varied group of writers and journalists in Theodore Dreiser's "studio" on West Fifty-seventh Street in New York. The following year he made a "public confession" of faith in the Communist cause when he marched down Broadway in his first May Day parade.

> I would never be more than a fellow traveler, yet I was an ardent one at the time, full of humility, the desire to serve, and immense hopes for the future. Because any disaster seemed possible in that year, so did any triumph. Suddenly the range of possibilities had widened and deepened, as had the picture of our relation to history. It was as if we had been walking for years in a mist, on what seemed to be level ground, but with nothing visible beyond a few yards, so that we became preoccupied with the design of things close at hand—friendships, careers, love affairs—and then as if the mist had blown away to reveal that the level ground was a terrace, that chasms lay on all sides of us, and that beyond them were mountains rising into the golden sunlight. We could not reach the mountains alone, but perhaps we could merge ourselves in the working class and thereby help to build a bridge for ourselves and for humanity.[4]

A common feeling among American writers in the thirties, Cowley says, was that the historical moment had arrived when "great" economic, political, and social changes *must* take place, and "it was our duty as writers to take part in them, at least by coming forward to bear witness."

In bearing witness in *The Golden Mountains* to what had happened thirty or forty years ago, Cowley impresses the reader as being confident in the accuracy of his memory of the animating idealism of the fellow travelers, which was to build a bridge to the future for "ourselves and humanity." Yet he acknowledges a certain ambivalence in the point of view from which he unfolds the story:

> I say "we" and "us" while conscious of their being treacherous pronouns; any reader is entitled to ask, "Who is *we*?" The question had been fairly simple to answer in *Exile's Return,* where the first person plural usually referred to those of my own age group with literary ambitions. . . . After 1930 most of my coevals were going their separate ways, and they also had younger rivals in the writing community, which was by then more than

usually rife and riddled with dissensions. There were still general statements to be made about the climate of opinion as it changed for all of us, but plainly the author of this new book would have to be more careful with his "we's," replacing many of them with a straightforward "I"—or even with "they," when he was thinking about the larger community of puzzled Americans. He would have to be more objective—and more subjective too, out of a feeling that one man is always representative when he gives testimony about what he has felt and observed.[5]

Endeavoring to be at once more objective and more subjective in offering testimony about what he "felt and observed" in the 1930s, Cowley seems at the beginning of *The Dream of the Golden Mountains* to wish to portray himself as a representative or characteristic figure in the group of writers who may be identified as fellow travelers. But straightaway he asks, what kind of person is "that author, that observer" who assumes in the 1970s that he can be "candid" about what he was like in the 1930s? Lacking both in intellectual sophistication and social credentials, Cowley says, the person who wrote *The Dream of the Golden Mountains,* compared to other writers he was associated with, was an unrepresentative figure of the times, "less typical, even of his own group, than he once fancied himself to be."

He had a farmer's blunt hands. "Look at the hands if you get a chance," that man of elegant letters, John Peale Bishop, wrote to his Princeton friend Edmund Wilson. "The plowboy of the western world who has been to Paris." The plowboy admitted that he was awkward, credulous, either rash or exuberant at moments, and usually persistent (or would you call it stubborn?). He never forgot that he came of people without pretensions, not quite members of the respectable middle class. He was slow of speech and had a farmer's large silences, though he was not slow-witted; people were fooled sometimes. He mentally revised his words, often until the moment had passed to utter them. Perhaps one might call him a wordsmith essentially, working at his forge and anvil, devoted to the craft of hammering his thoughts into what he had hoped would be lasting shapes.[6]

Though there is an element of truth in Cowley's self-portrait, it is largely a poetic fiction. He was not a farmer's son nor did he ever do any farming. His family lived most of the year in the industrial city of Pittsburgh, where his rather feckless father was a homeopathic physician with a modest practice. But Dr. Cowley did own a small farm located not far from the city, where the family would take up residence in the summers (the father coming out for weekends). Although he attended to no more than a few simple chores while residing on the farm, such as tending to the two horses on the place, Cowley liked to give the impression that his character as a writer owed a good deal to his having been brought up under the austere conditions of small-farm life, when the truth was that he lived most of each year in the city, attended good schools in Pittsburgh, and later went to Harvard. The fiction of a rural upbringing comported with his observation that, unlike "many of his colleagues," he was lacking in "worldly ambitions," not wanting to be rich or famous too soon, or occupy a place of influence, or be a leader. He "simply" had two ambitions: "to write better than others" and "to survive as a free man, an independent observer." [7]

In his self-conscious play on Bishop's satirical characterization of him as a lowly plowboy (who for sake of a metaphor is transformed into to a village blacksmith), Cowley implies a metaphorical connection between his role as a writer (a "wordsmith," a literary artisan) marching in the ranks of a revolutionary brotherhood of American workers and writers toward the golden mountains and the fabled power of America to redeem those who respond to the call issued at the end of the American Revolution by Thomas Jefferson and by his French contemporary St. John de Crèvecoeur: Come out of Europe and be saved. This appeal is best known in its classic formulation in *Letters from an American Farmer,* in which Crèvecoeur invites the European to free himself from the death-in-life that is the Old World—from "involuntary idleness, servile dependency, penury, and useless labour"—and to go to the New World to be "born again on his American freehold" and become a "new man . . . acting upon new principles," entertaining "new ideas," and forming "new opinions."

In broad poetic frame *The Golden Mountains*—in its way a deeply personal story about the author's experience of having been for a time caught up in the fable of the American as redeemer—turns on Cowley's ironic awareness of the fallibility of the redemptive role assumed by American writers, when, abandoning faith in the dream of finding literary and artistic salvation in Europe, they returned to their native land to dream of finding an alternative salvation in a dream of social redemption. As American artisans of the word, they would become participants in a great social revolution. Joining with the dispossessed farmers of the Dust Bowl, the striking coal miners in Kentucky, and the striking steelworkers in Pittsburgh, they would become part of a world historical revolutionary brotherhood marching toward the golden mountains singing "The International."

But although in their feeling of brotherhood with the workers the fellow travelers felt they were expressing their "deep concern" for the violation of "human values" by the capitalistic society, they had a hard time defining with precision the values they subscribed to. This was not only because they belonged to a society that, lacking a proletariat, a bourgeoisie, or an aristocracy of blood in the European sense, has always resisted definition in terms of Marxian analysis. It was also because they were not fundamentally interested in politics. Although they had exiled themselves in post–World War I Europe—which, everywhere in political and economic disarray, would shortly see the fateful rise of Stalin, Mussolini, and Hitler—they had by and large in the time of their exile taken no interest in Marxism or in any kind of political or economic ideology, revolutionary or otherwise. Like American writers before them—Henry James the most notable example—in coming to Europe they were basically moved by the desire to identify themselves with the life of a long-established literary culture. This was life of the culture formed and shaped by the secular community of writers during the past four or five centuries, and, in its ideal conception of itself, it constituted a realm of its own apart from state and church.

One of the most interesting facets of *The Golden Mountains* is that here, more than in his earlier inquiries into the twenties and thirties, Cowley exposes the connection between the faith of American writers in the realm of high art on the one hand and their faith on the other in a radical politics that led "most of the writers" he knew to regard "even the body of liberal opinion" represented by a Norman Thomas as "entirely too moderate." "They had been formed by the tradition of the 1920s, which was to despise the moderates and admire the authors who went to extremes: Flaubert, Dostoevsky, James Joyce. Now the standard of judgment was being extended to the political world, so that some of their favorite words acquired new meanings. 'Bourgeois' was one of the bad words, applied first to enemies of art and now to the enemies of the workers."

"'Revolution,'" Cowley continues, "had been a good word for writers in the 1920s." There had been "*la révolution surréaliste* and the Revolution of the Word"; now through the union of radical literary and social motives "there would be a total revolution."[8] Cowley's notion in *The Golden Mountains* that the "total revolution" produced by joining the Revolution of the Word (a twentieth-century version of the nineteenth-century Symbolist movement) to the political and social revolution of the thirties would seem to repudiate his conception in *Exile's Return* that the American literary exiles of the twenties discovered their initial inspiration to social engagement in the thirties in a reaction against the emptiness of a decadent European religion of art. The fellow travelers tended not so much to reject their dedication to the religion of art as, equating the literary artist's disdain for the bourgeois and the proletarian contempt of the bourgeois, to assimilate the religion of art to their new dedication to the revolutionary ethos.

We may single out two cogent illustrations of the union of artistic and socialist motivation in Cowley's essay-reviews for the *New Republic* in the thirties. One of these is a comment on a translation of *Flowers of Evil* by George Dillon and Edna St. Vincent Millay. Expressing his general dissatisfaction with this latest effort to render Baudelaire in English, the literary editor of the *New Republic* (who had begun his career as a student of the French Symbolists) devotes half his space to the bohemian social revolutionist Baudelaire, who was for six years "a comrade of the struggling poets and painters, . . . shared their hopes for overthrowing the bourgeois government," and "risked his life three times on the barricades." Although Baudelaire later became "aloof and conservative," the effect of his "revolutionary years," Cowley says, "survived in his life and in his poems."

> For him to turn violently away from politics was already one effect that he shared with other poets—indeed, the whole Symbolist movement was partly an outgrowth of the defeated revolution. But beyond this a new quality appeared and persisted in his work, a tenderness toward the poor and deep sympathy with people who suffer. It might even be said that the physical realism of his poems was connected with his revolutionary experiences; he sometimes writes with a direct earthiness very close to the spirit of the French working class. And that realism helps to explain his literary excellence.[9]

Another instance in his *New Republic* writings in which Cowley links literary artistry and the rejection of bourgeois capitalism is even more significant. Reviewing Franz Mehring's *Karl Marx: The Story of His Life* in 1936, he holds up Marx as a model of the revolutionary man of letters:

> As man of letters, Marx was a Romantic of the second generation, the spiritual contemporary of Baudelaire and Flaubert. Like them he toiled at his desk—corrected, recopied, recorrected—and published nothing till he was

sure of its absolute rightness. Like them he took pride in his isolation and his neglect by the conventional world: like them he despised the rabble of the half-educated. He reviled the bourgeois in a double sense, both as economic exploiters and as the enemies of honest writing. He suffered both as a rebel among reactionaries and as a genius among the philistines. The revolution he desired was one that would not only free the proletariat from its chains of wage slavery, but also the creative spirit from its chains of convention.[10]

Telling the story of the American writers in the early depression years as one man lived and observed them, Cowley presents a complex drama of conflicting motives in *The Golden Mountains*. The drama may be interpreted as deeply personal in nature. Indeed, only partially softened by the tone of mellow memorializing, Cowley's account of the thirties prompts tough questions about his motives in that time. What really made Cowley employ his literary skills in the grubby service of the workers' revolution? What exactly was the imperative that sent him to the dangerous coal fields of Harlan County, Kentucky, involved him in the National Hunger March on Washington, and directed him again and again to march in May Day parades in New York City; or what impelled him night after night in dingy New York meeting halls to propagandize for causes sponsored by the Communists before small audiences seated on rows of folding chairs he himself had to help set up and dismantle? But the most telling question readers of *The Golden Mountains* and its immediate predecessor, *And I Worked at the Writer's Trade: Chapters of Literary History, 1918–1978*, have asked is, why did Cowley remain committed to Stalinist Russia in the later thirties, when Edmund Wilson and other erstwhile fellow travelers had experienced a complete deconversion? Was his faithfulness to the cause of social revolution the result of folly compounded by stubbornness? Or was Cowley in actuality a hard-core Stalinist?

The latter possibility is so implausible that one may incline to the view that Cowley was in truth simply a singularly recalcitrant American "plowboy," who had stubbornly subscribed to a false dogma after the more sophisticated American literati had for the most part recognized its true character. But Cowley the "wordsmith" was not unsophisticated. Like his colleague Edmund Wilson, the author of *Exile's Return* self-consciously assumed that as a writer he was an agent of the moral government of society. It was an assumption that, descending through a long line of secularized, or humanist, scholars and critics, had achieved decisive expression in the relation between men of letters and the French and American revolutions. In the next century Marx and Engels, the inheritors of Voltaire and Condorcet, and of Franklin and Jefferson, conceived that a world historical socialist revolution would be the inevitable culmination of the quest for power in the name of liberty, equality, and fraternity. If, in identifying himself with the modern literary drive for power, the writer went no further than to alienate himself from the philistinism of the middle class, he might, like Joyce, transform the will to literary power into a desire to make the literary artist the godhead of literary art. But if a writer as "clerk" assumed the transcendent cosmopolitanism of the modern literary vocation and shared the conviction that the literary mind is the proper source and model of history, he might, like Eliot, identify himself with the alienation of classical-Christian culture from modern industrial and technological culture and become an advocate of the authority of tradition. Following the logic of Ezra Pound, such a writer might even project the championing of the fascist state as the emblem of the restoration of an authoritative cultural tradition. Another writer, estranged from his or her society by contempt for bourgeois values, might well find a sense of community in an identification with the workers of the world, who, as they are depicted in Marxism, are alienated from their work by the capitalist system. Such a writer, conceiving the socialist culture of Russia to be more in harmony with the work of the writer than the capitalist culture of the United States, might well believe that an association with the world mission of communism held the promise of the social empowerment of the writer.

In *Exile's Return* Cowley refers to "The Revolution of the Word," a manifesto published in 1929 in *transition* that asserted: "The literary creator has the right to disintegrate the primal matter of words imposed on him by textbooks and dictionaries." Reacting to the manifesto as simply another "funny" gesture of the time, Cowley did not sign it, and recalls that, according to his own testimony, Hart Crane was drunk when he did. But treating "The Revolution of the Word" more seriously in *The Golden Mountains,* Cowley in effect declares that the authors of the 1929 manifesto were participants in a significant quest for literary power. The manifesto's faith in the power of the word to create works of art that have "an organic shape," and thus are not only capable of a life "apart" from the lives of their makers but of "outliving" both their makers and the time of their making, was "transformed," Cowley says, into faith in the power of the word to inaugurate the revolution of the workers that will create a perfect social order. Moved by such a faith, writers—even those like him who were not Party members but were simply fellow travelers—renounced the exacting art of "making patterns out of words for the easier task of writing cautionary tales and artless sermons."

> [This] might possibly be explained by a parallel that was seldom mentioned, although it may have been present in many minds. Communism was antireligious, true, but even party members often pictured it as the new scientific faith that would take the place of Christianity. Hence, the two might bear the same resemblance as the opposite poles of a magnet. The millions who had already died for communism would be like the early Christian martyrs, while the works of the first proletarian writers would be like the Christian art of the catacombs. Still more, they would resemble the writings of the first church fathers, which was stiff, graceless, even barbarous by the standards of classical style, but which were redeemed by their power and fanaticism.[11]

Another proposition in the Manifesto of the Word states: "We are not concerned with the propagation of sociological ideas, except to emancipate the creative elements from the present ideology." The day will come, Cowley prophesied, when, like the church fathers who "overwhelmed the pagan rhetoricians" and saw the emergence of Christianity as the church triumphant, the proletarian writers would overwhelm the apologists for capitalism and witness the emergence of communism as the triumphant "Church of Earth." Thereupon "proletarian art would give way—as it already promised to do in Russia—to a universally human art endowed with the harmony and complexity of later Christian works like *The Divine Comedy* and the Cathedral of Chartres." Some of the fellow travelers, Cowley adds, recorded their experience of conversion to communism in language comparable to that of St. John of the Cross in describing the blessed assurance of the moment "when God takes your hand and guides you in darkness to a goal and by a way which you would never have found with the aid of your own eyes and feet." He refers in particular to a graphic description of the meaning of the conversion to Communism written by a now long forgotten Minnesota novelist, a young woman "of good family," Meridel Le Sueur, and published in *The New Masses*.

> It [i.e., the conversion experience] is difficult because you are stepping into a dark chaotic passionnal world of another class, the proletariat, which is still perhaps unconscious of itself, like a great body sleeping, stirring,

strange and outside the calculated, expedient world of the bourgeoisie. It is a hard road to leave your own class and you cannot leave it by pieces or parts; it is a birth and you have to be born whole out of it. The creative artist will create no new forms of art or literature for the new hour out of that darkness unless he is willing to go all the way, with full belief, into that darkness.

Some "promising" novelists, poets, and dramatists who began writing in the thirties, Cowley says, aspired to believe fully in the vision of a Meridel Le Sueur and perhaps even conceived that they would "be born whole" in the experience of entering the "darkness" of the "new hour." But although something akin to genuine religious fervor was at times evident in converts to Communism, or even more evident in converts to the ranks of the fellow travelers, it became evident as the decade of the thirties drew to a close that, save possibly for Steinbeck's *Grapes of Wrath*, faith in the social power of the word had by and large failed to create works of art that transcended their meaning as acts of social protest.

But the historical season changed during the waning years of the thirties. In *The Golden Mountains* Cowley recalls how German, Austrian, and Spanish refugees, at times wearing the look of "being reprieved from the grave," began to appear at parties and in the cafeterias of New York's Upper West Side. Each with a "tale about his narrow escape" and a "theory" to explain the collapse of Europe, they "gave a special atmosphere to the period." It was "the dusk of a late-autumnal day, after the leaves had fallen." Although "grand adventure and misadventures" were still to befall them, the writers of the thirties were no longer participants "in a confident dream." In recalling his counsel to refugee European writers and intellectuals arriving in New York City in the later 1930s, Cowley draws directly on an article he published in the *New Republic* in 1939 entitled "Exiles of the Arts." In this he warned refugees harboring the illusion that New York City is the gateway to a "really new world," a "world too robust for the diseases of old age that are attacking Europe," that, on the contrary, "New York is merely another great European city."

> It is younger than Paris or London; much too young to have developed the traditions of intellectual hospitality that have flourished in London since the eighteenth century and Paris since the Middle Ages. On the other hand, it has been a great city longer than Berlin, and it seems tired and

almost senile as compared with Moscow. It is a colony of European capitalism, a very old colony that has become a richer metropolis than any in the homeland, but without curing itself of the ills that capitalism suffers everywhere. The exiles ought to be warned that by coming here they will escape none of the problems that defeated them in Europe. On an unfamiliar battleground they will have to fight the same enemies.[12]

In their exodus from their homeland in the 1920s young American intellectuals and artists had been prompted by the illusion that they would find in Europe a society less materialistic and more congenial to their artistic aspirations. Seeing the exiles from Europe arriving in America a few years later, some of them at least thinking they had come to the promised land, Cowley confronted his misreading of a decade that had ended with an unholy pact between Russia and Germany, the one, in the "mythology of the 1930s," being a "good" country, the other a "bad" country.

The story of the fellow travelers in *The Golden Mountains* is edged with ironies and tragic nuances, none being more significant than the fact that in their involvement in the Communist movement the fellow travelers were driven by the underlying assumption—never explicitly, perhaps never even consciously formulated—that the "good" country and the "bad" country were both committed to world historical redemptive missions. Underlying the rhetoric of Cowley's somber admonition to the refugee literati that in leaving an old world they had come to no new world but to a colony of the old world is the recognition that the American writers who had lived the experience of becoming self-declared literary exiles in the twenties and thereafter returned to their homeland in the years of the Great Depression to become its self-declared redeemers had undergone a deeply disturbing psychic displacement. Rejecting the vision of America as a redeemer nation in favor of a vision of America as even yet a colony of European capitalism, American writers of his generation, Cowley suggests, had brought into question not only their faith in the efficacy of the Marxian interpretation of history but the interpretation of American history that had prevailed since the age of the Revolution.

The loss of confidence in the redemptive role of American writers in the later 1930s—symbolized in *The Golden Mountains* in Cowley's image of the autumnal mood induced in the fellow travelers by the arrival in New York of the dispossessed of Europe—is expressed more directly in his response to Edmund Wilson's study of revolutionary traditions in *To the Finland Station: A Study in the Writing and Acting of History* (1940). Agreeing with Wilson that Marx's dogmatic historical prophecies and what has since transpired in history are far apart, Cowley supports Wilson's underlying thesis that art and history are not necessarily—and, it is possible, not at all—complementary. He finds the most successful chapter in Wilson's book to be the one in which the author "considers *Das Kapital* as a work of art and Marx himself as a 'poet of commodities,' driven like other poets by selfless aspirations and obscure grudges." But Cowley could not entirely, not yet at least, consign Marxian social prophecy to the realm of art. The question in his mind was still, why did things go so wrong in the acting out of the Marxian vision of social revolution? Clinging to the belief that *something* did go wrong—that it *might* have been different—Cowley says that what is now needed is a historical routing *from* the Finland Station: a tracing of the "devolution" of the Communist ideal "in the writing and acts" of Lenin and his successors.[13]

When Cowley began his expansive account of the American twenties and thirties in 1973 with the publication of *A Second Flowering*, he was fully committed to the completion of what he regarded as his culminating work. In this he intended to present what he always regarded as the most significant aspect of his long literary career, the story of his participation, and the participation of his generation, in the history of the two crucial decades between the great wars of the twentieth century; and he would present this history as he saw it from the perspective he had attained on its meaning in living through three more decades of a tumultuous century. Such a perspective demanded that the major emphasis be not on the writers of the twenties and the brilliant achievements in literary art represented by *The Sun Also Rises*, *The Great Gatsby*, and *The Sound and the Fury*, but on the writers of the Great Depression decade who sought to equate art and social reform. Accordingly Cowley would devote two of the three volumes he planned to the time of the rise and fall (or the "devolution") of faith in Communism in the United States. But the volume that was to follow his account of the rise of this faith, in *The Golden Mountains*, was never completed. This was the part of the story, Cowley told me when he sent me a copy of *The Golden Mountains* upon its publication in 1980, that would be the most difficult to write: the part in which he would have to explain why he remained a fellow traveler in the last half of the thirties, when most American writers had not only rejected the Communist faith as represented by Russia but the faith itself. Although he published three or four episodes designed for the third volume in periodicals in 1982–1984, he seems never to have had in mind a firm structural plan for a book he wanted (or did not want) to write.

Cowley's failure to finish his account of the later thirties was forecast two years before he published *The Golden Mountains* in the tenth chapter of *The Writer's Trade*. In this he quotes at some length from his reply to Edmund Wilson early in 1940 after Wilson had charged in a "severe" letter that, by failing to renounce his affiliation with Communism following Stalin's pact with Hitler, Cowley had "given hostages to the Stalinists in some terrible incomprehensible way."

> I am profoundly disturbed by what has happened in the Soviet Union—as who isn't? I think that the Communists here [the United States] are tied to the apron strings of Russian foreign policy. They have ceased to play a vitalizing part in the American labor movement that they played in 1937, and they are now willing to destroy the United Front organizations they founded rather than lose control of them. You think that I should now frankly discard my illusions—but granted for the sake of argument that they are illusions, what is the good of discarding them for another set of illusions . . . ? And must I believe that Communists I saw working hard and sacrificing themselves are really without a single exception unprincipled careerists?

The situation demanded more, Cowley believed, "than simply deciding that what used to be white is now black and vice versa." We need to find out not only how the Russian revolution resulted in the present situation, whether Stalinism or Leninism or Marxism "is essentially at fault," but why democracy seems to have been left out of "all those directions for making a better society." We need to go further than Marxist theories based on history and economics and inquire into the question of whether or not anthropology affords a clue as to why the revolutionists misread the nature of the "human animal." But Cowley appeared to feel that what we most need to consider are "the faults of communism as a religion, for there can be no doubt that it has become a religion." Considering all the "heresies and inquisitions and excommunications" that have marked the history of Communism since the Russian Revolution, Cowley said, he was reminded "of nothing so much as the history of the Christian church during the first three centuries."

As a result of his loss of faith in the revolutionary cause, Cowley told Wilson, he was "left standing pretty much alone, in the air, unsupported, a situation that is more uncomfortable for me than it would be for you, since my normal instinct is toward cooperation." But "for the moment," Cowley declared, he simply wanted "to get out of every God damned thing"; the nasty quarrels among those who had once been united as fellow travelers reminding him of "a night a dozen years ago" when he had gone "on a bat with a lot of noisy and lecherous people" he "thoroughly despised," while realizing even as he did so that he "was one of them." After staying "a long time in a Harlem speakeasy, down in a cellar," he had come up the stairs to see "the doorman standing in the light of morning with his hands the color of cold ashes." "That is how I felt inside," and how, Cowley told Wilson, he felt now. Getting involved in "these feuds and vendettas of the intelligentsia" was "like being an unwilling participant in a Harlem orgy"; and it made him "wonder what the world would be like if it were ruled by the intellectuals."

> Some of them we know are admirable people, humble and conscientious, but intellectuals in the mass are not like that. A world run by them would be a very unpleasant place, considering all the naked egos that would be continually wounding and getting wounded, all the gossip, the spies at cocktail parties, the informers, the careerists, the turncoats. Remember too the character assassinations now so much in vogue (and even you are succumbing to the fashion, with your open letters to the *New Republic*) are nothing less than symbolic murders. They would be real murders if the intellectuals controlled the state apparatus. Maybe that is part of the trouble in Russia.

"Meanwhile," Cowley said, "I can't forget that all this business started with high purposes and dreams of a better society" on the part of radicals who were willing "to sacrifice themselves," swept, as he had put it in a poem, by the "flood of passage / toward the morning that is yours." But "we're all in a pretty pickle now," Cowley said, concluding his letter to Wilson with a suggestion for a "sequel to your present book describing the evolution of an idea to the moment of Lenin's arrival in the Finland Station." In this book Wilson ought to describe "the devolution of an idea from Marx to *The New Leader* and from Lenin to the latest editorial in *Pravda* on exterminating the Finnish bandits."[14]

In *The Beginning of the Journey*, Diana Trilling recalls the summer of 1931 at Yaddo when she and Lionel Trilling, under the tutelage of another Yaddo guest,

Sydney Hook, came to believe that "our best hope for the future" lay in communism, and bowing "to historical necessity," committed themselves to "the new revolutionary faith." Other guests at Yaddo that summer included Malcolm Cowley, who, she says, while he lacked "Hook's pedagogic energy," was by that time not only "an eager fellow traveler" but would "remain so for most of his long life."[15]

Diana Trilling's impression of the duration of Cowley's devotion to Communism is plainly a misinterpretation of the facts. Though he had repressed his feelings, his sense of disillusionment with the "movement" had been progressive since the Moscow trials and had become virtually complete in 1939. But it is interesting to read Diana Trilling's impression of Cowley in the light of his elegiac depiction in *The Golden Mountains* of the fellow travelers' loss of faith in Communism:

> It faded imperceptibly for some dreamers, perhaps for most of them; the golden mountains receded into the mist. For others, who had been more ardent, the dream was shattered in a moment of deconversion. It had exerted such power, though; it had risen from such a depth of national and personal confusion; it had answered such a need for faith that even those others clung to fragments of the dream—sometimes only to the single word "revolution"; they wanted to think of themselves as revolutionists long after their essential feelings had become conservative. Those for whom the dream merely faded were likely to persist for some time in patterns of behavior that their faith had imposed on them. They still went to meetings, they served on committees, and they signed open letters in spite of being dubious about what the letters said. Some of them must have felt that there was an emptiness at the center of their lives; once I described it as "The white egg-shaped motionless, speechless No."[16]

Cowley was not among those for whom the experience of being a fellow traveler faded easily and quickly into dream. He had no sudden moment of "deconversion"; and though he announced he was leaving the movement in 1940 by resigning from the League of American Writers (and was duly castigated for his defection in the pages of the *Daily Worker* and the *New Masses*), he did not engage in any dramatic act of repentance for the sin of having followed a false god. The vacuum of "the white egg-shaped motionless speechless No" in Cowley's life was created over a period of time by a slow diminution of what had been for a time an "absolute faith" in the ultimate triumph of a "revolutionary brotherhood" engaged in a salvational cause. Becoming engaged in the revolutionary cause, he had actually had the experience of being born again, and of establishing a sense of sacred comradeship, as he said in a poem, with those "nameless martyrs" around the world who had been born again and died "for having loved tomorrow,

> betrayed and bastinadoed, burned at the stake,
> slow starved in prison or exile, buried alive,
> beaten insensible, routed at the day's break,
>
> then hurried through the snow to execution,
> shot down in Florisdorf or Chapei Road,
> and now reprieved from prison graveyards, piled
> so high with victims that they overflowed.

"In the days of faith," Cowley says, he "had pictured the martyrs as a phantom army that would sweep the tyrants aside"; but as faith waned in the later thirties he had begun to experience moments of bitter wonder, "perhaps with many others, whether those millions had died in vain and whether the future might belong to their executioners."[17]

Eroded and finally brought completely into question by historical realities, Cowley's faith in the social power of the man of letters to interpret and direct the course of history gave way to nostalgic regret for his alienation from a vision of literary and intellectual comradeship he would not again know. He filled the emptiness of his silent "No" to the faith of comrades and martyrs by reasserting his old belief in the "hagiography and Book of Martyrs" of the religion of art. Admission to the realm of literary saints, he observed, depends on whether or not writers adhere to a moral code that "can be reduced to a very few commandments," the most powerful being the will of the writer, granted his talent, to believe in the absolute importance of his art. Although a writer may be alienated from the moral values of his society, the invariable characteristic of all true literary artists—Flaubert, James, Mallarmé, Joyce, Mann, Proust, Hemingway, Fitzgerald—is their profound obedience to the discipline—to the moral decorum demanded by their calling.

Taking Hemingway as an exemplary figure of the writer as artist, Cowley defines Hemingway's concept of the governance of art as a finely controlled tension in his consciousness between life and death. Striving ever to be in exact "harmony" with his subject, Hemingway sought a precise balance between style and emotion, as in the palpable evocation of a landscape "remembered with a sense of precarious joy." In the effort to achieve such precision, Cowley says, Hemingway followed his own dictum, "A writer should be of as great probity and honesty as a priest of God." Cowley was also strongly drawn to Marcel Proust as an exemplary personification of the life lived according to the "fable of *une patria perdue*," where writing, governed by the higher laws of art, is essentially a religious experience. He cherished the final scene in the life of the author of *A la recherche du temps perdu*, when, dying in Paris in his cork-lined room above the Boulevard Haussmann, the consummate literary artist broke off dictating to his aged housekeeper at 3 A.M. and concluded his lonely, intricate quest to achieve apocalyptic dominion over time with a self-conferred blessing on the work he had now completed: "Celeste, I think what I have made you take down is very good. I shall stop now."[18]

Though it existed under different historical circumstances, Cowley's sense of the situation of American writers in the 1930s may be compared to that which Henry James had defined, and made the major subject of his work, a generation earlier: the intricately ironic situation of the American writer who absents himself in Europe yet cannot but continue to share with his countrymen the dream of his homeland as a world-redemptive republic, purified of Europe and opposed to the Old World as innocence is to experience, as light is to darkness; who remains acutely aware that his homeland is the new nation that emerged from the American Revolution in the later eighteenth century yet in historical reality is part and parcel of the old and corrupt history of the European nations.

In late December 1978, in the eightieth year of his life, the former fellow traveler once again found himself in a meeting room in New York City facing "rows of strangers seated on folding chairs." The room in which Cowley spoke, however, was not an ill-lighted meeting hall on upper Broadway. He was before a session of the Modern Language Association in a convention hotel in mid-Manhattan, where a large crowd, comfortably seated on well-upholstered folding chairs, had gathered to pay him tribute and to hear him talk about the lost generation and the heroic life in letters. He spoke at length, so long in fact that he violated the MLA conventioneer's exacting slavery to the clock and a part of his audience began to steal away to other sessions, job interviews, cocktail parties, etc. The old performer had handled restless audiences before. He firmly called a halt, so that all who wanted to leave could do so. In the quiet that followed his gesture to MLA decorum, with only half his audience remaining, Cowley presented the climax of his remarks, an eloquent account of the mystery of dedication to the literary vocation as manifested in the life of his late friend Ramon Guthrie.

Like Cowley, Guthrie had entered the Great War as a volunteer in an agency connected with the French transport service. Later (as Cowley had attempted to do, only to be refused as physically unqualified) Guthrie had become a pilot in the fledgling American Army Air Corps, a service so perilous that Guthrie had come "to regard himself as, in effect, leading a posthumous life." But after the war he had found his way back into life, partly through teaching and literary scholarship devoted to Proust. He not only presented Proust in the classroom on a regular basis but reread *Remembrance of Things Past* each year for thirty-one years without skipping a word. But Guthrie's chief way of transcending war and death was his own poetry. In his later years he began an ambitious poetic composition that he thought would be his masterwork, but things went slowly and ill health came upon him with his book unfinished. Near death in a hospital—secured, as he himself put it, in a "frantic bramble of glass and plastic tubes and stainless steel" and struggling alternately against the abyss of coma and the hallucination that he was Marsyas being flayed alive by Apollo—he kept on writing *Maximum Security Ward*.[19] That the literary artist, in defiance of war and death and all the entanglements of history, may be born again in the isolated personal act of writing: it was his belief in this possibility that Cowley talked about in (so far as I know) his last appearance in a New York meeting hall.

As Cowley interprets the epoch of the fellow travelers in the history of American letters, it was marked by a division between two obligations in the mind of the writer who enlisted in the ranks of the fellow travelers. Both basically religious in character, the obligations were, on the one hand, to fulfill the faith in the power of the writer as an instrument of the world historical social revolution prophesied by Marx, and now in active progress; and, on the other hand, to keep the faith in the writer as an instrument in the fulfillment of the art of letters as a world-transcendent spiritual force. In *A Second Flowering* Cowley compares the 1920s to the time a century earlier when Emerson had pointed out to young American writers that "anything was possible." In the twenties, he says, young writers did not read Emerson but they did read Joyce and Eliot; and when *Ulysses* and *The Waste Land* appeared in the same year (1922), Cowley says, they responded to the exciting news that the writers of his generation had pushed "beyond the mountains" and were now opening "new territories for men of the new generation to explore." In their self-conscious dual role as actors in and observers of the history of their time—as "wordsmiths" committed to their "talent" and its realization in works of literary art—Cowley and his contemporaries had become "spinners and weavers" of the legendary heroes of a "cycle of myths for a century" that they "had felt from the beginning" was "to be partly" their own creation.[20] In the quality of their devoted participation to the act of creating their century, the spinners and weavers had created themselves as heroes of their time. And this was true, Cowley declared, not only of Hemingway, Fitzgerald, and Crane but of others who may now be deemed to be of lesser rank. In the chapter on Thomas Wolfe in *A Second Flowering*, Cowley says that during the years since he first read him, Wolfe had fallen off in his estimation. But in reading him again he had found a new respect for Wolfe, "one of the explorers who not only opened a new path but followed it to the end." "He had always dreamed of becoming a hero, and that is how he impresses us now: perhaps not as a hero of the literary art on a level with Faulkner and Hemingway and Fitzgerald, but as *Homo scribens* and *Vir scribentissimus*, a tragic hero in the act of writing."[21]

If Cowley does not resolve the uncertain relation in *The Dream of the Golden Mountains* between the "straightforward" "I," "we," and "us" and the ambivalent "he," "she," and "they," the sense of the ambivalence of his role in the story he tells in *The Dream* is less pronounced than it is in *Exile's Return* and *A Second Flowering*. As the eminently self-conscious bard of the spinners and weavers of the twenties in *Exile's Return* and *A Second Flowering*, Cowley had spun and woven himself into the legend of his heroes. If in *The Dream of the Golden Mountains* his sense of his role is less certain, this would seem to be not because he was reluctant to expose the nature of his role as a supporter of the Communist cause in the 1930s. It would appear to be more nearly because in looking back on this time he was never certain precisely what role he had in fact played.

More pointedly than *Exiles Return*, *The Dream of the Golden Mountains* dramatizes Cowley's conflicted awareness of the situation of the American writer, who, having cast himself in the twenties in the role of the writer alienated from politics and society, found himself in the thirties caught up in the role of the radical social reformer. In *The Dream of the Golden Mountains* he reenacts the role of actor in the story and the "independent observer" he plays in *Exile's Return*. But, as he indicates, it was harder to play this role in telling the story of a decade he saw as having been far more "turbulent" for the writer than the ten years preceding the bursting of the economic bubble. Though he was always "loyal to friends and institutions" in the thirties, he says, and "sometimes too loyal, it seems in retrospect," Cowley was at the same time an observer who was "especially curious about the behavior of people in groups: how they came together and how they tried to win each other's approval; 'That's the way things work,' he said to himself."[22]

But, Cowley adds, the way things work for writers can also be explained by the dream that each writer forms of his future: "Know a man by his daydreams." He fails to add that as night dreams may turn into nightmares, daydreams may turn into daymares. Know a man by his daymares, or his nightmares, as well as by his daydreams. But, although there were American writers who had bad dreams because they felt they had betrayed their vocation by their misguided faith in the unspeakable evil of a dictator who, in the name of the people, murdered them by the thousands, Cowley was not, I think, among them. After he had rejected Communism, he knew himself as a profoundly disillusioned but not, save insofar as he was guilty of gullibility, as a guilt-ridden man.

In a sense Diana Trilling was right in her impression of Cowley. He could never quite let go of the dream image of himself he had so ardently aspired to bring into reality as a fellow traveler. Contrary to that of the writer shaped by obedience to the decorum of alienation, this was the image of the writer shaped in "the days of faith" by the decorum of obedience to the role of the writer as an integral, even heroic, agent of the transformation of history.[23]

When I think of Malcolm Cowley's desire to assume an active role in the historical world of the thirties, two recollections flash on the screen of memory. In one a friend at the University of Texas in 1936 bounds into my room exclaiming, "Simpson, I've found a book you've got to read!" and thrusts a copy of *Exile's Return* into my hand. We lived under the pall of the Great Depression, but twenty-year-old youths in that particular time and place had no inclination to social radicalism. Instead, some of us of literary inclination read Hemingway and took refuge in the expatriates' bittersweet world of war, death, and art. So I read *Exile's Return* for the first time with no real grasp of its meaning as an explanation of Cowley's passage from alienation to social engagement, but with a vivid appreciation of his dramatic account of the suicide of Harry Crosby. In the other scene that resonates in memory it is an afternoon in Nashville, Tennessee, thirty-five years later, when I was a participant in a literary conference at which Malcolm Cowley was the chief speaker. Although I had carried on a correspondence with him, I had never met Cowley personally until, in response to a knock on my hotel door, I opened it to find the man who had known Hart Crane, Hemingway, Fitzgerald, Faulkner, Dos Passos, and all the others, saying genially, "Allen Tate tells me you've written something I must read."

The most moving passage I find in Malcolm's letters to me is one he dictated after he was unable to sit at his typewriter. He had always had "strong feelings," he said, "that a life should be a work of art and go out in a blaze of glory" rather than, as his was, "merely flickering out like a candle." Cowley was aware of the physical limitations that blocked the completion of his major work about the twenties and thirties, but he also was always aware, I suspect, of the possibility that a triumphant end to his long literary career had been effectively blocked long ago by the pathos of his involvement in the Communist faith in the thirties. Never fully made but strongly entertained, his subscription to this faith was antithetical to the sense of vocation that led him to think of himself, whether as poet, critic, or literary historian, as primarily affiliated with a transcendent faith in the art of letters. "In the background of the pattern" of Hemingway's stories, Cowley says, we find "death, loneliness, and the void," but "these are not his subjects." For example, in "A Clean, Well-Lighted Place," although the old waiter "seems to speak from the depths of nihilism," he suggests a remedy for the feeling of nothingness: "it is to sit all night in a pleasant cafe where he will be surrounded with order and decorum."

"Hemingway's real subject," Cowley says, "is the barriers that can be erected against fear and loneliness and the void." His stories represent "decorum in the broadest sense, in which it becomes the discipline of one's calling."[24] And for a wordsmith the discipline of one's calling is not to be found in seeking salvation, either personal or literary, in the pathos of the impossible dream of workers and wordsmiths united in the pursuit of the common goal of social justice. It is to be discovered in obedience to history enclosed in the self of the literary artist; to the decorum of alienation. In this obedience the writer is not deprived of his role as an actor in history, the writing of dreams and memories, or dreams of memories and memories of dreams, being an enactment of history. And in neither case is the writer deprived of dreaming of the writer in the role of hero. No more so than Scott Fitzgerald's Jay Gatsby, who in enacting the American dream was no doubt responsible for more than one murder. But, as his friend Nick Carraway says, there was nothing wrong with Gatsby's dream. It was the foul dust that floated in its wake.

I thought of Malcolm Cowley as a literary hero when I first read him in 1936, and now in a much later time, when the decorum of the writer is little esteemed, I still think of him as a hero of the literary art.

NOTES

1. Cowley, *The Dream of the Golden Mountains: Remembering the 1930s* (New York, 1980), 41. Cf. Cowley's 1941 essay "Communism and Christianity": "Apparently the progress of the race is not toward the eventual solution of class conflicts or any other conflicts, but rather toward their transformation and reappearance in new fields. And this chain of thought leads one to question whether the classless society for which Communists are working is possible either for the human species or would, if forcibly achieved, satisfy the specific human needs. Perhaps they have been sacrificing men and women to an unattainable ideal. Perhaps the Christian picture of human nature, which recognizes, if it does not solve, the problem of evil, is not only more emotionally satisfying but also, in the end, more realistic." Cowley, *The Flower and the Leaf: A Contemporary Record of American Writing since 1941*, ed. Donald W. Faulkner (New York, 1985), 24.

2. Hans Bak, *Malcolm Cowley: The Formative Years* (Athens, Ga., 1993), 438. An exhaustive and indispensable inquiry into Cowley's career in the 1920s that illuminates his whole career.

3. Cowley, *Exile's Return: A Literary Odyssey of the 1920s* (New York, 1951),

4. *The Dream of the Golden Mountains*, 83, 117.

5. Ibid., x–xi.

6. Ibid., xi.

7. Ibid.

8. Ibid., 111–12.

9. Cowley, *Think Back on Us: A Chronicle of the 1930s* (Carbondale, Ill., 1967), 285, 287.

10. Ibid., 105.

11. *The Dream of the Golden Mountains*, 247.

12. Ibid., 317; *Think Back on Us*, 167.

13. *Think Back on Us*, 184.

14. Cowley, *And I Worked at the Writer's Trade: Chapters of Literary History, 1918–1978* (New York, 1978), 154–57.

15. Diana Trilling, *The Beginning of the Journey: The Marriage of Lionel and Diana Trilling* (New York, 1993), 183.

16. *The Dream of the Golden Mountains*, 314–15.

17. Ibid., 316–17.

18. *And I Worked at the Writer's Trade*, 264, 265–66.

19. Cowley tells the story of Ramon Guthrie in *The View from 80* (New York, 1980), 58–74.

20. *And I Worked at the Writer's Trade*, 254.

21. Cowley, *A Second Flowering: The Life and Times of the Lost Generation* (New York, 1973), 189–90.
22. Ibid., xii.
23. *The Dream of the Golden Mountains,* 316.
24. *And I Worked at the Writer's Trade,* 28.

THE POET AND THE FATHER
Robert Penn Warren and the Redemption of Thomas Jefferson

> Fiction brings up from their dark oubliettes our shadowy, deprived selves and gives them an airing, as it were in the prison yard.
> —ROBERT PENN WARREN, "Why Do We Read Fiction?" (1962)

I recall being in a taxi en route from a downtown Washington, D.C., hotel to what was then called the National Airport. It was at first light on a summer morning sometime in the later 1970s, two hours before the morning rush would begin and three hours before the day's horde of seasonal pilgrims would erupt. The streets were nearly empty and almost silent. In the slowly growing light the buildings and monuments of the city, obscured by ground fog, seemed almost spectral: dream structures, one might fancy, of the pristine classical city the statesman and architect Thomas Jefferson had envisioned rising in the Potomac wilderness a few years before he had come to live for two presidential terms in the reality of the crude village that was the Washington of 1800.

We passed the Washington Monument and the Lincoln Memorial, both wreathed in mist; then, owing, I suppose, to some freakish quality of the early morning atmosphere, the Jefferson Memorial came into view with startling clarity.[1] I especially remember seeing, or perhaps not so much seeing, as having a vision of the statue of Jefferson standing in the elegant austerity of his porticoed chamber. I particularly remember that the figure seemed invested with an ineffable aura of loneliness.

Looking at the city pass below after my plane had taken off, I thought about how before long tourists would be lining up to take the elevator to the top of the Washington shaft, and others by the hundreds would be climbing the steps of the magisterial Lincoln shrine to stand in the massive presence of the Great Emancipator, while only a few would be making their way to the classically chaste Jefferson shrine. This did not mean that pilgrims to the capital city on that day would fail to pay their obeisance to Jefferson. They would do so at another shrine located in the National Archives, where—under the diligent scrutiny of uniformed guardians—they would pass in a silent line before a hermetically sealed case and, in the brief glance allowed each viewer, reverently try to make out a few of the familiar words of the preamble to the Declaration in which the Representatives of the United States in General Congress assembled in 1774 to announced to "a candid world" the birth of a nation:

> We hold these truths to be self-evident: that all men are created equal; that they are endowed by their creator with certain inalienable rights, that among these are life, liberty & the pursuit of happiness; that to secure these rights, governments are instituted among men, deriving their just powers from the consent of the governed; that whenever any form of government becomes destructive of these ends, it is the right of the people to alter or abolish it, & to institute new government, laying its foundation in such principles, & organizing its powers in such form, as to them shall seem most like to effect their safety & happiness.[2]

Americans believe in the abstractions Thomas Jefferson wrote of in that Philadelphia summer of 1776 and have died fighting for them, not only in the fateful struggle of colonials for freedom from the British Empire but in all the wars, declared and undeclared, they have since become engaged in. Ironically, these wars include not only the wars, which lasted until 1890, to complete the dispossession of the native peoples who were on the land we call our own thousands of years before we appeared on the scene; they include more than one conflict, however much we ignore the fact, related to our own imperial ambitions. Most ironically, the wars since the Revolution include one of the bloodiest in history: the one we waged against ourselves from 1861 to 1865, a war in which both sides claimed to be fighting for the sacred truths of the Declaration of Independence but were divided about the interpretation of the words in which these truths are stated, particularly the interpretation of the assertion that "all men are created equal." Yet in spite of this catastrophic disagreement, we yet regard the document authored by Thomas Jefferson—and ratified by the blood of the revolutionary army—as transcending the multiple ironies of our complex history. At the same time we still consider the sacred truths proclaimed by the Declaration to have been incarnated in the commander of the revolutionary army and look upon General George Washington as the father of our country. More recently, in the long aftermath of our bitter Civil War, we have also developed—if not universally, yet almost so—a strong sense of parental regard for the martyred leader of the Unionist cause in this war, who, in 1863, created another sacred American text when he echoed the Declaration of Independence on the battlefield of Gettysburg.

Yet, while the Declaration of Independence is absolutely central to our history, we do not hold in veneration a definitive image of its author as a father figure. In our general conception, I think it is fair to say, Jefferson, in contrast to George Washington and Abraham Lincoln, is a somewhat ambivalent presence. He is accepted as a father figure more by the convention that confers this status on all the founders of the Republic than by reason of our attachment to him as an iconic presence.

This is not to say that Jefferson is not universally present to us. Perhaps he is too close to us, the interpretation of his ideas too intimately a part of our ongoing, often turbulent history—too intimately a part of our psychic makeup, of our everyday hopes and fears as individual Americans—for us to hold him up for veneration. At least such a thought has often occurred to me, but in no way more insistently than in an effort over the years—not a notably successful one, I confess—to come to terms with one twentieth-century American poet's brooding involvement with the man who has been one of the most influential champions of freedom in modern history yet was a slavemaster all his long life. I refer to a long poem, the only poem of such length Robert Penn Warren wrote, *Brother to Dragons: A Tale in Verse and Voices.*

One problem in understanding this singularly strange and daring work is that it is made even stranger and more daring by the fact that thirty years after its first publication in 1953—and after it had been republished in six editions and had begun to acquire the aura of a classic—the poem appeared in 1979, to use Warren's own words, in a "very different version" that is "in some important senses" a "new work."[3]

In the foreword to the new version of *Brother to Dragons* Warren suggests that even as the first version was published he was unhappy about the fact that, owing to "some confusion," the publisher had failed to employ the text incorporating all his revisions. But a desire to correct this confusion, as Warren acknowledges in the foreword, was at best a secondary motive in his rewriting of the poem. Far from being a "patchwork reworking" of the first version, the second represents, Warren says, "a protracted and concentrated reliving of the whole process" of conceiving and writing the first version. We may, I think, interpret this statement to mean that the primary motive of *Brother to Dragons* II, as we may call it, is to be found in the poet's compulsion to return again and again to the question—poetic, philosophical, or it may be metaphysical—of his personal relation to Thomas Jefferson, especially as this was shaped by his knowledge of a lurid murder story associated with the region of Kentucky in which he was reared.

Known to Warren since boyhood in "garbled accounts," this story began in 1807, when Colonel Charles Lewis and his wife Lucy, a sister of Thomas Jefferson—together with their three sons and their three daughters—moved from the established world of Albemarle County, Virginia, to the frontier world of western Kentucky. Of some aristocratic pretension among the gentry of the Tidewater society, the Lewises presumably did not move by choice but were compelled by a pattern of hope that still urges Americans who have fallen on hard times to seek a promised land in the West. The leader of the Lewis family removal seems not to have been the father, Colonel Lewis, but two grown sons, Lilburne and Randolph. After the family arrived in Kentucky, it is not clear whether Colonel Lewis ever established himself on his own domain, but both Randolph (who does not figure in the murder story) and Lilburne bought parcels of land in Livingston County near the frontier town of Smithland and not far from the confluence of the Ohio and Cumberland Rivers. Lilburne chose a 1,500-acre site dominated by a bluff overlooking the Ohio. Here he erected what was for the time and place a rather grand house. Though in Kentucky his status was not, properly speaking, that of a planter but of a farmer, in the manner of the Tidewater planters he gave his house a name, "Rocky Hill." Assuming that Colonel Lewis did not buy his own property, Warren portrays Lilburne as presiding over something like a family dominion at Rocky Hill, the family consisting of his wife, Letitia, his parents, and the third brother, a somewhat feckless young man named Isham. (Warren leaves out the daughters in the Lewis family.) According to both the historical record and the poem, the Lewises were attended by several slaves, some of whom served as household servants, others as farmhands.

In contrast to the life the Lewises had known in Virginia, life at Rocky Hill was bleak. While they had not moved into a literal "wilderness," they had come to a community that had been established in a wilderness and still had a semi-wilderness quality. Thus, although it is an interpretation that is not necessarily supported by the life of the actual Lilburne, Warren sees him as one who, coming to the "wilderness" as "a light-bringer" and "herald of civilization," yielded to a darkness engendered in him by the harsh life of the place he had come to.

Whether this is what happened or not, the historical Lilburne, for whatever reason, was moved by a dark impulse, when—on the night of December 15, 1811, the night before the first tremor of the New Madrid earthquake, the greatest recorded earthquake yet to occur on the North American continent—Lilburne commanded his slaves to gather in a cabin that served as the plantation kitchen (Warren calls it "the meat-house"). And here, in the terrified presence of the huddled slaves, aided by Isham, Lilburne literally butchered a seventeen-year-old male slave. Called George, his real name, in the first version of *Brother to Dragons*, but for some unstated reason, called John in the second, the murdered slave was, as Warren describes him, "a sort of body-servant and handyman for Lilburne." George's death by the incredibly brutal act of the Lewis brothers was punishment for his having broken a pitcher prized by their mother, Lucy Jefferson Lewis, who had died a year earlier. Lilburne and Isham tried to hide their deed by having the slaves who witnessed it burn the body parts of George in the kitchen fireplace. But this disposal scheme was thwarted a few hours thereafter when the chimney of the fireplace collapsed onto the cabin during the first great tremors of the New Madrid quake. A second attempt to hide the murder by stuffing what was left of the flesh and bones of George in the masonry of a hastily rebuilt fireplace and chimney was confounded about two months later, when, as a result of the aftershocks of the New Madrid quake, the rebuilt chimney collapsed and George's remains were once again exposed. Additional grisly evidence came to light with the discovery not long after of George's head, which, unknown to Lilburne and Isham, had been carried off by a dog on the night of the murder. When the foul deed of Lilburne and Isham was revealed, they were arrested. (Slaves did not have the right to liberty and the pursuit of happiness, but they did have the right to life, at least in the sense that the law forbade their masters to murder them.) While on bail awaiting trial, the brothers concocted a scheme for a grand resolution of their predicament. According to the evidence set down in the legal record, they agreed to stand at their mother's grave and "present a gun at each others breast and fire at a word with an intention of killing each other" (*BD* I, 225n; *BD* II, 137n). But things went awry, when, as they prepared to fulfill their bizarre pact, Lilburne was accidentally killed. Unable to pull the trigger on himself, Isham fled. Soon caught, jailed, tried, and sentenced to death, he somehow managed to escape. His fate has never been known for certain, though it would appear that (as in Warren's poem) he eventually made his way to Louisiana, where he died in 1815 in the Battle of New Orleans.[4]

    Another problem in understanding *Brother to Dragons* is the relation between historical fact and myth. In telling the story of the Lewis family Warren in general follows the recorded story of the family. Only one person in the poem has no basis at all in fact, an ancient black slave named Aunt Cat, who is depicted by Warren as having been Lilburne's nurse when he was a baby. Yet in its total configuration the "tale" Warren tells "in verse and voices" is an elaborate fiction, which, in addition to the persons already mentioned, includes not only two major historical figures—Thomas Jefferson and the explorer Meriwether Lewis—but two persons who belong to the present. One is known only by the initials R.P.W. Described as "the writer of this poem," R.P.W. is in one sense the author of the poem and in another a persona of the author. The other living presence in the poem is R.P.W.'s eighty-year-old father.

In spite of the bizarre quality of Warren's adaptation of the history of the Jefferson and the Lewis family, *Brother to Dragons* is not a ghost story. Warren's intention was to make his poem represent historical reality. Recognizing that he was assuming a very broad poetic license in the tale he was telling, he prefixed the same italicized notation to each of the two versions:

> *The main body of the action lies in the remote past—in the earthly past of characters long dead—and now they meet at an unspecified place and unspecified time and try to make sense of the action in which they were involved. We may take them to appear and disappear as the urgencies of argument swell and subside. The place of this meeting is, we may say, "no place," and the time is "any time." This is but a way of saying that the issues that the characters here discuss are, in my view at least, a human constant.*

Warren, in other words, subscribed to the Faulknerian view that the historical past is not dead, it is not even past; and for the poet or the novelist to represent it as a costume drama is an artistic perversion. What he intended to do in his novels, and no less in *Brother to Dragons*, as he explained to Ralph Ellison in an interview not long after he had written its initial version, was to deal with certain "issues" in "a mythical form." Representing a "constant" not only in American history but in human history, these issues appear to have acquired a particular poignancy in America because of the "extraordinary romance" of a history so singularly rooted in the determination of Americans to be "self-sufficient": "You know, the grandpas and the great grandpas carried the assumption that somehow their lives and their decisions were important; that as they went up, down, and here and there, such a life was important and that it was a man's responsibility to live it." This compelling sense on the part of individual Americans, in Warren's view, was rooted in their faith that their nation was founded on the abstract promise that it would fulfill the "inalienable right" of each individual person "to life, liberty, and the pursuit of happiness." Established on this promise, America is different from all other nations, which had their origins in "the accidents of geography or race." It "is based on an idea"; and "behind the comedy of proclaiming that idea from Fourth of July platforms, there is the solemn notion, *Believe and ye shall be saved.*" How this "abstraction" sometimes becomes "concrete," Warren concludes, is a part of the American experience—and of the American problem—the lag between idea and fact, between word and flesh.[5]

In appealing to the notion that the conversion of the abstract idea on which the American nation was founded into concrete experience is represented in the story of Jefferson's connection with the Lewis family, Warren assumes the poetic license in *Brother to Dragons* of presenting as fact the myth that Jefferson was the sole author of the Declaration.[6]

> We suddenly had to define ourselves and what we stood for in one night. No other nation ever had to do that. In fact, one man did it—one man in an upstairs room, Thomas Jefferson. Sure, you might say he was the amanuensis for a million or so people stranded on the edge of a continent and backed by a wilderness, and there's some sense in that notion. But *somebody* had to formulate it—in fact, just overnight, whatever the complicated background of that formulation—and we've been stuck with it ever since.[7]

A further complication in understanding *Brother to Dragons* is the question of Warren's attitude toward its generic form. Warren himself says in the prefatory matter to both versions that it is "a dialogue spoken by characters." It has the initial apparatus we expect of a play text: a *dramatis personae* (or, the equivalent): "THE SPEAKERS *in the order of appearance*"; and a formal indication of the setting (or in this case, non-setting): "PLACE: *No Place;* TIME: *Any Time.*" Yet, even though his poem may look like a play, Warren advises the reader, "it is not a play, and must not be taken as such." Warren was emphatic on this point because he had gone through the process of attempting to conceive of *Brother to Dragons* as a play and deciding that it would not work on the stage. Finally, he "struck on the notion of using the form of a dramatic dialogue—not a play but a dialogue of all the characters." Warren might seem to have violated his own conception of his poem by later preparing a stage version of *Brother to Dragons* that saw several productions on the noncommercial stage in the sixties and seventies, but the stage production, he hoped, would be another way of fulfilling his intention of presenting, as the subtitle of both the poem and the play indicates, a poetic "tale in verse and voices," in which the voices are more important than the setting, and in a sense constitute the setting.[8]

The leading voices are those of Jefferson and R.P.W., who, though he appears in second place in the list of speakers, is described as "the writer of this poem" and is in fact the leading character and the major voice in *Brother to Dragons*. As the narrator of the tale, R.P.W. is present not only when he directly encounters the Jefferson family and others who belong to the realm of the past in the present but is an assumed presence in all of the encounters between persons who belong to this realm. It may not be too far-fetched to say that R.P.W. is something like a Dantean presence in *Brother to Dragons*. A devoted student of Dante, Warren—like Dante when he wrote his great poem in verse and voices, the *Divina Commedia*—was in mid-life when he wrote *Brother to Dragons*, and the tale Warren tells is not unlike a journey through secular visions of hell and purgatory toward a vision, though muted, of salvation through the self's acceptance of responsibility for history.[9] But the Dantean reference of the poem is indistinct until its conclusion, when, as I shall suggest, it becomes quite significant.

The more distinct frame of reference for *Brother to Dragons* is another poem in verse and voices. This, the source of Warren's title and to some degree of the form of *Brother to Dragons*, is the Book of Job. One of the "wisdom" books of the Old Testament, Job tells a tale in several voices of a righteous man who is in quest of the knowledge of why, when he has only "looked for good," evil has come to him; of why, when he has "waited for light," darkness has come. Job's search for the reason God has afflicted him represents a transformation of certain actual historical events into a tale that is fable, and in some ways, parable, but in the overall sense is a mythic record of an encounter between the soul, history, and the eternal. But unlike a New Testament book, which envisions history as a dimension of eternity, Job—ironically, like all the Old Testament, more "modern" than the New Testament—envisions eternity as a dimension of history. In *Brother to Dragons* a highly self-conscious modern poet imagines Job's story not as a direct source of the tale he wants to tell but as the shadowy frame for his transformation of certain actual events that occurred in the time of the early American Republic into a myth about a Thomas Jefferson who finally recognizes the evil of his overweening pride in the intellectual capacity of man to direct his own destiny. Coming into the knowledge that he and all men are by nature capable of evil as well as good, he accepts the limitations his Creator has imposed on his creation. The myth Warren imagines in *Brother to Dragons* is the symbol, we may say, not of an encounter between the soul and history in the all-embracing dimension of eternity, but of an encounter in a placeless historical present between history and what has replaced the entity called "the soul": the entity whose will to power is idealized and proclaimed—if not directly, by irresistible implication—in the Declaration of Independence: the autonomous secular individual, the self.

The feature of the dark story of Jefferson's nephews that seems to have struck Warren most forcibly is that, in spite of all the research devoted to Jefferson's life and thought, no scholar has found a single mention of the murder anywhere in his voluminous writings, public or private, nor discovered any record of his ever having mentioned it in conversation. Warren recognized that this apparent fact may at some time be proved to be untrue, but he was unconcerned about this possibility. As a poet, he said, he was interested in Jefferson's silence about the murder as symbolic truth, not as historical fact (see *BD* I, xi). What prompted Jefferson to in effect hide from himself a crime that was a matter of public knowledge? Was the author of the Declaration of Independence so blinded by the light of his delusionary belief that man is not innately evil but innately good that he was unable to face evidence of man's innate capacity for evil, especially when this was demonstrated by his own flesh and blood? What would have been the consequences, for himself and for the nation, if he had recognized and tried to cope with the meaning of the murderous behavior of his own sister's children? The reason why Warren eventually turned his hand to writing a second version of *Brother to Dragons* would appear to be that he more and more turned these questions inward. His search for the symbolic import of Jefferson's suppression of Lilburne and Isham's savage deed became a symbol of his quest for his own meaning—not only as an American poet and an American citizen but as an individual human being, a "self," existing in history. Warren had no choice but to keep on living with and remaking the original *Brother to Dragons*.

An understanding of Warren's struggle to create the second version of *Brother to Dragons,* as I think I have indicated, demands more than scrutiny of the two texts of the poem for editorial revisions and textual emendations. Our attention may well be directed, for one thing, to the relation between the two versions of the poem and Warren's non-poetic writings, especially essays and fiction written prior to the composition of the first version. I think particularly of Warren's remarkable essay on Joseph Conrad's *Nostromo* published two years before the first version of *Brother to Dragons* appeared. In spite of the tendency of critics to agree with Conrad's own evaluation of himself as "an imperfect aesthete" and "an imperfect philosopher," Warren argues in this deeply reflective essay that Conrad is to be defined "in the fullest sense of the term" as "a philosophical novelist." "Willing to go naked into the pit" over and over again "to make the same old struggle for his truth," Warren says, Conrad created in *Nostromo* "one of the few mastering visions of our historical moment and our historical lot."[10]

In placing a primary emphasis on the novelist as an individual—in asserting that Conrad created a "mastering" vision of the modern age out of the struggle "for his truth," for his own vision of history—Warren was seeking to delineate and to confirm his own literary motives as much as Conrad's. By the time he published his essay on Conrad, he had become a philosophical novelist in his own right. In no less than four distinguished novels—*Night Rider, At Heaven's Gate, All the King's Men,* and *World Enough and Time*—he had made his own struggle for visionary truth and had projected, if not a grand "mastering vision," a unifying vision of the American historical moment and the American historical lot—a vision centered in the perception that the underlying motive of American history is the fundamental motive Conrad had discerned in the history of the modern Western world: the assertion of the connection between intellect and self-will. Foreshadowed in Western literature in the legend of Dr. Faustus and made plain in Marlowe and Shakespeare, this motive has often been expressed in stories, like the tale of Prince Hamlet, that are symbolic embodiments of the self's struggle for identity in the historical context of the disturbing sense of the erosion of the traditional father-son relationship as a hierarchical society began to yield to the revolutionary forces signified by what Sir Francis Bacon called "the advancement of knowledge." In Warren's first four novels the father-son relationship is viewed as it has existed under the cultural circumstances of a national culture that had hailed the victory of the modern conception of the autonomy of the self by following Jefferson's recommendation to abolish the law of primogeniture. In each novel the son—an actor in the dialectical drama of the displacement in America of the traditional father-son relationship—discovers what Jack Burden in *All the King's Men* discovers: namely, that his only hope for salvation in his quest for self-identity is the recognition that he is a participant not only in the present but in the past, a past marked by the sins of his father. The implication is that if any sanity is to prevail in human relations under the governing terms of the redemptive promise offered by American history—the terms offered by the grand and noble, yet contradictory, equation between freedom and equality set forth by Jefferson in the Declaration—a dialectical tension between past and present, community and self, self and world must somehow be maintained.

But under the terms of life in American society how can it be?

This question haunts Jeremiah Beaumont in *World Enough and Time,* the novel that followed *All the King's Men.* In Jeremiah's case the question has become not the identity of the son as opposed to that of the father but the question of the relationship between a self that seeks its identity in what is praiseworthy by society and a self that refuses any familial or social role, a self that declares the self to be its "own truth."[11]

If the tale of Jeremiah Beaumont represents a climax in Warren's depiction in his first four novels of the willful self as a central, and at times destructive, force in American history, a deeper, more fundamental imagining of such a quest is suggested in the daring effort in *Brother to Dragons* to interpret the meaning of his own relationship to Jefferson, an effort that may be viewed as one climax in Warren's lifelong struggle to, like Conrad, envision not only "our" but his own "historical moment and . . . historical lot."

We discover the governing focus of this struggle in the well-known dictum set forth in the foreword to the first *Brother to Dragons* and repeated in the foreword to the second: "Historical sense and poetic sense should not, in the end, be contradictory, for if poetry is the little myth we make, history is the big myth we live, and in our living, constantly remake" (*BD* I, xii; *BD* II, xiii). Or, to put this more directly, the historian is a poet and the poet is a historian: history is poetry and poetry is history, the historian being no less a maker than the poet, who in the original Greek meaning of the term for poet is one who makes. Living the big myth of history, Warren says in effect, the poet or the historian makes and remakes history through making and remaking the little myth of poetry.

With respect to the drama of making and remaking embodied in the two versions of *Brother to Dragons,* it is interesting that in the foreword to the first version of the poem Jefferson is referred to as "the spiritual father" of "American history." But in the foreword to the second version he becomes simply one who "helped to found" the nation (*BD* I, xi; *BD* II, xii). The implicit contrast between the image of Jefferson as the spiritual father of the nation and the nominal image of Jefferson as only one of the nation's founders clearly suggests that as Warren relived the first version of *Brother to Dragons* he had become less certain about the significance of Jefferson's role in American history. The result is a heightened tension in the second version between Jefferson's identity in American history and the poet's sense of his own historical identity as an American poet.

We see this in changes made in the beginning of the 1979 version of the poem. In the initial encounter in the first version between R.P.W. and Jefferson, Jefferson starts to introduce himself:

> My name is Thomas Jefferson. I am he
> Whose body is yet under the triple boast
> On my green mountain—

He gets no further before R.P.W. interrupts:

> Yes. I've read your boast
> Cut in the stone where your body still waits
> On your green mountain, off in Virginia, awaiting
> I suppose, whatever fulfillment of the boast
> May yet be.
> (BD I, 5)

Whereupon Jefferson says:

> The boast—it was the boast
> That split my heart, the boast which I, in my late
> Last year, made, while my heart still hugged some hope
> That life had spoken and I'd heard it speak.
> It was that boast that split my heart. It split it
> As the vernal enlargement of life's green germ will split
> The dry acorn. My heart, it was only my heart—
> That old earth-fallen acorn, dry, but postulating
> Green germ and joy and the summer shade, and I said:
> Beneath that shade we'll shelter,
> Green grandeur and unmurmuring instancy of leaf,
> Through the heat of all the summer day.
> (BD I, 5–6)

Jefferson continues, explaining that if the boast split his heart, it was made neither "in pain" nor in "pride." It was made in a "pride past pride"—a pride in his "identity with the definition of man" that had been made in Philadelphia in 1776, when Jefferson and the other delegates to the Revolutionary Congress signed the Declaration of Independence. Those who signed "were only ourselves,"

> Packed with our own lusts and languors, lost,
> Each man lost, in some blind lobby, hall, enclave,
> Crank cul-de-sac, couloir, or corridor of Time.
> Of Time. Or self: and in that dark no thread,
> Airy as breath by Ariadne's fingers forged.
> No thread, and beyond some groped-at corner, hulked
> In the blind dark, hock-deep in ordure, its beard
> And shag foul-scabbed, and when the hoof heaves—
> Listen!—the foulness sucks like mire.
>   (BD I, 7)

Not only is Jefferson's introductory speech longer in *Brother to Dragons* II, it is divided into what Warren refers to as two "sections" separated by a stanza break; moreover, Jefferson speaks without interruption by R.P.W.:

> My name is Thomas Jefferson. Thomas. I
> Lived. Died. But
> Dead, cannot lie down in the
> Dark. Cannot, though dead, set
> My mouth to the dark stream that I may unknow
> All my knowing. Cannot, for if,
> Kneeling in that final thirst, I thrust
> Down my face, I see come glimmering upward
> White, white out of the absolute dark of depth,
> My face. And it is only human.
>
> Have you ever tried to kiss that face in the mirror?
> Or—ha, ha—has it ever tried to kiss you? Well,
> You are only human. Is that a boast?

R.P.W. makes a more succinct response to this question than he does in the first version:

> Well, I've read your boast
> Cut in stone, on the mountain, off in Virginia.

Jefferson's reaction to R.P.W.'s abbreviated remark is:

> What else had I in age to cling to,
> Even in the face of knowledge?
> I tried to bring myself to say:
> Knowledge is only incidental, hope is all—
> Hope, a dry acorn, but some green germ
> May split it yet, then joy and the summer shade
> Even after age and the tangle of experience
> I still might—
> Oh, grandeur green and murmuring instancy of leaf,
> Beneath that shade we'll shelter. So in senility
> And moments of indulgent fiction I might try
> To defend my old definition of man.
>
> (*BD* II, 5)

In abbreviating R.P.W.'s response to Jefferson's question "Is that a boast?" and in altering the tone of Jefferson's rejoinder, the poet, I take it, emphasizes the rather dire implications in the beginning of *Brother to Dragons* for the tone and movement of the whole poem. The omission of R.P.W.'s provisional "whatever fulfillment of the boast / May yet be," together with the introduction of the idea that the Jefferson of the poem repudiated the real Jefferson's "definition of man" in the Declaration of Independence, foreshadows Warren's reduction in the second version of his allowance for "hope" for the amelioration of the human condition that is implicit in the three accomplishments Jefferson "boasted" about on the tombstone he designed for himself the year or two before he died in 1826: his authorship of the Declaration of Independence and of the Virginia statute for religious freedom and his fathering of the University of Virginia. The relatively more severe attitude in *Brother to Dragons* II toward such a fundamental spiritual trait of humankind as hope for the future—a trait that has often been considered to be the very essence of the American—evidently results from Warren's increased sensitivity in the second version of the poem to his lifelong search for the meaning of the self. A more intense concern for the role of the self is evident in Warren's introduction at the beginning of *Brother to Dragons* II of an image that is not present in the first version: Jefferson's image of himself kneeling to drink from the Lethean stream, and thus to "unknow / All my knowing," only to see rising "out of the absolute dark of depth" his own face; whereupon he asks R.P.W., "Have you ever tried to kiss that face in the mirror?" As he comes into his existence in "No Time, No Place," Jefferson's desire to "unknow" all his "knowing"—his knowledge of the Enlightenment definition of man as a rational being capable of making his own world—is confounded by the narcissistic self-image that emerges even from Lethe's black depths.

Of course, there is nothing startling in the discovery that the central motive of *Brother to Dragons* is a search for the definition of self-identity. This, Warren's subject throughout his novels and poems, is, to be sure, the American literary subject: indeed, if we consider poetry in a generic sense as encompassing all literature, then American literature—including our central poem, the Declaration of Independence—is a metaphor of the quest for the meaning of the relation between time and self, history and self. Or, more precisely, for the meaning for the equation of history and self. Or, more precisely still, for a way to assert the identity of self and history.

In both versions of *Brother to Dragons* Jefferson's appeal to the myth of the Minotaur represents such an equation. At the time of the American Revolution, he says "every manjack of us" was "lost" in "some blind alley" of "Time" or "Self"; and there encountered "hock-deep in ordure" the Minotaur, the man-beast born as a result of the lust awakened in Pasiphae, queen of Crete, for the Cretan god-bull by Aphrodite as a punishment for disobeying the goddess, as some sources say; or, as other sources say, as a punishment of her husband, King Minos, for disobeying Poseidon. The king orders the supremely cunning artificer, Daedalus, who has built the device which enables Pasiphae to mate with the bull god, to construct an intricate labyrinth, in which he concealed himself, Pasiphae, and the Minotaur. Obviously Warren's employment of the myth of the Minotaur bears a certain relation to his interpretation of Jefferson's lifelong silence about the testimony to the innate evil of man offered by his own blood kin even as he offered his own testimony to the triumph of man's innate rational virtue.[12]

The myth of the Minotaur bears a relation also to the "more significant role" Warren gives Meriwether Lewis in *Brother to Dragons* II (*BD* II, xiv).[13] Although he was a native of the former domain of the family of Colonel Lewis, Albemarle County, Virginia, Meriwether was not, as Warren says in the foreword to *Brother to Dragons* I, "the first cousin of Lilburne and Isham Lewis." Warren rectifies this error in the second version of the poem by referring to Meriwether simply as "the cousin" of Lilburne and Isham. (He may in fact have been a distant one.) In the second version Warren is also more cautious in his description of the relationship between Jefferson and Meriwether Lewis, changing this from "cousin" to "kinsman." But, aware of the importance of kinship, however remote, in the society of the time and place, Warren had no reason in the second version to change the description of the relationship between Jefferson and Meriwether he had made in the first. It was, he says, a "filial" relation (*BD* II, xiii).[14] In both versions, to be sure, Warren implies another and stronger justification for the appointment of Meriwether to lead the expedition to explore the vast western territory the second president of the Republic had succeeded in adding to the national dominion: it involved the trust a father might place in a son. If in manipulating the Louisiana Purchase Jefferson had pursued tactics that willfully defied his own conception of the proper limits of the constitutional powers of his office, he justified his transgression of his own principles not primarily by the political, economic, and military importance of bringing the western territory under the dominion of the new nation. The Lewis and Clark Expedition was a climactic moment in a vivid desire that, whether he was in office or out of office, ruled Jefferson all of his life: the desire to illuminate the darkness of the world with rational knowledge. He entrusted Meriwether not so much to head an official government expedition as to fulfill what was for him a compelling personal mission: that of bringing the vast Louisiana Territory under the dominion of mind.

Two years following the completion of the expedition when, by Jefferson's appointment, he was serving as the governor of the Louisiana Territory, Meriwether Lewis, at the age of thirty-five, died a violent death in the Tennessee wilderness while on a journey from St. Louis to the national capital. The circumstances were somewhat mysterious. One story is that he was murdered, but the more likely story is that, hounded by officials in Washington and unrespected by his subordinates, the "Governor of Louisiana, of all the West," as he ironically refers to himself in the poem, fell into a state of extreme depression and took his own life (*BD* I, 182; *BD* II, 113). This was the story the historical Jefferson accepted, attributing Meriwether's suicide to "hypochondriacal affections."[15] In his enlarged role in the 1979 *Brother to Dragons*, Meriwether Lewis—whose brains, R.P.W. says, "Stare out like one great eye, / Winking in blood"—becomes a crucial influence in the redemption of Jefferson from the ideology of the Enlightenment to what may be called the knowledge of the blood: the saving knowledge of that original and permanent stain of sin that entered the human blood stream when Cain murdered Abel (*BD* II, 109). Seeking a rational explanation for Meriwether's suicide, Jefferson's ghost says it resulted from Meriwether's being falsely accused of wrongdoing after his appointment to the territorial governorship. But, when he confronts Jefferson in the climactic scene of *Brother to Dragons,* Meriwether says that the truth is that he was "murdered" by Jefferson's "lies" about the goodness of human nature (*BD* I, 176–77; *BD* II, 109). When Jefferson cries out, "No! no, my son!" the very exclamation is an admission of the truth of the accusation (*BD* II, 115).

Warren's basic conception of the relationship between Meriwether Lewis and Jefferson, which remains the same in both versions of *Brother to Dragons,* is hardly more significant than his conception, which also remains the same in both versions, of the relationship between R.P.W. and his eighty-year-old father, Robert Franklin Warren. In the poem the father twice accompanies R.P.W. on visits to the town of Smithland, Kentucky, and the country thereabout, where the Lewises had settled. The first visit to the scene of the long-ago murder is based on actuality, the second would seem to be imagined. During the second visit Robert Franklin Warren tells R.P.W. about how his father (i.e., Robert Penn Warren's paternal grandfather), with the return of spring each year, ritualistically administered to his sons a dose of bitter tonic made from the root of percoon and the bark of "prickly ash," the purpose being to "unthicken" their blood and make them less inclined to devilment.

> "Percoon, what's that?" I said. And he: "Why, Son,
> It's just some sort of plant they called percoon."
> "But what's it like?" I said. And he: "Why, Son,
> I just don't recollect. But it's percoon."
> (*BD* I, 205; cf. *BD* II, 127)

Although the real Robert Franklin Warren does not appear to have accepted original sin as doctrine, the poet uses his father as the voice for a folksy tale about a homemade tonic that may be taken as an ironic symbol of a truth beyond questioning, at least for many in the world in which his father had been reared, the blood knowledge of original sin. But R.P.W.'s natural father is conceived by the son, the maker of *Brother to Dragons,* as standing not in contrast to Jefferson, the sophisticated foe of king and priest and all emblems of what he considered to be superstition, but, in his folksiness, as a figure apposite to Jefferson. Both the living parental presence of the aged gentleman who rides to Smithland with his son and the ghostly presence of Thomas Jefferson haunt the poet's imagination of his parentage. To him both the author of the great Declaration and the teller of the tale about the percoon are themselves poets—poets of a people, many of whom, though not all, believe at once in original happiness and original sin; and of a people who are all deeply and inextricably involved in the past yet believe they are free from the past. The author of *Brother to Dragons,* explicitly in one case and by implication in the other, stands in a filial relation to both.

But the primary filial relation in *Brother to Dragons,* the one at the center of the poem, is the implied relation existing between R.P.W. (and Warren himself) and the historical Jefferson. In both versions of the poem Warren transforms what he takes to be the real Jefferson from a devotee of the Enlightenment into a lapsed *philosophe,* who, in a psychic dominion somewhere, engages in a struggle for redemption from a terribly destructive innocence. Eventually, as Warren has it, the ghostly author of the Declaration of Independence—having, through the agency of the living poet R.P.W., relived in No Time and Any Place a part of his life that he refused to acknowledge in his earthly life—comes to the realization that his redemption is dependent on his acknowledgment of his intricate entanglement in the drama of good and evil that is human history. But, more importantly—in a way reminiscent of Jack Burden, the teller of the tale in *All the King's Men*—R.P.W., in his involvement with the story of Jefferson, is telling the story of his own quest as a twentieth-century American poet for a redeeming vision of the meaning of history.

It is not, I think, an incidental fact that Warren finally managed to complete and publish the second version of *Brother to Dragons* during a period when his poetic output was at its height, a time when, I remember, Cleanth Brooks remarked to me, "Red is writing poems by the yard." A year after he published the second version Warren published a collection of striking lyrical poems written in the short span of three years, 1977–1980. Bearing the significant title *Being Here,* this volume concludes in an unusual way with an appended prose notation, entitled "Afterthought," in which Warren says that, representing "a fusion of fiction and fact in varying degrees and perspectives," the poems herein collected constitute "a shadowy autobiography." He does not suggest what may be fiction, what may be fact in the poems, saying only that as a question may be more significant than the answer, "fiction may often be more deeply significant than fact." "Indeed," he adds, "it may be said that our lives are our own supreme fiction."[16]

In effect, in the "Afterthought" to *Being Here* Warren recognizes that his writings, early and late, bear the tangible, if not always distinct, imprint of a lyrical, a deeply subjective or autobiographical motive. The imprint of the subjective motive is plain in the ambiguity of the setting Warren seeks to establish for *Brother to Dragons*. In both versions it is clear that Warren conceives the setting in "No Place, Any Time" to be a way of getting a perspective on Our Place, Our Time. It is not quite so clear that in a more subjective sense Warren conceives the setting to be "My Place, My Time." The setting, in other words, is not a metaphysical context beyond but the historical context of the poet's life during the time of the composition, and recomposition, of his poem. This was the time of the greatest crisis in our national identity since the Civil War: the agonizing epoch that began in the American response to North Korea's invasion of South Korea, that reached a climax in the disastrous historical trap of the misadventure in Vietnam, and that, as daily events unmistakably indicate, now reaches toward its culminating historical expression in the American imperial spirit's drive toward the "globalization" of American culture.

The setting becomes explicit in R.P.W.'s meditation on the prosperity of Smithland when he returns for his second visit to the community associated with the long-ago crime of Lilburne and Isham. In *Brother to Dragons* I, and in *Brother to Dragons* II with a few nonessential changes, this reads:

> And paint is on the houses, and new stores,
> And gas pumps are a rash that's worse than measles.
> And Ford and Plymouth vie to make you happy,
> And money jingles in the local jeans.
> That's fine. I don't begrudge such solvency,
> And who's to blame if there is some correlation
> Between it and the dark audit of blood
> In some Korean bunker, at the midnight concussion?
> Yes, who's to blame? For in the great bookkeeping
> Of History, what ledger has balanced yet?
> And every entry is a scrawl of blood.
> (*BD* I, 206; *BD* II, 127)

The ultimate rationale in the making and remaking of *Brother to Dragons*, it may be suggested, lies in Warren's need to resolve his vexatious sense of the connection between his own identity and the identity of the poet, who in writing the Declaration of Independence, became the maker, the father, of the American

Republic, and so of all American poets since. Responding to the ironic feeling of alienation from the standard image of Jefferson as the man of reason, Warren attempted to transcend his ironic reservations about the Jefferson of historical fact by creating a fictional Jefferson he could identify with, a Jefferson immanent in his [Warren's] imagination of his own historical moment. The attempt to create this Jefferson was bold not because it involved the device of imagining the present in terms of a world outside historical time and place yet consonant with it. It was bold in that, although he may not have yet set it down in explicit formulation, Warren followed the dictum stated in *Being Here* that one's own life is the supreme fiction one lives. In the making and remaking of *Brother to Dragons*, he attempted nothing less, you might say, than to incorporate the supreme fiction that was Jefferson's life into the supreme fiction that was his own life—to fuse the Jefferson of historical fact and a fiction of *his* redemption with the fact of the historical R.P.W. (or the poet himself) and a fiction of *his* redemption. Whether or not the poet is successful in this endeavor depends on how convincing we deem it to be.

In his final appearance in the poem, Meriwether says, "All is redeemed, / In knowledge," and Jefferson responds, "But knowledge is the most powerful cost. / It is the bitter bread. / I have eaten the bitter bread. / In joy, would end" (*BD* II, 120). But do we believe he will indeed end in joy? Do we believe that Warren's Jefferson, having eaten of the bitter bread of knowledge, has truly transcended the bitterness of the knowledge the earthly Jefferson hid from himself?

This question receives its answer as R.P.W.—in "the last light of December's, and the day's, declension"—contemplates the meaning of his final leave-taking from the site on the bluff of the river where Lilburne had built his house and where he and Isham had committed the heinous act the historical Jefferson could not hide from the world but could and did hide from himself. R.P.W.'s thoughts become a meditation on the nature of joy, when (in both versions of *Brother to Dragons*) they lead to the introduction of an intimate personal reflection.

> And I think of another bluff and another river.
> I think of snow on brown leaves, and below
> How cold and far was light on a northern river,
> And I think of how her mouth and mine together
> Were cold on the first kiss. We kissed in the cold
> Logic of hope and need.

Who is to name delusion when the flesh shakes?

So in this other year by another river,
Far in Kentucky there, I raised my eyes
And thought of the track a man may make through Time,
And how the hither-coming never knows the hence-going.
Since then I have made new acquaintance
With snow and brown leaves.
Since then I have made new acquaintance
With the nature of joy.
(*BD* II, 129)

Continuing his meditation, R.P.W. thinks "of the dead beneath my feet," and

Of Lilburne on his mountain here,
Who brought no light into the dark, and so died.
And of another mountain, far away,
In Albemarle, where Lilburne's kinsman sleeps,
And thought of all
Who had come down the great river and are
Nameless. What if
We know the names of the niggers hunkering by the wall,
Moaning? For yes, we know each name,
The age, the sex, the price, from the executor,
Who listed all to satisfy the court.
(*BD* II, 130; cf. *BD* I, 208–12)

R.P.W. thinks too of other things we know: "the names of all who went with Meriwether / To lie on night-mats in rain, and hear the utterance of ocean." This knowledge, together with the knowledge embodied in his recollection of a transforming moment in his own life, are the immediate reference for the basic question R.P.W. thereupon propounds about the relation between knowledge and redemption: "But what is knowledge / Without the intrinsic mediation of the heart?"

Although he has never returned to the scene of the long-ago murder, R.P.W. says at the end of *Brother to Dragons*, he has held this "landscape in his heart" ever since he "crossed the evening barnlot, opened / The sagging gate," prepared "To go into the world of action and liability."

> I had long lived in the world of action and liability.
> But now I passed the gate into a world
>
> Sweeter than hope in that confirmation of late light.
> (BD II, 132)[17]

It would seem that in the conclusion of *Brother to Dragons* Warren's reference is no longer to the Book of Job but to the *Divina Commedia,* especially the conclusion. His vision of a world sweeter than hope echoes Dante's imagination of his passage from the state of hope in the *Purgatorio* into the state depicted in the *Paradiso.* As would be expected in the case of a poet who assumes the metaphysical tradition of Christianity, the poet of the *Divina Commedia* finds that his imagination fails him utterly in the presence of the vision that comes to him at the end of his journey, when his love for his spiritual guide, Beatrice, is transformed by a vision of the unity of the triadic God. To describe the ineffable, transcendent state of consciousness, beyond history and beyond imaging as a world his vision represented, was not, the poet says, "a flight for my wings: / Except that my mind was struck by a flash / In which what it desired came to it." In this flash he knows that his "desire" and his "will" are "being turned like a wheel, all at one speed, / By the love which moves the sun and the other stars."[18]

What R.P.W. says at the end of *Brother to Dragons* obviously strikes a more consoling note in the breast than Jack Burden's austere statement at the end of *All the King's Men* about going "out of history into history and the awful responsibility of Time." Certainly R.P.W.'s valedictory is far more consoling than the terrifying question Jeremiah Beaumont leaves dangling before the reader at the end of *World Enough and Time,* "Was all for naught?" Yet, we may ask, is the resolution of the story of Jefferson and R.P.W. and their involvement in the murderous act of Lilburne and Isham Lewis effectively resolved in R.P.W.'s vision of passing into "a world / Sweeter than hope"? A world, that is, pervaded by the Dantean sense of love? For all his long struggle with *Brother to Dragons,* does Warren's conclusion to the second version—although more economically and sharply presented than in the first version—transcend the ironic sense of history and human nature that pervades the poem as a whole? Considering R.P.W.'s comment immediately preceding his vision of a "world sweeter than hope," does Warren intend for us to think so?

> We have yearned in the heart for some identification
> With the glory of the human heart. We have devised
> Evil in the heart, and pondered the nature of virtue.
> We have stumbled into the act of justice, and caught,
> Only from the tail of the eye, the flicker
> Of joy, like a wing-flash in thicket.
> (BD II, 131)

Is not the Dantean moment of the transcendent vision of joy in *Brother to Dragons*—the effort of the poet to imagine a world sweeter than hope—subject to the pervasive sense of irony that pervades the poem as a whole? We may think of the dragons in *Brother to Dragons* as pride, especially intellectual pride, and the other deadly sins, but in sum there would seem to be one dragon, the dragon of self—the desiring, willing self. I would not at all make Warren out to be a Freudian, but there is strong suggestion in his vision of the later Freud's depiction of structure of the self (libido, ego, and superego) of the tragic opposition that exists between the ego and the ruthless superego. This situation in the Freudian drama of human nature is not treatable by analysis, the alienation of the ego and the superego being permanent, having no remedy whatsoever. Some such sense of the irremediable nature of the human condition haunts the tale of R.P.W.'s quest for his historical self-identity in his dramatic encounter with the persons he summons into the present from the history of the time of the making of the nation.

That this is the case is pinpointed in the change of one word in the second part of *Brother to Dragons* II. Jefferson speaks to R.P.W.:

> I have long since come to the considered conclusion
> That love, all kinds, is but a mask
> To hide the brute face of fact,
> And that fact is the un-uprootable ferocity of self.
>   Even
> The face of love beneath your face at the first
> Definitive delight—even that—
> Is but a mirror

> For your own ferocity—a mirror blurred with breath,
> And slicked and slimed with love—
> And even then, through the interstices and gouts
> Of the hypocritical moisture, cold eyes spy out
> From the mirror's cold heart, and thus
> Self spies on self
> In that unsummerable arctic of the human lot.
>
> (*BD* II,33)

Compare the last line of the passage I have quoted with the last in the same passage in the 1953 poem, in which we read, "In that unsummerable arctic [not of "the human lot" but] of the human alienation" (*BD* I, 47). The term "human alienation" suggests that the self somehow recognizes its compulsion to seek its own aggrandizement at the expense of all other selves, and therefore conceivably has some control over its behavior; in substituting the term "human lot" in the second version Warren has his author of the Declaration of Independence conceiving the isolate condition of the self as absolute and beyond alleviation. Does *Brother to Dragons* II suggest that the search for the meaning of the self in history is to be discovered in the self's ferocious yet futile rebellion against the realization of its isolation in history; or, to put it in a contrary yet complementary way, against its discovery of the isolation of history in the self—in, as Warren bleakly puts in "Why Do We Read Fiction?" the "prison yard" of the self? But, we note, in this same passage Warren shows an inclination to alleviate the bleakness. According to its "own nature," each self may get a chance "to participate . . . in the life which fiction presents." When we read *Crime and Punishment*, "something in our nature participates in the bloody deed, and later, something else experiences with murderer Raskolnikov, the bliss of repentance and reconciliation."

Since Warren, and more than once, weighed each word with great care in his revision of *Brother to Dragons*, we would appear to be justified in saying that his depiction of the ferocity of the self is more intense in the second version. But in either version it is sufficiently intense—is it not?—to cast the shadow of a dark question over the theme of redemption in *Brother to Dragons*: After such an austere and forbidding vision of the demonic nature of the self, what redemption for Jefferson, for Lilburne, for Meriwether, for R.P.W.? Or for their creator, the poet Robert Penn Warren?[19] Concluding with R.P.W.'s vision of "a world / Sweeter than hope," does not the poem end in ironic ambiguity?

Yet, paradoxically, in the ambiguous resolution of the redemptive—which is to say, the autobiographical—motive in *Brother to Dragons* lies the success of this singular poem, for it opens up an instructive vision of considerable scope and power.

Jefferson's frightening meditation on love and the "un-uprootable ferocity of the self" is not only a metaphor of the fate of the self under the specific conditions of American history. In the larger sense Warren's effort to interpret the meaning of the silence of the philosopher and poet who wrote the Declaration of Independence about a murder committed by his nephews assumes the character of an ironic metaphor of the character of the self in modern history generally. Signifying the complicity between self and the modern power of secular mind, it represents a psychic situation that Marlowe and Shakespeare intuited, that Francis Bacon, although without quite realizing what he was doing, set forth in *The Advancement of Learning* and elsewhere, and that John Donne, the most sophisticated English poet and intellectual of his age, explicitly delineated in 1611 in his poem "Anatomy of the World":

> And new philosophy calls all in doubt . . .
> Prince, subject, father, son, are things forgot,
> For every man alone thinks he hath got
> To be a phoenix, and that then can be
> None of that kind, of which he is, but he.[20]

Donne saw that in willfully identifying itself with the greatly enhanced powers of the rational intellect that were coming into play in the age of Francis Bacon the modern self would identify itself with the mind of God and increasingly seek to assume a preemptive role in history. Perhaps Donne's vision in the early seventeenth century of the destruction of the traditional father and son relationship may be conceived of as foreshadowing its fulfillment in a visionary manifesto, by a late-eighteenth-century American philosopher, poet, and slavemaster, proclaiming all men—all selves—to be free and equal. Perhaps we may even take Donne's vision to foreshadow the twentieth-century American poet, novelist, and historian who would struggle for half his literary life to write an interpretation of the anatomy of the Jeffersonian world, a world that he saw as reaching a culmination in his own world—our own world; a world that is at once a symbol of the triumph of the Jeffersonian faith in the union of the human will and the human intellect, and the most violent period in human history. Whatever else we may learn from Warren's long pursuit of his personal relationship to Thomas Jefferson, we learn that we ourselves are not done with Jefferson, nor, most assuredly, is Jefferson done with us.

We are reminded of this fact in the final evocative moment of the story of Warren's life, which occurred on Sunday, October 8, 1989, when in a private ceremony an urn containing his ashes was buried in a lonely country cemetery not far from his beloved summer home at West Wardsboro, Vermont. I had some account of the last rites for Warren in a telephone conversation with his friend and bibliographer, James (or as we know him, "Bo") Grimshaw. When, in accordance with his wishes, the earth of a New England burying ground that had not been disturbed for a hundred years was opened for Warren, this act expressed the vision of "a place to come to" (as the title of his last novel, the story of Jed Tukesbury, puts it) for a storyteller for whom the mystery of personal identity was deeply fused with the mystery of place; for a poet who was an unmoveable nonbeliever yet always knew the yearning to believe; for a poet who was southern to the bone—who knew that he could never be at home save in the South—yet knew that he could never come home again. As I listened to Bo Grimshaw's quietly eloquent description of the farewell to Warren in distant Vermont—including one particularly graphic detail, a reading, amid the burgeoning color of a New England autumn, of Warren's Louisiana poem "Bearded Oaks" by the distinguished poet and friend of Warren, John Hollander—a thought I have expressed before came to me with singular force. I refer to the idea that between New England and the South there has been a fateful symbiotic relation, this subsisting in the ironic mystery that southerners are, or once were, spiritual New Englanders; and conversely that New Englanders are, or once were, spiritual southerners. It is an idea fraught with tragic implications; but in remembering Red Warren I took comfort in it. In no way more so than in recalling that Warren was a contemporary of William Faulkner, who identified himself with his most compelling creation, the Quentin Compson of *The Sound and the Fury* and *Absalom, Absalom!*, the southern youth who, haunted by the defeat of the southern nation, so emphatically protested to his Canadian roommate at Harvard that he did not, did not hate the South before he drowned himself in the Charles River.

NOTES

1. I of course write about the memory of a time before the symbolic configuration represented by the Washington Monument, the Lincoln Memorial, and the Jefferson Memorial was drastically altered by the addition of the Vietnam and Korean war memorials.

2. See Pauline Maier, *American Scripture: Making the Declaration of Independence* (New York: Knopf, 1997), for an authoritative text of the Declaration.

3. *Brother to Dragons: A Tale in Verse and Voices* (New York, 1979), xiii–xiv. Hereinafter this volume will be referred to as *BD* II, and *Brother to Dragons: A Tale in Verse and Voices* (New York, 1953) will be referred to as *BD* I, in parenthetical references in the text. Both versions of the poem have been widely discussed. After making an extensive gathering of critical interpretations down to the early 1980s, James A. Grimshaw, Jr., concluded that his collection proves "there are indeed more than thirteen ways of looking at a blackbird." *Robert Penn Warren's "Brother to Dragons": A Discussion* (Baton Rouge, 1983), 10. Discussions subsequent to Grimshaw's collection support his conclusion. See especially the distinguished readings of the poem in John Burt, *Robert Penn Warren and American Idealism* (New Haven, 1988), 199–218; and Hugh Ruppersburg, *Robert Penn Warren and the American Imagination* (Athens, Ga., 1990), 38–78. Also, see the references to the poem in William Bedford Clark's valuable study focused on the Americanness of Warren, *The American Vision of Robert Penn Warren* (Lexington, Ky., 1991).

4. For a definitive historical account of the Lewis family, its relation to Thomas Jefferson, and the murder of the slave by Lilburne and Isham Lewis, see Boynton Merrill, Jr., *Jefferson's Nephews: A Frontier Tragedy* (Princeton, N.J., 1976). Concerning *Brother to Dragons* Merrill comments (p. 427) that "in its unique literary and artistic quality it stands alone among other works based on the Lewis tragedy." But Merrill indicates that he is not entirely in agreement with Warren's statement in the foreword to *BD* I that since he is "trying to write a poem and not a history," he has had "no compunction about tampering with facts." Warren has "succeeded admirably, both in his poem and in tampering with the facts," Merrill observes, though he adds that it may be "ventured that facts usually do stand in the way of poetic expression and artistic triumph, such as Warren has achieved." In the foreword to *BD* II Warren refers appreciatively to Merrill's "scholarly and conscientious account" of the history of the Lewis family and the murder of the slave by Lilburne and Isham Lewis. But he makes an indirect response to the ironic tone of Merrill's remarks about *BD* in the fillip to be found in the foreword to *BD* II (which was published three years after Merrill's book): a poem can "be totally accurate as history and still not be worth a dime as a poem" (*BD* II, xii–xiii).

5. Ralph Ellison and Eugene Walter, "Warren on Fiction," in *Talking with Robert Penn Warren*, ed. Floyd C. Watkins, John T. Hiers, and Mary Louise Weaks (Athens: University of Georgia Press, 1990), 38.

6. The highly significant role of the Congress in writing the Declaration of Independence is authoritatively examined by Pauline Maier in *American Scripture: Making the Declaration of Independence*.

7. *Talking with Robert Penn Warren*, 38.

8. See Robert Penn Warren, "The Way It Was Written," *New York Times Book Review*, August 23, 1953, 25. For an excellent account of the dramatic productions of *BD*, see Victor Strandberg, "*Brother to Dragons*: Poem / Play / Film," *Southern Quarterly* 33 (Winter–Spring 1995): 187–96. There is no

published version of the play text. For the script of the television production, see "*Brother to Dragons: A Play in Two Acts*," *Georgia Review* 30 (Spring 1976): 65–138.

9. According to Joseph Blotner's biography of Warren, Warren's interest in Dante led him to begin a reading of the *Divina Commedia* in the original in the summer of 1939 during a month-long voyage to Italy on a tramp steamer. At that time he was devoting a great deal of time to completing a play he called "Proud Flesh." Based on the story of Huey Long, this work was partly in verse. Warren had no luck in getting the play published, let alone produced, but it was later transformed into his most successful novel, *All the King's Men*. The epigraph for this novel is a line from the third book of the *Purgatorio*. See Blotner, *Robert Penn Warren: A Biography* (New York, 1997), 176.

10. Warren, "'The Great Mirage': Conrad and *Nostromo*," *Selected Essays* (New York, 1958), 31–58.

11. *World Enough and Time: A Romantic Novel* (New York, 1950), 320.

12. See George Garrett, "The Function of the Pasiphae Myth in *Brother to Dragons*," in James A. Grimshaw, ed., *Robert Penn Warren's "Brother to Dragons": A Discussion* (Baton Rouge, 1983), 77–79.

13. In the foreword to *BD* II Warren associates the enlargement of the role of Meriwether with "the off-and-on process" of preparing the poem for the stage. This may have given him the idea of heightening in *BD* II the dramatic relationship between Lilburne and Meriwether that he says he had simply suggested in *BD* I. "Both Lilburne and Meriwether Lewis," he says, "entered the wilderness as heralds of civilization, as 'light-bringers,' and my story is about the difference with which they performed the role and their tragic ends" (*BD* II, xiii). Yet the Lilburne-Meriwether relationship is hardly more explicit in the second version than in the first. One reason may be that the ghost of Lilburne in both versions says very little, coming to us mostly through what others say about him, and Meriwether says nothing about Lilburne.

14. See Merrill, *Jefferson's Nephews*, 211–12.

15. See Jefferson's biographical sketch of Meriwether Lewis in *Writings of Thomas Jefferson*, ed. Andrew A. Lipscomb and Andrew Ellery Bergh (Washington, D.C., 1905), 18: 159–61.

16. *Being Here* (New York, 1980), 107–8.

17. Cf. *BD* II in which the stanzaic pattern into which these lines fall is altered and the last four lines of the conclusion of the poem (not quoted above) are cut:

> I walked down to the car where my father had been waiting.
> He woke from his cold drowse, and yawned, and said,
> "You finished what you climbed up there for, Son?"
> And I said: "Yes, I've finished. Let's go home."

As is the case in the cutting of various other lines that appear in *BD* I, the elimination of these lines would seem to have been done for the sake of poetic economy and force.

18. *All the King's Men*, Bantam edition (New York, 1980), 438; *World Enough and Time*, 512; *The Divine Comedy*, trans. C. H. Sisson (Chicago, 1981), 498. Cf. the epigraph for *All the King's Men*, which is from the second book of the *Divina Commedia* (the *Purgatorio*): "Mentre che la speranza ha fior del verde" ("As long as hope has any touch of green"). The treatment of hope in *BD* lends credence to the interpretation that the setting of *BD* is in some sense a vision of Hell, Purgatory, and Paradise. (Cf.

note 9 above.) Like the experience of Jack Burden, who in *All the King's Men* is in a way the persona of Warren, R. P. W.'s experience in *BD* bears an ironic relation to a spiritual journey for which Dante provides the archetype.

19. In the foreword to both editions Warren says poetry, being "more than fantasy," is obligated to try to "say something about the human condition." In changing the term "human alienation" to "human lot" Warren may be said to conform more strictly to his general vision of poetry in relation to history (*BD* I, xii; *BD* II, xiii).

20. Donne, "An Anatomy of the World," *Major British Writers* (New York, 1959), 1: 383.

LIONEL TRILLING AND ALLEN TATE
The Agency of Terror

The following remarks, I realize, have an informal, even at times a personal tone. This is owing to two circumstances. One is that, although I did not know Lionel Trilling personally, for fifty years he has been a part of my life as a teacher, historian, and editor in the field of American letters. The other circumstance is that I did know Trilling's older contemporary, Allen Tate, with whom I shall seek to bring Trilling into a certain degree of relationship, especially with respect to the way in which they regarded the nature of the literary vocation.

My sense of obligation to Trilling goes back to the time when, following the completion of the lengthy and tedious process of intimidation called getting a Ph.D. a year or so after the end of the Second World War, I began—though always by choice confined to the campus—to try to get an education I might reasonably certify as my own.

In this effort I was inspired by Trilling's exemplification of education as a continuous and open-ended process. The books by Trilling I associate most particularly with my own effort to fulfill this process are: *The Liberal Imagination* (1950); *The Opposing Self* (1955); *Beyond Culture* (1965); *Sincerity and Authenticity* (the Norton Lectures at Harvard in 1970, published in 1972); and *Mind in the Modern World* (the inaugural Jefferson Lecture of the National Endowment for the Humanities in 1972, published in pamphlet form the same year). But, although I shall put considerable emphasis on *The Liberal Imagination* and *The Opposing Self*, I am here concerned in a central way with Trilling's notebooks, a work not known publicly until the posthumous publication of selections from the notebooks in the 1980s.[1]

On the surface Tate and Trilling appear to be opposites: Tate was a southerner who was a prominent contributor to the 1931 Agrarian manifesto *I'll Take My Stand* (a title, incidentally, that both Robert Penn Warren and Tate deplored, and for which Warren wanted to substitute "Tracts Against Communism"); Trilling was a New York Jew, who in the time of the Agrarians was briefly attracted to the American Marxist movement. Although Tate and Trilling had in common a connection with the Kenyon School of Letters in the time when its founder and director, John Crowe Ransom, was at Kenyon College in the 1940s and 1950s, and on occasion exchanged letters, the connection that may be discovered between them in the literary and cultural history of their age is deeper than their incidental personal relationship.

In the late 1930s, when Trilling's Matthew Arnold (1939) and Tate's novel The Fathers (1938) were, for American literary intellectuals anyway, notable current events, Tate's close friend John Peale Bishop wrote to Tate that he was reading Trilling's Matthew Arnold. It "stinks," Bishop said. Later a letter from Tate to Bishop mentioned a review Trilling had done of The Fathers in the Partisan Review. He liked the comment on the book, Tate said, "as well as I could like any Marxist view." But in his public response to Trilling's review Tate did not dismiss Trilling so cavalierly. In one of the most penetrating notices the novel received, Trilling had observed how Tate, "a traditionalist in his literary as well as his social preference," had within "the limitations of strictest form" created "a fable" of violence, which, in the author's delicate control of the tone of his story, suggested the existence of a fundamental tension between the desire to refer social order to an explicit societal code—"under which people . . . live by a culture and not by a morality"—and the recognition of the possibility that the society of the Old South destroyed itself from "lack of mind." This interpretation hit home, getting at a problematical situation in Tate's vision of order that he not only failed effectively to refute in his response to Trilling's review of The Fathers (Partisan Review 6, no. 2 [1939]) but would in fact never resolve.[2]

Tate might have been more convincing in his reply to Trilling's comment on The Fathers if he had not been fixed on the notion that Trilling was a doctrinaire Marxist. This fixation directed Tate to assume a narrow attitude toward Trilling's perception of the relation between politics and culture even as he professed his admiration for Trilling's review as the "ablest and most interesting" analysis of The Fathers he had seen. Tate's unfavorable opinion of Trilling was also influenced by another fixed attitude Tate assumed, an acute disdain of the academic man of letters. In the same letter to Bishop in which he mentioned Trilling's review, Tate also remarked on something Trilling had just written about Hemingway. It is, he declares, "foully written," adding, "But when you get the English Department mentality combined with the Marxian dialectic, the result is a Y.M.C.A. secretary."[3] The bantering tone of Tate's depreciation of Trilling marks an antipathy to English departments so firm (though not so inflexible as Edmund Wilson's) that for years only economic necessity forced Tate onto the campus for temporary stints of teaching. Eventually this necessity led him to accede to a permanent association with the English department of the University of Minnesota, where he was granted tenure and the eminence of a chair.

Ironically Tate's objections to Trilling on either the political or academic counts were distinctly wide of the mark in two respects. For one thing, Trilling's attraction to Communism lacked conviction. Although in 1931 he and Diana Trilling had, as she puts in her memoirs, under Sidney Hook's "guidance . . . bowed to historical necessity and embraced the new revolutionary faith," they never shared in the enthusiasm of fellow travelers like Malcolm Cowley.[4] And by the mid-thirties (as a notebook entry for June 13, 1936, affirms) Trilling not only had come to doubt "that the future will be a certain—Marxian—way," but felt that his doubt of the Marxian way was "symbolic" of a fundamental change of life. He was, he told himself, "acquiring a new dimension," or "a new emotional response to all things"; in doing so he was developing a larger "sense of life—of the past and present"—"a sense that I do not have to prove anything finally and everlastingly" ("Notebooks," *Partisan Review* 51, no. 4, 503).

Tate was also wrong about Trilling's commitment to the academic pursuit of letters and learning. Although in outward appearance Trilling had a long-lasting and harmonious connection with Columbia—where he acquired an awesome reputation as the occupant first of the George Edward Woodberry chair and later as the occupant of the still more distinguished seat of University Professor—and although he never seems to have imagined himself outside the academic life, or for that matter, outside Columbia, Trilling was always a doubting, at times recalcitrant, resident of the campus. In truth the published excerpts from his notebooks demonstrate that for a long time he was apprehensive that the university would be the damnation of his talent and indeed that he was never more than partially reconciled to the academic profession. For a number of years, the notebook entries indicate, he excused his employment as an instructor in English at Columbia on the basis of economic expediency: teaching was something he was doing "in order to get started with my work of writing" ("Notebooks," *PR* 51, 499). Yet as early as 1933 Trilling was bitterly accusing himself of violating his own motive. He records that he has seen a "crazy letter" Hemingway sent to Clifton Fadiman. Written when Hemingway "was drunk," Trilling says, the letter is "self-revealing, arrogant, scared, trivial, absurd." Nevertheless, he declares, it shows "how right such a man is compared to the 'good minds' of my university life—how he will produce and mean something to the world . . . how his life which he could expose without dignity and which is anarchic and 'childish' is a better life than anyone I know could live, and right for his job. And how far-far-far I am going from being a writer—how less and less I have the material and the mind and the will." The entry ends on a note of almost despairing prophecy: "A few—a very few—more years and the last chance will be gone" ("Notebooks," PR 51, 498). The pathos of his half-patronizing yet anguished jealousy of Hemingway's life as a freelance novelist is enhanced when we realize the force of the term "dignity" in Trilling's lament. Even though he was still in his twenties, Trilling did not have, and had never had, the Bohemian option of "exposing" his life "without dignity" by writing a letter when he was drunk. For one thing, he came from the discipline of the middle-class Jewish culture of New York City, a heritage not necessarily more repressive but far more closely structured than that of the boy from Oak Park, Illinois. Another, and, I believe, more conclusive, reason why Trilling could not conceive of taking the Bohemian option was that the Trilling self who longed to identify with the Hemingway self—the self of the intense literary artist indifferent to or disdainful of society—was opposed by another Trilling self, a self that identified with the writer as man of letters as critic of society. This self was the proponent of literature as the representation of the moral reality of human existence. In the service of the realm of letters, the critic was responsible to literature, even at the expense of becoming in some measure alienated from society.

Trilling the man of letters and critic, it would appear, existed in unhappy conjunction with Trilling the "creative" self. Indeed for years the "critic self" was under the reproachful censure of the "creative self," which, according to the value system of the modern literary culture, was, especially when it deliberately alienated itself from society, spiritually the superior self. On July 3, 1961—nearly thirty years after his first anguished comparison of his own career to Hemingway's—Trilling made another entry about Hemingway in his notebooks:

—Death of Ernest Hemingway. Except Lawrence's 32 years ago, no writer's death has moved me so much.—who would suppose how much he has haunted me? How much he existed in my mind—as a reproach? He was the only writer of our time I envied. I respected him in his most foolish postures and in his worst work (except *The Old Man and the Sea*). ("Notebooks," PR 52, 10)

The basic conflict in Trilling between the critic and the novelist—or in the generic sense of the term, the poet—informs other moments in the notebooks when, as in the comment on Hemingway, Trilling either overtly or implicitly recognized the unfolding inward history of his own life. In 1928, at the age of twenty-seven, he describes an awareness that shadowed all the moments of his life: "Being a Jew is like walking in the wind or swimming: you are touched at all points and conscious everywhere" ("Notebooks," PR 51, 496). In the spring of 1936 his consciousness of being a Jew became acute, when Trilling, who had by then been an instructor at Columbia for four years, heard that he would be dismissed. "The reason for dismissal," he recorded in his notebook, "is that as a Jew, Marxist, Freudian I am uneasy. This hampers my work and makes me unhappy" ("Notebooks," PR 51, 498). But, as we know, Trilling was not fired by Columbia. In 1939 (through the intervention of Nicholas Murray Butler, the president of Columbia) he became an assistant professor; and in five more years he reached the associate professor rank. Obviously, however, some members of the professorate at Columbia were as uneasy with Trilling as he was with them. Whether or not in 1936 the fact that Trilling was a Jew was in any overt way a factor in his relationship with his colleagues or with the administrators of the college or the university (that is, was more important than his professed Marxism and Freudianism) is not clear. But in a time when anti-Semitism was still explicit in America and when at the more refined levels of American academic life—none being more refined than the life at the Ivy League universities—Jews were kept in a segregated state by a "gentleman's agreement," Trilling's Jewishness undoubtedly colored the attitude some of his senior colleagues took toward him. But if their dissatisfaction with his teaching—based on what they regarded as the violation of academic decorum implicit in his Marxian-Freudian bias toward "literature as sociology and psychology"—reflected an anti-Semitic attitude, it was one governed by something more subtle than simple racial prejudice. Trilling had in effect gone further in his effort to escape his Jewishness than the two deracinated men of letters, Marx and Freud, he had taken as his models. Choosing deracination, they had become high priests of the secular-spiritual culture of modernity; but in electing deracination, Trilling had repudiated his Jewish heritage by very self-consciously seeking to identify himself, as Marx and Freud had not, with the Western intellectual tradition associated with the university, an institution that even yet, in the time of the "multi-university," still substantially reflects its effective origin as a secularized embodiment of the medieval ecumene of the Christian mind. If some of his colleagues felt that Trilling was in violation of academic decorum, they may well have been expressing their feeling of resentment against him for having come into the academic halls to get out of the wind of his Jewishness, when he should have stayed in his place. However they may have expressed it, he was a disturbing presence, the outsider who sought to become an insider.

Yet Trilling's situation presented more of a problem to himself than to Columbia, being complicated by the fact that, even though he was concerned about his status on the Columbia faculty, he felt that the academic profession was antithetical to what he regarded as his true vocation, that of the writer, or more specifically, of the novelist. Yet after an early association with the fraternity of liberal Jewish intellectuals represented by the *Menorah Journal,* Trilling—in spite of a deep and continuing feeling for the rabbinic tradition he expressed in his notable essay on "Wordsworth and the Rabbis"—did not want to be considered as belonging to the company of secularized Jewish novelists like Malamud, Singer, and Bellow, declaring in the *Contemporary Jewish Record* in 1944: "I do not think of myself as a 'Jewish' writer: I do not have it in mind to serve by my writing any Jewish purpose. I would resent it if a critic of my work were to discover in it either faults or virtues which he called Jewish."[5] Having also by this time rejected an association with the Marxist community of intellectuals, Trilling, it may be suggested, spent the rest of his life seeking a convincing self-identification with the sense of the vocation to letters he conceived Hemingway to represent.

Trilling's search for a way to connect himself to a sustaining faith in the vocation to writing, one conjectures, encouraged him to develop the affinity he early on sensed with the Victorians and eventually to choose Arnold for his dissertation subject at Columbia. This was a way of connecting himself with the last embodiment of the amalgam of classical, Hebraic, and Christian strains referred to as Renaissance Christian humanism. Arnold stressed the moralism of this tradition as a necessary resource in carrying on a cultural program designed both to hold the Philistines at bay and to assist in the moral progress of society. In highly principled Victorians like Arnold, Mill, Carlyle, and George Eliot, Trilling identified the literary vocation with a transcendent obligation, singularly and severely incumbent on the individual writer, always to make "duty" the preeminent rule of life. One of Trilling's favorite anecdotes was the story told by the Cambridge scholar F. W. H. Myers, who, walking with George Eliot in the Fellows' Garden of Trinity College in the gathering gloom of a rainy May evening, heard this "austere sybil" pronounce the dictum that while God is inconceivable and immortality unbelievable, duty is "beyond question" the "preemptory and absolute" mandate of one's existence.[6]

Yet the Victorians could not hold Trilling forever in their thrall. The self of the artist struggled against them. Whereas, to pick up with another moment in the notebooks, he had discovered at the beginning of the 1930s that John Stuart Mill is "enormously rich and exciting," fifteen years later, in 1945, he confided to his journal: "The Victorians have lost all charm for me—they make my *parent* literature, the reading of with which I was most cosily at home—I could feel their warmth and seemed always to know my way among them—now they bore me utterly—I cannot read them—I cannot teach them with any conviction.... Dickens is the exception—possibly Newman" ("Notebooks," *PR* 51, 505). That Trilling might exclude Cardinal Newman from the charge of boredom does not indicate any tendency to turn toward Rome; it intimates the drastic nature of Trilling's repudiation of his feeling of community with the social progressivism of the Victorians. Another notebook entry in 1945 makes this explicit. "In three-four decades, the liberal progressive has not produced a single writer that it itself respects and reads with interest. A list of writers of our time shows that liberal-progressivism was a matter of contempt or indifference to every writer of large mind—Proust, Joyce, Lawrence, Eliot, Mann (early), Kafka, Yeats, Gide, Shaw—probably there is not a name to be associated with a love of liberal democracy or a hope for it." Trilling solidifies this reactionary declaration by pointing to "the enormous breach" between the "'serious' journalism of liberalism" and the "important works of the imagination in our time." It is well, he told himself, that the breach exists, thereby somewhat enigmatically implying that the writer who, under compulsion of the "liberal-democratic ideal," attempts to join imagination and action contributes to the "spiritual collapse" of his age ("Notebooks," *PR* 51, 505–6).

At this point Trilling was engaged in the preparation of two books. The critical work, *The Liberal Imagination*, was to give him fame; the other, *The Middle of the Journey*, a novel, was to give him some credibility as a novelist but would likely have been little noticed save that it was taken to have been written as an exposé of the fallacy of the author's commitment to the radical politics of the 1930s. Both works are, it seems to me, fundamentally devoted to the same theme, which may be summed up as the illusion of a "continuity between imagination and action," and both seek the true relationship between criticism and fiction, or between ideas and poetry.

How much and at what depth the problem of the relationship between imagination and action preoccupied Trilling in the period from the middle 1940s to the 1950s—how much this question presented itself to him as an urgent crisis of vocation—cannot be dealt with at length here. But I think the nature of Trilling's "career crisis" is presented in what may be the most intensely personal, the most dramatic, and it may be the most enigmatic passage in the published notebook selections. This entry was made in 1946.

> I meant to write here a note that I had just got over a period of about 6–8 weeks of insatiable desire for praise & notice—nothing satisfied and the more I got the more I wanted—grew by what it fed on—I had to make conscious effort to check this & not allow it to be publicly seen—I would *court* affirmation and flattery—also about this time a period of terrible sleeping, in which consciousness seemed increased in sleep & nightly problems were presented to me which *had* to be solved—I could see-smell-feel the aura of philosophy—the classroomy, textbooky aura of abstraction, terribly engaging, terribly repelling—life depended on solving the abstract problems presented to me—I would wake with a hideous sense of desolation and loss—absolutely hopeless—dominant in my thoughts the desire for children—one night near the end of this period a great sense of being on the point of *connection*—the connection between 2 things never before connected, which if reconciled would be of incalculable good—it all depended on my mental effort—but I could not do it—desolate at the same time (end) a great sense that by not doing criticism, not using my "mind" I was losing all force and poetry whatever—giving myself only to the novel was making me go all soft and nothing—at the same time the novel was beginning to open up, but almost to seem too easy—this association of events came suddenly of itself & is almost too pat!—facing sexual scenes of novel—sexual fantasy in connection with them. ("Notebooks," *PR* 51, 506–7)

A "great sense of being on the point of *connection*—the connection between 2 things never before connected, which if reconciled would be of incalculable good": Did Trilling—at a point when he was working with equal assiduity both as critic and novelist—envision the possibility of resolving his divided career as writer? Does the traumatic experience of his recurrent dream suggest a painful but blessed union of critic and poet? We are struck by the likelihood that this may be the import of the Freudian nightmare he records. Whether or not we hear an echo of the Shakespearean imperative, "Let me not to the marriage of true minds admit impediment," we feel in Trilling's portrayal of his inner history a passion for the marriage of the mind of one self to that of the other. Trilling—is it too much to say?—sought a union in which the passion of the critic not only matches that of the poet but incorporates critic and poet. Is he suggesting even more than this? That through writing a criticism of poetry that is a poetry of criticism he himself will become the embodiment of a whole and transcendent literary self? I would not argue that *The Middle of the Journey* in any precise way comes off as an attempt to unify criticism and poetry in the form of a novel. But both his novel and *The Liberal Imagination* suggest that in associating himself with the literature of social ideology promoted by the American "liberal progressivism" of the 1920s, while at the same time being drawn more and more to the "non-rational" literature of the great modern writers, Trilling became, like Allen Tate, the critic as both actor in and interpreter of the literary myth of modern history. I mean the actor in and the interpreter of the story, the drama, of self and history that is so much the inward substance of history as history was interpreted in the age that ended in the twentieth century, the "modern age."

It would seem to have been at least partly through Tate that Trilling began to be aware of the broad, mythic context of the conflict he experienced between the rationalist literature of political persuasion and the works of imagination in the twentieth century. In *The Liberal Imagination* Trilling, referring to Carlyle's observation that Shakespeare was "the product of medieval Catholicism *at the distance at which Shakespeare stood from it*" and that this had "much to do with the power of Shakespeare's intellect," says:

> Allen Tate has developed in a more particular way an idea that has much in common with what Carlyle here implies. Loosely put, the idea is that religion in its decline leaves a detritus of pieties, of strong assumptions, which afford a particularly fortunate condition for certain kinds of literature; these pieties carry a strong charge of intellect, or perhaps it would be more accurate to say that they tend to stimulate the mind in a powerful way.[7]

Trilling has pointedly in mind here an essay on Emily Dickinson in Tate's *Reactionary Essays on Poetry and Ideas* (published in 1936), in which Tate, describing this eminently self-conscious descendant of the New England Puritans as "acting out her part in the history of her culture," asks: "What is the nature of a poet's culture?"

> A culture cannot be consciously created. It is an available source of ideas that are imbedded in a complete and homogeneous society. The poet finds himself balanced upon the moment when such a world is about to fall, when it threatens to run out into looser and less self-sufficient impulses. This world order [the Puritan world order] is assimilated in Miss Dickinson, as medievalism was in Shakespeare, to the poetic vision: it is brought down from abstraction to personal sensibility.

In Emily Dickinson, Tate says further, "There is no thought as such at all; nor is there feeling; there is that unique focus of experience which is at once neither and both." Like Shakespeare, she had no opinions but "had all the elements of a culture that has broken up." Her poetry comes from "an intellectual life towards which it feels no moral responsibility."

Trilling, it would seem likely, also read another essay in Tate's *Reactionary Essays*, "The Profession of Letters in the South." In this classic analysis Tate refers to the "peculiar historical consciousness" of the southern writer, which he defines as "the curious burst of intelligence that we get at a crossing of the ways, not unlike, on an infinitesimal scale, the outburst of poetic genius at the beginning of the sixteenth century when commercial England had already begun to crush feudal England."[8] Identifying the motive of the subject of the contemporary southern writer with the seventeenth-century transition to modernity—the age that announced the effective destruction of the corporate community of Christendom by the forces of science, finance capitalism, and individualism—Tate suggests a parallel between the southern writer and Marlowe and Shakespeare. In *Hamlet* or *Richard III* in particular Shakespeare dramatizes the psychic consequence of shifting the apprehension of existence from the traditionalist to the historical mode, and prophesies the results of the experience of individuation—comic, pathetic, tragic—that would occur as the society of assigned status fragmented. He not only intuits but establishes the subject of literature for the next five centuries: the modern self's emergence as a historical entity and its struggle to define its existence—pulled on the one hand by the will to autonomous meaning and on the other by the recollection of its origin in the dissolution of hierarchical order.

Tate's depiction of Emily Dickinson impresses us as curiously ascribing to her an ambivalent, even contradictory, character: on the one hand, being devoid of opinions, she is nonintellectual; on the other hand, she is intellectual in that her poetry derives from "an intellectual life." But the intellectual life Tate refers to is not of course her own life; it is what is still left of the "great idea" of puritanism—the necessity of absolutely purifying the relationship between God and the individual soul, which rested on a sophisticated theology devised by a highly learned body of Puritan theologians (or intellectuals). Tate's acute discernment of Emily Dickinson's situation, we judge, is not the greater because he is an intellectual and a critic than because he is a novelist and poet. We see in Tate the clear lineaments of that hybrid being who came into existence in the seventeenth century in response to the poet's need to explain his cultural situation to himself. I refer to the critic who defines the culture on the poet's terms. Abstracting the elements of the culture, he describes and explicates what the poet once assumed as given but now must seek to understand. In other words, he is a poet-critic, who makes poetry out of his search to understand the cultural situation. The line of poet-critics extends from Ben Jonson and Donne to Dryden, Pope, and Samuel Johnson; and on to Wordsworth, Coleridge, Shelley, Carlyle, Arnold, Poe, Whitman, Baudelaire, Henry James, Eliot, Edmund Wilson, and R. P. Blackmur. We can say, too, that the line extends to writers whose overt critical activity is incidental but whose critical sensibility—encompassed in their historical sensibility—is a primary governing force in their poetic accomplishment: among them, Flaubert, Yeats, Joyce, Hemingway, and Faulkner. In fact, it is hardly too much to claim that all poetry—all work of the imagination—from the age of Donne on displays a tension between the critical and the poetic. The initial documentation of such a claim is Donne's magnificent poem "Anatomy of the World," which is a direct critique of his culture—the culture of science and history—and is a more exact intimation than anything in Shakespeare of the subject of modern literature as defined by Trilling: "the selfhood which culture cherishes as its dearest gift." Donne's brutal metaphorical vision of the dissection of the anatomy of the medieval cosmology—exemplified by the work of Copernicus, Kepler, and Galileo—mirrors the disintegration of what had formerly seemed to be a divinely willed social structure. Yet, in his sensitivity to the new condition of being—in his awareness of the isolation of the self in history and the isolation of history in the self—Donne suggests that the poet will find new force of being. Displaced from the bardic community of myth and tradition, he will, through his own will, relocate poetry in the dominion of the individual consciousness.

Donne created his poems and his sermons out of the depths of his experience of willing himself as a poet to recognize the new condition of the modern self even as he, a priest of the church, celebrated the community of man in the Christian faith. Yet Donne's career largely testifies to the loss of the very tension it exemplified. The consequences of this loss are of course central to any grasp of Western literature in the past several centuries. And in none more than the twentieth, when it would be reflected in the pathos of the effort to reimagine the meaning of such a tension. Reflected most directly, one might say, in the work of a T. S. Eliot. But it is present in many twentieth-century writers, one striking instance, as I have no doubt all along suggested, being afforded by the pathos of Lionel Trilling's struggle to define his vocation. Its duration is indicated in a graphic moment in his journals in the late 1960s:

> Whether or not the artist derives his powers from neurosis, he certainly derives them from a species of insanity, from megalomania, from his absurd belief in his own myth. This is what accounts for the achievement of Mailer and Bellow and even Malamud. They believe they are great men, they insist on being the center of their universe: all revolves around them. To impose, to impose: this is their single aim; it acts as a real thing, though it arises out of absurdity. I defeated myself long ago when I rejected the way of chutzpah and mishagass in favor of reason and diffidence. ("Notebooks," PR 52, 13)

One can hardly fail to see that these remarks strike a distinct note of Trilling's envy of three Jewish contemporaries who had achieved fame as novelists since he had written his moving essay on "Art and Neurosis" in the 1940s. But this note is incidental to the implication the passage bears for Trilling's final rejection of programmatic liberalism and its accompaniment, the programmatic pursuit of literature. This rejection, one realizes, indicates how deeply sensitive Trilling the critic was to the life of the author of the "works of the imagination of our time"; how little, in spite of his great success as a critic, he could justify—let alone transcend—his rejection of art in favor of reason. In a sense an easing of the struggle between the programmatic and the imaginative occurred when Trilling abandoned the notion that he must somehow interpret history as an ideological struggle; or, to put this in a different way, when he came into the knowledge that literary power is never vested in ideas conceived as categorical concepts but in ideas conceived as emotions.

I do not think we can uncover any wondrous epiphanic moment when the fallacy of rational constructs of history came to Trilling. The transformation of his vision of history, occurring uncertainly and slowly (and never completely) is most strikingly evidenced perhaps by his inner doubt and pain about his continuing affiliation with the academic world. In 1948 he appraised the meaning of his promotion to a full professor in terms not only of self-deprecation but almost of self-loathing, writing in his notebooks that he feared he was each year growing "weaker & weaker, more academic, less a person." He adds with unequivocal desperation: "Suppose I were to dare to believe that one could be a professor and a man! and a writer!—what arrogance and defiance of convention. Yet I deeply dare to believe that—and must learn to believe it on the surface." In 1951 Trilling took the most decisive gesture he ever made toward attaining his freedom from the university system: he gave up his identification both with his major subject matter field, American literature, and his status as a graduate professor and went back to undergraduate lecturing. As any university teacher knows, a voluntary renunciation of one's status as a member of a graduate faculty—even though in Trilling's case it did not involve going back to freshman composition—is almost inconceivable. Even more than his resignation from the graduate school, Trilling's rejection of American literature as an academic subject can be taken as a last-ditch effort to separate the self of the critic from that of the imaginative writer. Contending with himself in the privacy of his notebooks, Trilling declares that he must get away from specializing in American literature because this "denies my being a part of it." This objection is juxtaposed with the idea that "as a subject" American literature cannot be dealt with in a systematic way through the study of its individual authors. It must be studied as a "history of culture." Yet Trilling reveals he is not thinking about an objective, systematic interpretation of American literature in its relation to cultural history. He has in mind, he says, an approach that is subjective—one that will require not only "subtlety & complexity" but "a total intellectual and emotional involvement." This, he protests, he cannot dedicate himself to.

The ambiguity of his diagnosis of his connection with the literature of his own country enhances the element of pathos in Trilling's situation. Had he not in truth reached the point when he must acknowledge to himself that both the circumstances of his life and the limitations of his talent dictated that, though he was touched by the poet, his literary role would be largely that of the critic? Did he not want to obviate the pain of recognizing that he would never cut a figure as an American novelist? At the same time, did he not somehow understand that in his very attempt to fulfill his aspiration to be "a writer"—to be an author of works of the imagination, and thus a "part" of the literature of America—he had been living out the question put by Tate, "What is a poet's culture?" Did he not understand that, enmeshed in a detritus of pieties, he had been living his own version of the "crossing of the ways," participating in the repetitive experience of writers since Donne and discovering in his own way what Tate says Poe and Hawthorne discovered a hundred years before, the essential modern subject, "the isolation and frustration of personality"?

By 1949, when he wrote "The Meaning of a Literary Idea" for a conference on American literature at the University of Rochester, Trilling had, I think, formulated a poetic, dramatic, and dynamic idea about the nature of literary ideas that would provide the foundation for a poetics of cultural criticism.

> What comes into being when two contradictory emotions are made to confront each other and are required to have a relationship with each other is . . . quite properly called an idea. Ideas may also be said to be generated in the opposition of ideals, and in the felt awareness of the impact of new circumstances upon old forms of feeling and estimation, in the response to the conflict between new exigencies and old pieties. And it can be said that a work will have what I have been calling cogency in the degree that the confronting emotions go deep, or in the degree that the old pieties are firmly held and the new exigencies strongly apprehended.

At the end of the essay in which this definition of the "literary idea" is made Trilling says that when we learn to "think of ideas as living things, inescapably connected with our wills and desires, as susceptible of growth and development by their very nature, as showing their life by their tendency to change, as being liable, by this very tendency, to deteriorate and become corrupt and to work harm, then we shall stand in a relation to ideas which makes an active literature possible."[9] During the years following the writing of this essay, Trilling composed the series of compelling meditations on the idea of the modern self that constitutes his major achievement and—although he himself may never have quite known this—fulfills, as far as he could do so, his desire to be the author of works of the imagination. Significantly these meditations were composed in nearly all instances as occasional pieces—being written in response to an invitation to give a paper somewhere, provide an introductory comment for a new edition of a book, etc. Moreover, save for *Sincerity and Authenticity,* a small volume composed of the

Norton Lectures, Trilling wrote no more book-length works. Although leading the regular life of the classroom lecturer, he took on jobs like a freelance essayist, taking up topics as the literary demand arose; living apart from the academic tendency to deprecate the essay in favor of the book-length work, Trilling solidified his fame with two collections of essays published ten years apart. The first of these (the other is *Beyond Culture*, 1965), *The Opposing Self: Nine Essays in Criticism*, was published in 1955, the same year in which Tate brought out the volume that in the overall sense is his most significant collection of essays, *The Man of Letters in the Modern World*.

This book, I take it, is in Tate's career what *The Opposing Self* is in Trilling's career, the crucial, the central work. Devoted to essays, or meditations, on Keats, Dickens, Tolstoy, Wordsworth, Orwell, Flaubert, and (in spite of his declaration about American literature) on two Americans, Howells and James, *The Opposing Self*, the author points out in a prefatory essay, deals with "episodes in the literature of the last century and a half." In the case of each writer he considers, Trilling says:

> I speak of the relation of the self to *culture* rather than to *society* because there is a useful ambiguity which attends the meaning of the word culture. It is the word by which we refer not only to a people's achieved works of intellect and imagination but also to its mere assumptions and unformulated valuations, to its habits, its manners, and its superstitions. The modern self is characterized by certain powers of indignant perception which, turned upon this unconscious portion of culture, have made it accessible to conscious thought.[10]

In his declaration of the capacities of the modern self Trilling united the poet and the critic and by implication established the definition he had long sought of his own vocation to literature. But the cost of fulfilling this vocation—of obeying the self's powers of perception—is high; as the last essay in *The Opposing Self*, a disturbing meditation on *Mansfield Park,* makes clear, the expense is nothing less than the self's terrorizing of the self. I quote at some length from the key passage in the essay on Jane Austen's novel:

> It was Jane Austen who first represented the specifically modern personality and the culture in which it had its being. Never before had the moral

life been shown as she shows it to be, never before had it been conceived to be so complex and difficult and exhausting. Hegel speaks of the "secularization of spirituality" as a prime characteristic of the modern epoch, and Jane Austen is the first to tell us what this involves. She is the first novelist to represent society, the general culture, as playing a part in the moral life, generating the concepts of "sincerity" and "vulgarity" which no earlier time would have understood the meaning of, and which for us are so subtle they defy definition, and are so powerful that none can escape their sovereignty. She is the first to be aware of the Terror which rules our [the writer's] moral situation, the ubiquitous anonymous judgment to which we respond, the necessity we feel to demonstrate the purity of our [the writer's] secular spirituality, whose dark and dubious places are more numerous and obscure than those of religious spirituality, to put our lives and styles to the question, making sure that not only in deeds but in *decor* they exhibit the signs of our belonging to the number of the secular-spiritual elect.

She herself is an agent of Terror—we learn from her what our lives should be and by what subtle and fierce criteria they will be judged, and how to pass upon the lives of our friends and fellows. Once we have comprehended her mode of judgment, the moral and spiritual lessons of contemporary literature are easy—the metaphysics of "sincerity" and "vulgarity" once mastered, the modern teachers, Lawrence and Joyce, Yeats and Eliot, Proust and Gide, have but little to add save in the way of contemporary and abstruse examples.[11]

In his conception of Jane Austen as the initial agent of the terror of the secular spirituality that defines the self of the modern writer, who, having internalized history, is imprisoned in his or her only moral resource, Trilling's irresolute search for vocational identity, or so I would argue, reaches at least a momentary resolution when his own power of indignant perception became luminous to itself, and poet and critic coalesced in a poetics of criticism.

In the remarkable prefatory essay to *The Man of Letters in the Modern World*, Allen Tate says we may scarcely hold that the moment of indignant perception bears a weight akin to that of the peripety of tragedy, the moment when the last seal on the tragic hero's ignorance of his condition is broken and the knowledge of his fate is fully revealed to him. Tate may be said to have in a general sense spoken for Trilling as well as for himself in his conclusion that the "act of criticism . . . is a crisis of recognition always" and is not without a certain tragic ambience in that, for all the effort put into it, criticism yields no certain nor finally any knowledge at all. What the practice of criticism gives the critic in the end is the certain knowledge "that as literary critic one knows virtually nothing."[12] By the time Tate said this he presumably knew a vision of existence beyond tragedy. He had been a Roman Catholic for five years, having formally accepted in 1959 what he had always believed to be true, namely that religion must be the condition of literature.

Tate no doubt would have scorned the idea that the modern critic qualifies as a tragic hero. But we may doubt that Trilling would have done so. He could never believe other than that it is "an impropriety to try to guarantee literature by a religious belief." For Hegel, Trilling says in *The Opposing Self*, moral and aesthetic standards are no longer joined "in the old way," one, that is, that makes "morality the criterion of the aesthetic." On the contrary, "the aesthetic is now the criterion of the moral," so that "not merely the deed itself . . . is . . . submitted to judgment," but the "entire nature, the *being*, of the agent."[13] Fundamentally all that Trilling could use to validate—to authenticate—his vocation to literature was the quality of his devotion to it. On the basis of his witness to his own vocation in his own writings, we can point to his sense of this as comparable to the sense of vocation he attributes to Jane Austen when he speaks, in his essay on her in *The Opposing Self*, of her novels as having answered to the demand of the moral standard of our secular spirituality described by Hegel. This requires that we not only bring our deeds but the style of our lives into question. In the latter years of his life Trilling developed his idea about the quality of the agent still more intensely, elaborating in *Sincerity and Authenticity* an intricate distinction between the "sincere self" and the "authentic self." We may think with some assurance that he was impelled to elevate the concept of authenticity by his understanding of what disappears when religion is lost: this is, he says, nothing less than reality, "the imperative actuality of life." This observation occurs in *Sincerity and Authenticity* at a point when we might not expect it, in a discussion of Freud, for whom religion was an illusion. But Trilling read Freud as a great tragic poet, who in his youth, Trilling recalls, chose John Milton "as a favorite poet" because, "Although the idea of redemption could mean nothing to him," he shared "Milton's appalled elation . . . in the ordeal of man's life in history."[14]

For Trilling such an astringent but vividly dramatic, and immensely humanizing, attitude toward history guaranteed the continued meaning of literature. He had authenticated this attitude through his own experience of being a writer—his criticism at its best being, like the work of Jane Austen or D. H. Lawrence, an expression of the terror of the modern literary insight into the relation between history and the individual human being; he himself—a defeated novelist, a defeated poet—being a troubled, and compassionate, agent of the terror he beheld in our unremitting self-consciousness of our existence in history.

NOTES

1. *Partisan Review* 51, no. 4 (1984): 496–515; 52, no. 2 (1985): 7–17. References to passages from the *Notebooks* will be incorporated in the text.

2. *The Republic of Letters in America: The Correspondence of Allen Tate and John Peale Bishop*, ed. Thomas Daniel Young and John J. Hindle (Lexington, Ky., 1981), 148; *Partisan Review* 6, no. 1 (1938); 6, no. 2 (1939).

3. *Republic of Letters*, ed. Young and Hindle, 148.

4. Diana Trilling, *The Beginning of the Journey: The Marriage of Diana and Lionel Trilling* (New York, 1993), 183.

5. As quoted in William M. Chace, *Lionel Trilling: Criticism and Politics* (Stanford, Calif., 1980), 10.

6. Trilling, *Sincerity and Authenticity* (Cambridge, Mass., 1972), 117.

7. Trilling, *The Liberal Imagination* (New York, 1950), 284–85.

8. As reprinted in Tate, *Essays of Four Decades* (Chicago, 1968), 293, 533–34.

9. Trilling, *The Liberal Imagination*, 283, 287.

10. Trilling, *The Opposing Self* (New York, 1959), x.

11. Ibid., 228–29.

12. Tate, *Essays of Four Decades*, 625.

13. Trilling, *The Opposing Self*, xii.

14. Trilling, *Sincerity and Authenticity*, 157.

DIANA TRILLING:
A Poetic of Cultural Politics

In the issue of *Newsweek* for January 11, 1993, Diana Trilling made a twofold appearance. In one instance she was featured with, among others, James A. Michener, Gore Vidal, Arthur M. Schlesinger, Jr., and William Styron, as a contributor to a special retrospective section entitled "The World War II Generation and How It Changed America." Adapted from her long-awaited book *The Beginning of the Journey: The Life and Marriage of Lionel and Diana Trilling* (which would be published later in 1993), her particular contribution was a remembrance of a dark moment in our post-1945 history called "How McCarthy Gave Anti-Communism a Bad Name." In her other appearance in the January 11, 1993, *Newsweek*—less conspicuous, though hardly less important—Diana Trilling was cited in an article about the release of Jean Harris from the women's correctional facility in Bedford Hills, New York, as the author of a book (title not given) about the notorious Harris case. At the time of her release Jean Harris, the former headmistress of the exclusive Madeira School for girls in McLean, Virginia, had served twelve years of a fifteen-to-life sentence for the 1988 murder of her lover, the then famous "diet doctor" Herman Tarnower of Westchester, New York.

The fact of Diana Trilling's appearance in two places in a single issue of *Newsweek*—as a featured writer in a carefully planned special section and in an article about a breaking news event—was obviously pure coincidence. Yet to one interested in the motives of her long career in American letters the coincidence seemed suggestive. Why did a highly sophisticated and politically conscious New York intellectual like Diana Trilling develop a compelling interest in the Harris case?

In spite of holding a position of some eminence in the educational field, Jean Harris, like most educational administrators in America, was hardly in any strict sense an intellectual. Nor was she, as we say, a "political person," nor was Dr. Tarnower; and in his murder one finds, in the usual sense, no imputation of a political motive. The Jean Harris story, to be sure, seems to be no better than a good soap about upper-middle-class America. Is *Mrs. Harris: The Murder of the Scarsdale Diet Doctor* (1981) to be taken simply as an effort by a member of the literary elite to write a popular, saleable book? The quality of the thought and feeling in Mrs. Harris plainly refutes such an unkind notion. The book reflects an interest in the murder of the "diet doctor" so strong that it led its author not only to the considerable trouble of faithful day-by-day attendance at a lengthy trial, but to become engaged in a painful struggle with herself about the meaning of this event—a struggle so demanding that after she had finished a book about the case she felt compelled to reconsider and rewrite the book.

At the risk of seeming to make a forced point, I would suggest that Diana Trilling's attraction to the case of Jean Harris in 1980 bears a significant relation to her compulsive interest in the subject of her *Newsweek* essay, the antics of an opportunistic red-baiter, whose flagrant efforts to expose a Communist conspiracy within the American government a quarter of a century earlier had led eventually to his own investigation and censure by his colleagues in the Senate of the United States. Pursuing this notion, I find myself offering the suggestion that, like her other books, Diana Trilling's *Mrs. Harris* bears an integral relation to the shaping motives of a career, that, like that of her eminent husband, Lionel Trilling, is integrally related to the history of the American literary intellectuals who came of age in the 1930s and entered into their intellectual maturity in the age of the cold war.

Diana Trilling herself offers a succinct description of the nature and meaning of her career at the beginning of the *Newsweek* essay.

> From the '40s onward, after a brief period as a communist sympathizer, I was engaged as a writer in what is called "cultural politics," that area of the intellectual life in which issues of national policy, especially in foreign affairs, are most intimately associated with culture. Today we celebrate the collapse of Soviet communism as not only the victory for democracy which we hope it will be, but as if it were specifically an American victory, brought about by the unified will of the American people. But the fact is that this country has been much divided on the issue of communism. I know this myself because I was that villainous creature, an anti-communist. This was often an isolating experience.

The encapsulation of her career in *Newsweek* leaves one with the impression that Diana Trilling clearly regarded its chief motive to have been a long and passionate quarrel with other American intellectuals, who, like her, were liberals who opposed communism but, unlike her, for a good part of the century just ended were nonetheless dupes of Soviet communism.

The charge that they were dupes may well seem exaggerated. Certainly being a communist in America once singled one out as a major villain, but how could being *against* communism in a nation generally committed to this opposition have made one into a socially isolated villain? In actuality, Diana Trilling is speaking of a special rather than a general situation in American society. When she refers to the division of the Americans on "the issue of communism," she assumes a sense of identity between Americans in general and the elite group with whom she explicitly associated herself, the American literary and intellectual class. Her reference to herself as an "anti-communist villain" recalls a particular historical moment: the time in the period of the cold war, when, as she says, within the ranks of American intellectuals being an anti-communist liberal involved one in the irony of opposing a "lie" that was "promulgated" by the very persons with whom, by professional commitment, the opposer most closely identified, the dominantly "liberal" element among those of superior education—"writers, university teachers, journalists." In her summation this lie—"one of the towering lies of history in this century"—simply held that within the Soviet Union "there was to be found a fairer distribution of the decencies of life and a corrective to our faulty society."

As the economic depression signaled by the collapse of Wall Street in October 1929 grew into the Great Depression, this view of the Soviet system offered itself to a good many American liberal intellectuals with the force of a new revelation. This was not because, being intellectuals, as the popular attitude held, they had a natural proclivity for exotic and alien ideologies. It was because they had once, consciously or unconsciously, assumed the truth of the myth of the American Republic and so assumed that they were participants in the fulfillment of the world historic revolution that had been inaugurated by the American Revolution. Witnessing the world in the grip of the Great Depression—a world in which the American self-interpretation of history had proved to be wrong—they sought to transform desperation into hope by in effect believing that the Marxist-Leninist version of history had replaced the capitalist, corrupted American version. For American idealists—and American intellectuals were generally idealists, aware that the nation had come into historical existence as an "idea" of history—it was a heady moment, a chance to participate in the redemption of a world historical promise. Commitment was demanded: the vision of America as the embodiment of the moral progress of mankind was at stake.

Yet for some American intellectuals the moment of belief in the Russian Revolution as the redemption of history was brief. Diana Trilling indicates she and her husband were actively engaged "with the radical movement of the early thirties" for less than a year before abandoning it in 1933. All it took to destroy their faith in communism—and transform them into thorough-going anti-communists—was an association for a few months in 1932–1933 with a communist-front organization called the National Committee for the Defense of Political Prisoners. A "firsthand knowledge of the authoritarianism and dishonesty of the Party and its cynical betrayal of its own proposed goals" shocked them into an immediate "understanding of the nature of the Soviet dictatorship and of the workings of communism throughout the world." Their inability to close their minds to the complexity of history, one surmises, made for their quick grasp of what other fellow-travelers understood more slowly, or never got at all.

But for her and her husband, Diana Trilling observes in *The Beginning of the Journey*, this also made their communist moment as profound as it was brief, insuring that their short experience as fellow-travelers in the 1930s would have "a deep and lasting effect" on their "thinking about politics and society and on the kind of work" they did for the rest of their lives.

The effect, however, was not registered in quite the same way in retrospective evaluations of the decade of the thirties by these two former fellow-travelers. As time went on Lionel Trilling was inclined to see the thirties as an age of innocence, whereas Diana Trilling was consistently to regard this time as an evil age. For her it remained a time when, overlooking or dulcifying the positive evidence of the great Moscow purge of the mid-thirties, many American liberals—the majority in her opinion—kept on believing that the Soviet system was more desirable than either German fascism or American capitalism. Subsequently American intellectuals ignored the crucial revelation of historical reality attendant upon the signing of the Molotov-Ribbentrop pact and the Russian invasion of Finland. "Far from being the most moral decade of this century, the quickest and most irradiated with right feeling," Diana Trilling wrote in 1979 (in a review of Samuel Hynes's *The Auden Generation*), the decade of the "ideological thirties" was "almost entirely built upon self-deception and the deception of others." In their self-deceit about the meaning of Stalinism, she charges, the company of fellow-travelers left "a legacy of debilitating ignorance."

The legacy of the thirties, according to Diana Trilling, was more or less ignored by the opponents of communism in the 1940s. The fact that they were outnumbered did not produce in the anti-communists of this decade the feeling that they were "excluded" from the liberal "intellectual mainstream of the country." The experience of alienation came only with the rise of Senator McCarthy. "A great gift to Stalin, indeed, the greatest gift our country could have made to the Soviet Union," McCarthy "robbed anti-communism of its base in liberalism and brought upon it the opprobrium which properly attached to his own mode of operation." "I was against both communism and McCarthyism," Trilling says. "They were enemies of each other, but I was the enemy of both." But she found that although it is not "so difficult to hold two opposing views in one's mind at the same time," her position was suspect to those who either couldn't do so, or refused to do so. Like "all anti-communists, liberal no less than illiberal," she became "vulnerable to the demeaning charge of McCarthyism."

In concluding her recollective comment in *Newsweek,* the author recalls two critical events in her life. (These are recorded more fully in *The Beginning of the Journey.*) One is about the time in 1933 when she was asked by Whitaker Chambers—whom she knew to be a communist agent—to "become his drop" (receive mail for him). Although she was by then on the verge of leaving the radical movement, she was "enormously flattered" that Chambers, "this man of the world," indeed "this man of two worlds," thought her to be "capable of his treasonable assignment." Yet because she realized that her personal "pleasure had little to do" with the radical politics she had been espousing, she refused to serve as a drop for Chambers. The other event Trilling recalls is an evening when, as a twelve-year-old girl in Brooklyn, she joined two other girls in a daring little venture "to pick up boys" on Ocean Parkway. When a car stopped, occupied not by boys but three men, and one pointed to her and said of the three girls he would take her, she fled back to the safety of her home a block away. She had been flattered, she remembered, by being chosen: "But the point is, of course, that I did not surrender to the flattery. My upbringing was stronger than the seduction." Pointing up a somewhat cumbersome moral, Trilling says that "the seductions of the former Soviet Union have been gravely entrapping of us in the democracies." Not only have we "paid a big price for conspiring in the lie that communism represented," we continue to pay it; for "despite the collapse of the Soviet Union, our most-conscious social egalitarians steadily grow in self-confidence and even—shall I say it?—in moral smugness." It is as if anti-anti-communism has given them "moral rectitude." As in the case of "all refusals of truth," their "measurable self-deception" must "impair our perception of political and social actuality."

From Trilling's adaptation of her memoir in *Newsweek* one derives at least two distinct impressions. One is that of a strong-willed, independent critical mind. The other impression is that Diana Trilling's career has been controlled by her sensitivity to her involvement in the opposition in America of anti-communism and anti-anti-communism. It is somewhat disconcerting to find these impressions do not entirely accord with the fuller treatment of her career in *The Beginning of the Journey*. Reading the *Newsweek* essay one assumes that the Diana Trilling of the 1930s was, like her husband, a youthful, highly self-conscious New York literary intellectual. But in the memoir she is at some pains to explain that at the time when she was a fellow-traveler she did not consciously identify herself as an intellectual. She was still in training for a musical career, and even after this career became improbable, she says, she did not think about turning to a literary career. According to her memoir, this fateful turn was a happenstance.

> I became a writer by accident early in 1941 as the result of a telephone call to Lionel from Margaret Marshall, the literary editor of the *Nation;* she was calling to inquire whether he knew someone who could write the brief unsigned fiction notes for her magazine. I overheard Lionel's end of the conversation: he told her he would look around for a possible candidate. When he hung up I offered myself for the job. I have no idea of why I was moved to make such a suggestion. Until that moment it had never occurred to me to be a professional writer, least of all a critic.

Questioning the accuracy of Trilling's own account of the origin of her writing career is no doubt impolite, but on the basis of other things she says in *The Beginning of the Journey*, and more importantly on the basis of her other writings, one is led to ask if in truth she was an accidental writer. The evidence would seem to indicate that early on she recognized her endowment with literary talent. This had expressed itself in "skits and lyrics for our camp songs," and in the early years of her marriage continued to express itself in "plays and stories," though she says she wrote these "only to fill the time." But while she had experienced no real challenge to seek her identity as a playwright or novelist, in becoming a critic Diana Trilling was responding to a deep need to resolve what was, in the fullest sense of the cliché, an "identity crisis."[1]

We may well consider Trilling's insistence in *The Beginning of the Journey* that she became a critic by accident in the light of another passage in her memoir in which she says that she was actually deeply attracted to the intellectual life well before Margaret Marshall's phone call. "Back in the thirties," when she had married and "had entered Lionel's world" and made his friends her chief company, her "career as a critic lay in the future," but "unconsciously," she says, "I may have been preparing for it." Although the persons she "was now getting to know" were "not easy companions"—tending to be "overbearing and arrogant, excessively competitive," she recalls, and "often lacking in magnanimity" and "often [even in] common courtesy"—they were "intellectually energetic to a degree" she "had not previously encountered." They were "particularly" impressive in their attitude toward "cant": "A received idea was an idea to be resisted; piety in thought was the equivalent of non-thought." But Trilling also says in her memoir that she was not intimidated by such austere intellectuality. "Curiously enough" while she "had not even heard of the books on which they [her husband's acquaintances] had cut their critical teeth," she "never doubted" her competence to "judge their work," anymore than she had doubted her competence when she was engaged in "reshaping draft after draft" of Lionel Trilling's *Matthew Arnold* (1939). To quote directly from the memoir:

> I was not undertaking to shape ideas other than as style is inevitably an extension of thought. Lionel never resisted this intervention. Indeed until he no longer required it, he welcomed it, counted upon it. . . . Behind my confidence that I knew good writing when I saw it lay a considerable if unexplained faith in my ability to judge the whole of a literary performance. This was now much bolstered by Lionel's willingness to recommend me for the *Nation* position; if he had indicated any doubt of my ability to do the work, I would have withdrawn my candidacy, and I would not today be the person I am.

The last statement seems unequivocal. Yet even as she insists on her reliance on her husband's judgment about her ability to do the job for the *Nation*, Trilling recalls she "was worried that Margaret Marshall had engaged me without proof of my competence, out of regard for Lionel," and that this had led her to exact a promise "through Lionel that she would not keep me on because of him."

One senses an intriguing ambiguity in Trilling's discussion of her motive in assuming the vocation of the critic. On the one hand, she virtually says her identity as a writer was conferred on her by her husband; on the other hand, she asserts an unmitigated confidence in the relationship between her intrinsic talent and her literary identity. In the tension in her memoir between these attitudes her love and respect for Lionel Trilling would seem to be the controlling attitude. Does this account for the fact that, although she has much to say about herself in her memoir, including frank accounts of various psychic difficulties, she gives comparatively little attention to her own writings?

Prior to the publication of her memoir, Trilling had published three books in addition to *Mrs. Harris:* her *Claremont Essays* (1964), *We Must March My Darlings* (1977), and *Reviewing the Forties* (1978). Of these books, all essay collections, only one, *Reviewing the Forties*, a selection of the reviews of current fiction she wrote from 1942 through 1949 as fiction critic for the *Nation,* is given more than cursory attention in *The Beginning of the Journey.* And then only indirectly—that is, although she does not refer to *Reviewing the Forties*, she comments specifically on a few of her *Nation* essays during an illuminating discussion of her years with what was then one of the more important periodicals in the America.

Published late in the author's career, with an introduction by Paul Fussell, *Reviewing the Forties* might give the impression of simply being a retrospective recognition of Diana Trilling's critical apprenticeship. But in reading the essays in the volume, one discovers that they are hardly what we expect from an apprentice. As Fussell comments in his introduction, not only do they sound more like the work of a critic than of a weekly book reviewer, they indicate a critic with a broad cultural orientation: a critic who was "not satisfied to leave literature sitting there uninterpreted in its fullest psychological, social, and political meaning"; a critic who perceived that "literature is no mere decoration of life but an index of the health or sickness of society." If his evaluation of the *Nation* essays somewhat exaggerates the quality of some of the week-in-and-week-out reviewing Trilling did for seven or eight years, Fussell is correct in stressing that from the first she was a critic of unusual psychological, social, and political range and perceptiveness. In a more particular sense, we may say, the *Nation* essays are the work of a complex critic, who perceived American literature to be the index of a society that has been adversely influenced by a malformed liberal tradition. In writing them, as she says in her memoir, "My anti-communism was seldom far from the surface."

On occasion the *Nation's* literary critic self-consciously assumed that the role of the critic was to be a stern moralistic judge and prophet pronouncing imperious, sweeping self-righteous judgments on self-righteousness (i.e.: "Present-day liberalism, in all its astigmatism and self-righteousness, has many important cultural as well as political sins to account for at the day of judgment"). At other times, and more often than not, Trilling conceived of the critical task as demanding a less strident and more subtle voice. One of the more arresting essays in *Reviewing the Forties* is on Edmund Wilson's notorious novella *Memoirs of Hecate County* (1946). Comparing *Hecate County* with Wilson's earlier *I Thought of Daisy*, Trilling sees the two stories as together constituting a "record of American artistic and intellectual life" in the twenties, thirties, and forties. In the two stories, she says, Wilson presents "an enormously valuable document of social change," and of the impact change "must have on the thought and emotion of the artist and intellectual." But in taking a "highly subjective attitude" toward the stories he tells, Wilson fails in the primary duty of the artist and intellectual, which is to keep the "creative will" from being at the mercy of history. Opposing reality to idealism, he finds that the idealistic outlook is "morbidly diseased." This discovery results in a "breach between sensation and emotion" in the protagonist in *Memoirs of Hecate County*. He is an intellectual without compassion.

> Clearly, I do not mean . . . to say [Trilling remarks in the conclusion to her comment on Wilson] that it is the job of the intellectual to go about doing good in a bad world. But we do, I think, have the right to ask that he maintain, amid disorder, some principle of private order from which a principle of general order could be adduced—that he keep, for one thing, a sound integration between head and heart, which itself of course is another way of asking that he distinguish between sensation and emotion. For if he allows himself to be disordered by his disordered society, all he will generalize is mess, whereas if he maintains personal order within a disordered society, he will at the least have a tragic—which is to say, a meaningful—experience of pain. And that is everlastingly the intellectual's job: to be meaningful, despite and above his social situation.

Wilson could not achieve a sense of personal order to offset social disorder, Trilling argues, because in the decade of the forties the American intellectual was still trapped in a "sad recoil from the broken promises" of the thirties. Although her time with the *Nation* was in the pre-McCarthy age—before the term "liberal" became one of opprobrium and one could still distinguish without rancor between "anti-communist liberals and fellow-traveling liberals"—Trilling saw the recoil from the thirties beginning, through the preemptive self-righteousness of "politically correct" liberals, to work itself out in a more repressive future for the critical mind in America. The most arresting example of her insight into this process is a comment on Jean Paul Sartre, who in the forties was at the beginning of his influential reputation in America. Referring to Sartre's *The Age of Reason,* she says in *The Beginning of the Journey* that she "outraged" the publishers of "the leader of the French Existentialists" and "no doubt many of the *Nation*'s readers as well" by interpreting Sartre to say in effect that, although the individual must resist a "fascist dictatorship" to the death, his "final act of freedom" is "the free choice to give up all purely personal freedom" to the power of the state as vested in a "proletarian" dictatorship. "While one hesitates," Trilling says, "to conjecture that the very fierceness of the Existentialist protest against authority may disguise a longing for it, we recall that Heidegger, the German Existentialist, became a Nazi."[2]

Trilling's sensitivity to the motives of Wilson and Sartre reflects the discovery and development in her *Nation* essays of a quest that, either directly or indirectly, would engage her throughout her career. Highly self-conscious, and, I think, eminently personal, Diana Trilling's search for the identity of the literary intellectual necessarily demanded an effort to define the relation between modern society and the intellectual. Her ultimate inspiration was no doubt her self-conscious experience of the company of the New York intellectuals in the early days of her marriage. And we may deduce another, at once more particular and less definable, source: her intellectual and emotional involvement in the writing of her husband's book on Matthew Arnold—a work that reflects a variety of motives but is essentially a response to the cultural politics of the 1930s.

Tracing the character of this response in Diana Trilling through the *Nation* essays into *Claremont Essays,* we find that the pieces in the latter, although largely written in the McCarthy decade, are still based on the animating premise of the *Nation* essays: namely, that the individual intellectual is the embodiment of the social power of reason.

> While I find in myself small impulse to challenge the contemporary premise that society is more incoherent than accessible to reason, more destructive of the individual than designed for his uses, I remain convinced that it is yet susceptible to rational processes, and—what is more important in this context—that even while the terms of its organization radically alter, it has an anatomy in whose study we discover some of the main lines of our individual growth. Far from believing that the self is best comprehended or realized apart from society, I am of the older opinion that it is society

which provides the self with its best possibilities of ascendancy, even of transcendence.

But if Trilling saw herself in her *Claremont Essays* as still adhering to the "older opinion" that reason should govern the relationship of the individual and society, she at the same time intimated her awareness of "prognosticative phenomena" pointing to the deepening crisis in the situation of the intellectual that she would explore in the essays she wrote "roughly" from 1965 to 1975 and collected in *We Must March My Darlings*. For the most part these essays qualify, even reject, the possibility of maintaining adherence to the eighteenth-century rational humanism, with its vision of controlling the connection between the individual and society through the social power of reason.

For Trilling the final sign of the loss of the classic American liberal concept was the abrupt and tragic end of the presidency of Jack Kennedy, whose election she had seen as heralding the revival of the classic liberalism. Her deeply felt elegy to Kennedy, the first essay in *We Must March*, has a compelling force.

> A man, a president, who believes in history and in the continuity between past and future but who even in the view of the most intransigently young cannot be written off as a "square"; a national leader whose personal aura is one of heroism, romance, gaiety, and even a certain rakishness—and it ignores the obvious not to note the erotic element in Kennedy's charm, with what this was bound to add to his image as a champion of freedom—but who has the stern substantiality of mind and character to guide his country in international crisis and to propose new paths of domestic enlightenment; a modern who is a traditionalist; a traditionalist who is the very essence and image of the contemporary—what more could we have asked in reassurance that life was solid under our feet despite our uncertainties, and that the present was not only dread and isolation? To give us this reassurance, to dispel our loneliness: for some time now this has been the burden refused by the artist and unmet by the politician. Kennedy enlarged the political profession to provide just such an answer to the needs of the spirit.

In addition to the assassination of President Kennedy, the essays in *We Must March* unfold a whole procession of highly disturbing occurrences: the rise of the drug culture, the rise of the radical women's liberation movement, the quest for a radical sexual freedom, the riotous protests against the Vietnam war, the disruption of American campuses, followed by a falling off in post-Vietnam college students of a sense of meaning and purpose. Here were happenings of great consequence; yet, while each had "its full dramatic or . . . melodramatic moment" in the mind, it was no more than this, each development being "virtually wiped from memory by a next event, a next dramatic moment." No longer "something that might be relied upon for evidence of cultural continuity," history became "non-history." What she had still "taken for granted" in *Claremont Essays,* the sense of "historical time," Trilling says in the introduction to *We Must March,* has "vanished" in the new collection of essays.

Searching for a metaphor of the cultural situation that manifested itself in the sixties and early seventies, she likens the loss of the sense of history to the disappearance of what painters used to call "negative space," that distance left "between such objects as were represented in a picture" so as "to permit the introduction into the painting, if the artist desired it, of any other objects which might in reality occupy the space." *Claremont Essays,* a volume which—even though it dealt with "prognosticative phenomena" like "the moral radicalism of Norman Mailer" and the "meaning of the meaninglessness of Albee's *Who's Afraid of Virginia Woolf*"— was, Trilling says, based on the assumption that "there was still space in which the life of culture had its relatively orderly growth." As she had pointed out in the foreword to *Claremont Essays,* the very title of that book was taken from the name of her street in the Columbia neighborhood and refers to the concept that "even in an unsatisfactory society the individual is best defined by social geography." But the title *We Must March My Darlings*—borrowed from the well-known first stanza of Walt Whitman's "Pioneers! O Pioneers!"—implies the "ironic" rejection of the spatial concept of culture. Originally conceived as the title of a projected book about "Radcliffe, my old college," Trilling says, *We Must March My Darlings* became the title of both one section of the 1977 collection and of the whole collection.

The projected book on Radcliffe was presumably never completed, but the fragment in *We Must March* serves the purpose of reporting on the author's discovery, during a period of close association with undergraduates at Harvard and Radcliffe in 1971, that, for all the celebrated radicalism of the youth of the Vietnam era, the students she associated with not only lacked a sense of generational and personal identity but basically displayed a strange passivity toward the future. Their attitude suggested to her "the possibility that it is the younger and not, to borrow from Whitman, 'the elder races' who 'droop and end their lesson.'" In the 1950s man had been depicted by cultural diagnosticians as coping with modern life through his Protean ability to make infinite changes—to, like the artist, conceive negative space on a canvas as a symbol of the "social and moral possibility" that may be introduced "into the canvas [that is, into our vision of society] without violating its circumstantial accuracy." Since "space and time are in important ways inseparable," if space has been "blotted out" by an acceleration of time so sharp as almost to "constitute a mechanism," the possible "obliteration" of man is suggested.

The most compelling essay in *We Must March* is "On the Steps of Low Library." Its enabling perception is the link Trilling perceived between the march on the Pentagon in the fall of 1967, as told in Norman Mailer's essay "On the Steps of the Pentagon" (which appears in *Armies of the Night*) and the disorders at Columbia University in the spring of 1968. To her these events "were acts of civil disobedience initiated by people who regard the law as the arm of a despised form of social organization."

> Both . . . dramatized drastically opposed ideas of what is meant by social responsibility and both had the intention of forcing on us a new examination of the workings of democracy: the discrepancy between democratic theory and practice. Both proceeded by, or at least began in, outrage of the conventions of educated speech and behavior. And both events faced us, whether or not we were prepared to look at what was being shown, with the capacity for hatred and violence which many of the educationally privileged left-wing young share with those they most condemn on the score of their hatred and violence. This is no small likeness. The two occasions, indeed, can significantly be separated only in terms of their practical outcome and the emotions consequent on their differing capacity for effectiveness.

Yet in their deepest relation, in their most fundamental resemblance, Trilling felt, the march on the Pentagon and the Columbia disorders could not be separated. She refers to Mailer's characterization of the Columbia situation as "existential," observing that for him, "who for some years has served faithfully at the ceremonies of experience," this was a "criterion of the worthwhile." But, she says, "the word 'existential' is also in fairly general use to describe the improvisational character of our contemporary revolution, its disdain of ideology and program, and its appeal as an instrument of personal definition." Mailer's "honorific designation" may be more precisely applied, therefore, to the situation at Columbia than to a preplanned, symbolic march that had been deliberately designed to make a statement. Exploding in an unrehearsed "release of social bitterness and rage," the action at Columbia invoked a response that "quite precluded" Trilling's own further emotional involvement in what had taken place in Washington a short time before: "Touch with hostile hands the building which houses the Department of Defense and you perhaps flick the soul of your nation but the building and your nation remain intact. Touch a university with hostile hands and the blood you draw is prompt, copious, and real. There may be disagreement on the quality of the blood, it may be good blood or bad blood, pure or impure blood, but as to the actuality of the wound you have inflicted, there can be no question."

In Trilling's effort to deal with the Columbia disorders the tension between the possibility of a rational approach to the problem and the doubt of it was virtually eclipsed by the power of the existentialist impulse. "One's own existential moment yields to no other," she says. But the obligation of the intellectual to develop a rational analysis of a given situation does not entirely disappear in her account of the insurrectionary attempt to take over the university. She brings up the question of whether or not a rational historical explanation of the "Columbia revolution" may not be discovered in the irony of a "democratic self-criticism" that has at once condemned the failings of American democracy while "exempting communism . . . from the shortcomings of industrial modernity." But the invoking of this problem in "On the Steps of Low Library" strikes one as being not much more than a gesture. Not only in this essay but throughout *We Must March*, the belief in the rational capacity to define moral responsibility and act on it is haunted by the anxious doubt—always strongly implied, if not overtly stated—that such a definition is no longer possible. Finally, in the conclusion of a reflective narrative that takes on a more and more meditative quality as it proceeds, the anxiety of doubt is resolved in a cathartic recognition of the tragic ambiguity of what had happened at Columbia. This comes in an appeal to an event that, although it had no immediate connection with the Columbia situation, was profoundly relevant to it—the assassination of Robert Kennedy.

Drawing on newspaper accounts, Trilling re-creates the poignant scene the night before the funeral of the second Kennedy to be felled by an assassin's bullet, when, as the body lay in state in St. Patrick's Cathedral, none other than Tom

Hayden—the dedicated leader of the SDS, who, although he was not and had never been a Columbia student, had been a major participant in the uprising—came to the Cathedral, which was "dark, empty save for the guard around the coffin," to mourn the death of his sworn enemy.

> Holding in his hand the field cap which reputedly was given him by Castro, Hayden sat alone in the shadows, weeping, until someone who saw him invited him to stand a watch at the coffin, which he did, probably glad of the invitation—in moments of grief, it is helpful to be part of the ceremony. The question this newspaper report raised in my mind—and it refuses to be answered—was, how can the strong emotion which brought Hayden to St. Patrick's in the middle of the night to mourn for Robert Kennedy so totally divorce itself from the ideas which govern the SDS and Hayden as one of its chief leaders? After all, everything that Hayden most significantly lives and works for is directed to the destruction of everything that Kennedy most significantly lived and worked for. One can truly love one's political enemy, and not only in the way dictated by Christianity. But to the degree that one weeps for him alone in the night? And when the political difference is so nearly absolute? It can be put simply: Kennedy believed in the possibility of our society and Hayden believes that our society must be destroyed. These are antithetical principles. Do they not generate antithetical emotions, or at least require some distancing in personal feeling?

Answering her question, the author recalls that earlier in her essay she had spoken "of the ambiguousness of Mailer's Pentagon story, in particular of the ambiguousness which resides in supposing that a higher reasonableness will be reached by acts of unreason, a more reliable condition for peace by acts of violence." But she now extends her comment on Mailer to observe that "perhaps more than we can readily recognize, Mailer's ambiguousness is also the ambiguousness of our apparently most single-minded insurrectionary students and their leaders, of all our intellectuals and all our enlightened population which welcomes the student revolution; the ambiguousness, in fact, of our moral and spiritual times."

Whereas she had once talked about the "moral confusion" of our age, Trilling now spoke of its essential moral ambiguousness. Nor does she speak in the abstract. In "On the Steps of Low Library" she implies her intense personal experience of discovering the pervasive moral equivocalness in the contemporary American cultural situation resulting from the loss of faith in the interlinked modes of moral and intellectual perception developed by the high culture of the Enlightenment as the transcendent reference of civilized order. With the disappearance of the perception that had guided the instigators of the American Revolution and the founders of the Republic, she further implies, the definition of self-deception has become impossible. Therefore—is this the most drastic implication of the cultural situation depicted in *We Must March?*—the assertion of the betrayal of liberalism in America through the yoking of liberalism and Marxism has become meaningless.

In the essays in *We Must March* a controlling opposition present in Diana Trilling's writings from the beginning threatens to disappear: I refer to the stress between a commitment to the idea that through the agency of rationality intellectuals will ultimately triumph in human affairs and a persistent suspicion that intellectuals, possessing no greater capacity for virtue than anyone else, are prone to betray their vocation. Yet, we must note, although Trilling's faith in the educated mind's capacity for reason came under severe stress in the crisis of the sixties and seventies, *We Must March* does not represent a full surrender to the existentialist imperative. Of the two pieces in the collection that were originally contributions to *Partisan Review* symposia, the most important of these, "Liberal Anti-Communism Revisited," represents a rewriting of what Trilling had said in 1967 on the problem of the relationship between American policies in Vietnam and the attitudes of American "anti-Communists of the Left." In its rewritten form a trenchant reply to Lillian Hellman's criticism of the Trillings in *Scoundrel Time* (1976), this essay is also Diana Trilling's most cogent and expansive analysis of the effect on American literature and thought of the struggle between the anti-communists and the anti-anti-communists: When "liberalism" was destroyed in the conflict between the "liberal" ("left-wing") partisans and the "liberal" ("left-wing") opponents of communism, it created a "great intellectual rift" in the American mind. That she locates the origin of this split in the 1930s, not in the 1950s, when it became overtly manifest, suggests with vivid certainty her recognition of her own intellectual origin.

> Although the term "anti-anti-Communism" dates from the fifties and specifically refers to the split among left-wing intellectuals on the McCarthy issue and what has followed from it, the concept was in preparation as far

back as the thirties when, with the rise of Nazism in Germany and with the Spanish Civil War, the newly radicalized intellectuals in the democracies were so successful in capturing the antifascist cause and identifying it with the communist cause. Put most summarily, what happened was that throughout the thirties the Communist Party with great energy and skill organized "innocent" groups, people committed to certain presumed goals of the party but not party members or necessarily even fellow-travelers, into movements against war and fascism, a maneuver by which Communism became intimately associated in the minds of people of progressive political impulse with these dedications. As a consequence of this maneuver, whoever put himself in opposition to Communism came to be regarded as of the Right or even as an "objective fascist."

But obviously in her clear-cut analysis of the fate of "liberal anti-Communism"—which concludes with the hope that "if we indeed have a working liberal-intellectual class and not merely an intellectual lobby for moral self-certification," liberalism can be "rethought" and made to function once again—Trilling had not reached the point of writing off the historic equation between reason and liberalism.[9] If in "On the Steps of Low Library" she felt that the vocation of the intellectual had become involved in a struggle with ambiguities that destroy the efficacy of mind, Trilling did not abandon her faith in the continuing possibilities of intellect.

While in comparison to her other writings, *Mrs. Harris: The Death of the Scarsdale Diet Doctor* may seem to be an exotic performance, its basic, shaping motive is Trilling's continuing preoccupation with her commitment to the view that the cultural critic is a moralist, whose duty it is to serve as a monitorial voice both in the realm of his or her peers and in the general society. This motive is not overtly expressed in *Mrs. Harris*. It may not have been quite available to the author's grasp of her own intentions in writing the book. But it is a motive of which the book itself is a symbol, its presence being unmistakable, for instance, in Trilling's description of the inner drama of her reaction to the growing presence of the defendant in the courtroom.

> From hour to hour my own judgment of her would drastically change—I'd swing from an extreme of sympathy to an extreme of disenchantment. When she was charming, I was charmed. When malice took over as it so

often did without her being at all aware of it, I scarcely remembered that I had ever felt anything but dislike of her—I would think, how can anyone fail to see that this woman is dangerous? Perhaps these swift shifts of feeling attest to her lack of a firm emotional core; certainly hers was a strange power for someone to exercise who sobbingly described herself in a metaphor of emptiness.[10]

We come close to the compelling motive of her fascination with Jean Harris in the next moment, when Trilling returns (though with no reference to her prior use of the same notion in *We Must March*) to the concept of negative space in a painting. In contrast to her first reference toward the possibility of using negative space, her attitude has become positive: "On the canvas of Mrs. Harris's personality there is much negative space, room for what hasn't been painted in." The power of Jean Harris in the courtroom that Trilling observes was the way in which she responded to the challenge to fill the emptiness, to conceive her life not as a metaphor of closure to interpretation but of openness to it.

Published in 1981, a year after the trial, *Mrs. Harris* is what Trilling fills in the negative space Jean Harris represented to her. The book not only sets forth a detailed account of the day-to-day courtroom scene as the trial proceeded but—drawing on the author's assiduous personal investigation and analysis of the circumstances surrounding the murder of Tarnower—effectively locates the Harris case in its social context.

The murderer of the "diet doctor" was not simply a schoolteacher: she was the administrator of a respectable educational institution. Her victim was not only a wealthy cardiologist: in a country that takes dieting as seriously as football, he was the author of the best-selling *The Complete Scarsdale Medical Diet* and thus in a sense a figure of national renown. Another important facet of the Harris case is a widespread doubt that justice was well served by the conviction of a woman who, even though she bore the responsibility of a voluntary relationship with her paramour, may have been as much his victim as he was hers.

The motive for the murder seemed to be the jealous resentment of the fifty-seven-year-old Jean Harris. After a long liaison with Tarnower that had once held the promise of marriage, she had been rejected by her sixty-nine-year-old lover for a younger woman. Her bitterness toward Tarnower was extreme, yet, according to her own account of the murder, Harris went to his fashionable home in Westchester on the night of March 10, 1980, carrying a pistol she intended to use not on him but on herself. Tarnower's death, she testified, was in effect accidental. This defense did not convince the jury, which convicted her of murder in the second degree. Nor later on was her story convincing to Governor Mario Cuomo, who refused Harris's plea for clemency (or the recognition of her right to parole) three times. When he finally did grant clemency—and followed this action three weeks later by ordering that Harris be paroled—Cuomo may well have responded not to the plea for justice but to an immediate need for humanitarian expediency. At any rate the granting of clemency was coincident with Harris's need for heart surgery. Then, too, Cuomo's action may well have been influenced to some extent by what the *Newsweek* article refers to as the "changing attitude toward emotional abuse" in America. Reflected over the years in thousands of letters received by the governor's office on behalf of Harris—including one from the trial judge upon his retirement from the bench—this attitude was also evident, *Newsweek* observes, in several books relating to the Harris case, among them not only the three books pleading her own case Harris wrote while in prison, but also books "sympathetic" to Harris by Shana Alexander and Diana Trilling.

The pairing of Diana Trilling's book with Shana Alexander's is, however, a gross oversimplification. Although, like Shana Alexander's book, it is in the mode of "personal journalism," *Mrs. Harris* is a far more complex narrative. A troubled inquiry into the moral drama of the author's response to the Harris case, it bears the aspect of a record of Diana Trilling's own self-conscious participation in it. Initially, she says, her interest in Jean Harris was inspired by the "great upwelling of feeling" across the nation for a woman who had been grossly wronged by a cruel and tyrannical man. When the realization came to her after she had written the first draft of her book that her perception of the tangled motives involved in the case had been obscured by the influence of doctrinaire feminism, she discarded the manuscript and began again. As in her struggle against the anti-anti-communists, she resisted ideological conformity: "Was I a child of my ideological times? Maybe, but not to the extent of allowing any system of ideas or feelings to obscure immediate truths."[3]

Comparing her to Emma Bovary and Anna Karenina, both of whom violate their status in society by doing something they are not supposed to do, Trilling finds in the Jean Harris story an exemplification of the difficult relation between fact and fiction. Seeing Harris solely in her actuality—"in the raw state of life where we have only the making of art, without its seamlessness"—wondering "how this unprepossessing woman, whose life and love had been of such uninspiriting quality, could create around her such an air of superbness," she "put her in the company of large persons in literature and in life." Yet, Trilling says, it would have been "wrong not to emphasize the ordinariness in which her extraordinariness begins." The answer to the problem of how Jean Harris created "the air of superbness" lies in the more or less indefinable thing theater people call "star quality." This is not something with which one can be invested by others. Like Marilyn Monroe, Jean Harris inherently possessed this "mysterious ingredient" and drew "strength from it." This is why everyone who has heard of the tragedy of Jean Harris "wants to speak about her and hear about her."

> Her elusiveness tantalizes, her personality is like a hall of mirrors: one loses one's way in it. She has become everyone's story. Everyone claims her, everyone claims to understand her, to have solved her mystery. But the mystery is of course not solved or to be solved. People aren't solved. Even women aren't to be solved, though they sometimes act as if it were a desirable consummation. In one of the novels of Anthony Powell he has a character say, "When I read about *crimes passionels* in the papers, I am struck not by the richness of the emotions, but by their desperate poverty. On the surface the people concerned may seem to live with intensity. Underneath, is an abject egotism and lack of imagination." Yes, this could be said of the Harris case too and of Mrs. Harris herself except . . . except that whatever the abjectness of Mrs. Harris and self-boundedness, these are not the aspects of her character that, at the last, remain with us. I'm far from sure that Mrs. Harris is a worthy person, an admirable person, a lovable person, a person we would wish to see replicated in our society. Not any of these. But she's a person who for some reason sparks the imagination and who has her place in our imagination of this time.

The shifts in perspective implied in the movement from "one" and "everyone" to "I" and "our" in this passage may be regarded as no more than a conventional rhetorical gesture aimed at identifying the mythical general reader with the author; at, so to speak, bringing the unknown reader into the authorial embrace. Yet is not this simple device a key to the question of Trilling's compelling attraction to the Harris case? Her solicitation of the reader assumes the presence of a particular kind of reader, a member of the audience she identifies with and for whom she has always written, namely, her peers, the members of the intellectual class, in particular, as she describes them in *Claremont Essays*, "the people I know best, the academic and literary intellectuals of New York."

If in the writings of Diana Trilling we seem to feel at times a more confining New York provincialism than in the writings of Lionel Trilling, we do not experience this as markedly inhibiting. She shares with Lionel Trilling the cosmopolitan conviction that the right motive of the critic as an actor in the drama of history is Arnoldian. The critic has the moral duty always to sit in rational, responsible judgment; for in truth—at least in the Western world, where we have traditionally conceived that the civilizing process is inseparably tied to the culture of letters— the fate of civilization depends on the conscientious performance of the critic's task. Yet Diana Trilling also shares with Lionel Trilling a sense of the fragility of the critic's sensitivity to the burden of responsibility for the use of letters. Like him she expresses an ever-present awareness of conflict in her own mind between the assumption that the vocation of the critic imposes a mandatory obligation to be the moral agent of society and the recognition that this obligation is not self-defining.

As a highly self-conscious, dedicated intellectual, Diana Trilling assumes in *Mrs. Harris*, as she has always, that the role of the critic implies an instructive or admonitory self-representation of the critic's own moral character. Does she not assume also that she is less concerned in *Mrs. Harris* with the moral character of the person who shot Dr. Tarnower than she is (to employ an adjective she uses elsewhere) with the "moral-intellectual" character of her own personal response to Tarnower's killer? Considering this implication in *Mrs. Harris*, I think the book may be compared to a novel in which, in the conflicted struggle to tell the story of a hero or a heroine, a first-person narrator in effect becomes the protagonist. At times it seems that the goal of the implied protagonist in *Mrs. Harris* is to come up with a reasoned, objective analysis of the Harris case. But this possibility is constantly tempered by the narrator's recognition of the limits of reason in the pursuit of the truth of human behavior. Having meticulously pursued the duty of the reporter to get at the facts about Jean Harris, the narrator-critic discovers finally that "without the armature of fiction," her story will become "a clinical study"—a perversion of the fundamental truth about human beings, which is that they "cannot be solved." She refers the meaning of the story of Jean Harris to the realm of "imaginative writing, where . . . Freud learned, as we learn, about characters in conflict."

By the time Trilling wrote *Mrs. Harris* the struggle between the anti-communists and the anti-anti-communists had ceased to be an active issue. But the capacity of American intellectuals for self-deception remained for her what it had always been, a fundamental issue in American cultural politics. One may refer especially to two passages in *Mrs. Harris*. Both are concerned with culture in relation to taste and moral values in Jean Harris's life style. In one passage the author presents her as "a values lady," who, "in her system of values," holds "intellectual honesty" as the "first principle."

> As witness after witness took the stand for the defense, Arunou [Joel Arunou, Harris's lawyer] would ask the same stilted question: what about the headmistress's reputation for "veracity"? The question became silly. It had to be plain to anyone that for Mrs. Harris veracity is a moral imperative. Aurnou's client reeks of truth. There's an important sense in which she's sick on truth—if she didn't over-estimate truth for its own sake and be pledged to stay true to her ideals, she wouldn't have to resort to denial as disastrously as I believe she did and does. Mrs. Harris tells the truth even when she lies. In a way this is what is meant by denial: the process of self-deception spares one the need to lie just as it spares one the confrontation of truth.

Here is the other passage in *Mrs. Harris* concerning culture and taste one may refer to:

> In the trial Harris was at considerable pains to consolidate her own social and cultural position by the way she pictured Dr. Tarnower, her social companion for so many years. She made him into a fitting partner of the superior intellectual life she led as member of the academic profession. She told us that when she first met him, Tarnower talked with her of Russia and instructed her in Jewish history. She said he was the kind of man who "read Herodotus for fun" and that the two of them had never argued except "over the use of the subjunctive.". . . In adducing a moral style from a style of life, I was perhaps more generous with Mrs. Harris than with Dr. Tarnower: although I was embarrassed by her intellectual boasts, her gifts of mind were sufficiently striking so that I could at least suppose she had a better foundation for her cultural vanities than he had. . . . Expanded from a two-page diet sheet, [Tarnower's] book spoke more than a volume's worth

of social pretension to anyone who was willing to read it as something other than just a guide to weight loss.

Is it an exaggeration to say that Diana Trilling, assuming that the critic has the novelist's privilege of employing the preemptive imagination of the artist, creates Jean Harris as a kind of parodic figure of the American intellectual, a figure with whom she herself is, however, deeply empathetic? Something like twenty years before she wrote about the case of Mrs. Harris, she had remarked (in *Claremont Essays*) of the Profumo affair in England:

> Ours is an era of "cases" starting with the Sacco-Vanzetti case in the 1920s, proceeding through the Hiss and Oppenheimer cases, to the Rosenberg case, the Chesman case, the Eichmann case, and most recently culminating, if we can call it a culmination, in the Profumo case. That in 1963, our great confrontation between opposing social principles began with the discovery that a government official has been engaged in illicit sex was opportunistically manipulated by the party in England that is supposed to speak most firmly for the liberal—by which we mean decent—values, and was brought to the semblance of moral resolution by the suicide of a man of the character of Stephen Ward, should remind us that the life of reason continues to have its difficulties.

Trilling's rhetorical understatement about the cultural politics of England dramatizes a failure of reason by the presumably educated mind in England so fundamental that it suggests not merely a lack of diligence on the part of those who are responsible for the education of the nation but, to use Julien Benda's famous term, a "betrayal of the clerks," an act of treason by professors, philosophers, and critics, those who are responsible for the uses of mind. While the case of the headmistress of the Madeira School had nothing as such to do with the involvement of American intellectuals in communism, like the Profumo affair it had to do with sexual misbehavior by a person in a position of public trust, which is to say with the cultural politics of sexual behavior. In Trilling's complex vision of it, the Harris case is altogether a symbol of the incapacity of the moral imagination of the American intellectual class (which properly in a participatory democracy must include all its teachers). In a large and poetic sense, Trilling's book about Jean Harris—which locates the story about her misconduct in the context of the author's personal struggle to imagine the life of the intellectual in "this time"—in our time, in the time of the author of *Mrs. Harris*—can be read as part of a fable of twentieth-century American cultural politics, the animating motive of this being the ironic betrayal of the basic motive of American history, i.e., the struggle for national self-definition, by a willed self-deception about the ends of this struggle.

I am not sure at all how one may reconcile the independence and brilliance of Diana Trilling's career and her disposition at times in her memoir to attribute her career to Lionel Trilling's influence. In view of the independent character of her own career, is it not both more comfortable and more logical to seek the nature of the remarkable relationship between the two minds not in the dependence of one mind on another but in the mutual intensity of their dedication to the responsibility of the critic? I find myself remembering an essay on the character of Lionel Trilling's work I wrote several years ago, in which I refer to Allen Tate's notion that criticism is invested with an ambience of the tragic, the "act of criticism" always being a tragic action in that it finally and imperatively presents a "crisis of recognition." What exactly does the critic, the interpreter of meaning, recognize? He recognizes finally that the only "certain knowledge" he possesses is that he "knows virtually nothing."

Writing about Jean Harris would seem to have been for Diana Trilling a way of recovering from the despair of meaning that she describes in *We Must March*. The recovery is not based on a renewal of an assured faith in her capacity as an intellectual to serve as an agent of order. She had never had this. *Mrs. Harris* indicates a restoration of what Diana Trilling had preeminently shared with Lionel Trilling—a dramatic tension in her vision of the world between faith in the capacity of the critic to be an agent of reason and the threat of being overwhelmed by despair about this possibility; a tension, in her own words, between "an intellectual life in which we define ourselves by our manifest responsibility to reason and the consequences of thought" and "a world in which we validate our sensibility by our apocalypticism."

We recall Trilling's homily on the meaning of Edmund Wilson's career in her review of *Memoirs of Hecate County*. "Amid disorder" in "a bad world," she says, the intellectual must maintain "some principle of private order from which a principle of general order might be adduced." The critic must maintain "a sound integration between head and heart, which of course is another way of asking that he distinguish between sensation and emotion." Having failed to integrate head and heart, Wilson has in effect betrayed the vocation of the literary intellectual by failing to sustain a sense of "personal order within a disintegrated society," thus making it impossible for him "at the least to have a tragic—which is to say, a meaningful—experience of pain." He has thus failed in what "is everlastingly the intellectual's job, to be meaningful despite and above his social situation." An experience of pain that transcends society as the ultimate measure of the critical achievement: As far as I am aware Trilling never explicitly repeated this austere poetic criterion for evaluating the worth of the critic, but her career exemplified her recognition of the irony that was its inspiration: the irony of a long career spent in the impossible but necessary attempt to imagine the vast spiritual and intellectual disorder of our times, while at the same time endeavoring to imagine a sense of personal order strong enough to oppose her imagination of disorder. We of course see in Diana Trilling's participation in the drama of the struggle for order in the twentieth century the influence of Lionel Trilling, but it is more to the point to see that the two critics share in the same effort; and in doing so share in the same desperate effort by all the best literary minds of this century.

NOTES

1. It may be noted that I ignore the question of the relation between the literary identity of Diana Trilling and the fact that she is Jewish. Doing so, I follow her own insistence—so contrary to the present-day preoccupation with ethnicity—on the unimportance of the ethnic factor either in her life or in Lionel Trilling's life. She says in her memoir: "Like Lionel but unlike most of the Jewish intellectuals of our generation, I had the childhood of an American who happened to be a Jew, not that of a Jew who happened to be an American." This made a great deal of difference. It also made a difference that by the 1920s, as Irving Howe has explained, the cosmopolitan intellectual life in New York City encouraged Jews with intellectual aspirations to adopt "secular and universalist values." Of the time Lionel Trilling began his career William Phillips has observed: "One thought less of one's ethnicity than of one's internationalism and concerns for humanity as a whole. We thought of literature and our literary profession not as Jews, but as heirs of the Western tradition." A good summation of the question of Lionel Trilling's Jewishness is in Stephen L. Tanner's *Lionel Trilling* (New York, 1988), 10–17. Also, see an earlier comment on this question in Lewis P. Simpson, "Lionel Trilling and the Agency of Terror," *Partisan Review* 54 (Winter 1987): 18–35.

2. Trilling's insight with respect to Sartre is supported in Tony Judt's brilliant study, *Past Imperfect: French Intellectuals, 1944–1956* (Berkeley, Calif., 1992).

3. Diana Trilling's complex ideas about what she calls the "American feminine fate" deserve exploration at length. See especially her essays in *We Must March My Darlings* in the section labeled "Women's Liberation" ("Female Biology in a Male Culture" and "The Prisoner of Sex") and the section called "We Must March My Darlings" (the record of the author's return to Radcliffe in 1971).

A CHARLESTON JEW AND THE SHAPING
FORM OF MEMORY
Louis D. Rubin, Jr.

> We are our memory.
> —LOUIS D. RUBIN, JR., *Small Craft Advisory*

"In my end is my beginning," T. S. Eliot proclaims at the end of "Burnt Norton." In a sense Louis Rubin has followed this dictum in writing the three book-length memoirs he has published to date. The first, *Small Craft Advisory: A Book about the Building of a Boat* (1991), is a lyrical celebration of the fulfilling interrelation Rubin has discovered between his passion for writing and publishing, along with his establishment of the Algonquin Press in 1982, and the building in 1990 of a cabin cruiser he named the *Algonquin*. Built for pleasure yet constructed on a wooden hull (instead of fiberglass) configured like the "many hundreds" of workaday craft that ply the waters of the Carolinas, this boat was designed by Rubin himself and commissioned to be individually crafted by an old-time, semiretired professional boat builder of Harker's Island, North Carolina. The second volume of Rubin's memoirs, *An Honorable Estate: My Time in the Working Press* (2001), tells the story of his effort to fulfill his passion for writing and printing through his association with several newspapers in the 1930s and 1940s; and, briefly, records the crucial change in his career when, seeking a richer fulfillment of his passions, he turned from the vocation of journalist to that of academic literary scholar and critic. The third volume of his memoirs, *My Father's People: A Family of Southern Jews* (2002), records Rubin's experience of recovering the meaning of the history of the family of Charleston, South Carolina, Jews in which he grew up. His focus is on his father and his father's three brothers, along with one of their sisters, the children of immigrant parents, Hyman Levy and Fannie Rubin, East Prussian or Lithuanian Jews, who in the mid-1880s took up residence in the old port city of Charleston. Here in 1923 Louis Decimus Rubin, Jr., was born into the family of the youngest of the four Rubin brothers.

None of the Rubin family followed the sea or seems to have had any inclination to do so; and in the earlier years of his boyhood Louis was conscious of the marine environment in which he lived—the "ships, boats, the harbor, the water everywhere about Charleston, the ocean that lay out beyond Fort Sumter and the jetties"—simply as "inaccessible territories." But by the time he had reached the period we now call the "preteens," he had fallen under the spell of a romantic sense of the mystery of the ships moving up and down the Ashley River, which was visible across the wide tidal marsh that fronted the Rubin home on Souci Street in what, as the city expanded, came to be known as Uptown Charleston. This sense was expressed for him in a glee club song:

> I never see a sail afloat but in my heart's a song
> To guide it on its willing way and bring it back erelong.
> I'd leave the harbor far behind if one would wait for me,
> But as I wait and vainly hope, I know 'twill never be.

Then there came the moment when, having discovered in a volume of the *Book of Knowledge* the picture of a small boat with a boy seated in it, Louis hit upon the idea of actively participating in the life of the marine world by building a similar craft, launching it in the marsh creek, and sailing in it to the edge of the river, where the ships went up and down. How, with the aid of a friend, Louis actually built this tiny, "coffin shaped" boat out of "scrap" lumber (appropriated from nearby work sites), gave her the name *First Boat,* and christened her with Kool-Aid; how he and his friend launched *First Boat,* only immediately almost to lose her because the seams were not properly caulked; how eventually Louis added a crude sail and ventured a little way onto the expanse of the Ashley River—this story constitutes an altogether charming boyhood idyll. But the building of *First Boat* represents for Rubin more than the memory of an idyllic—and, to be sure, perilous—boyhood enterprise, since he could not swim.

> Building and using that little boat was one of the more satisfying accomplishments of my life. I have thought about it with pleasure many times, and have written fiction about it. It was, I think, deeply emblematical. For it was the first time I had ever done anything of my own accord to *change* my life. I wanted to go out on the water—leave the land, free myself from

the restrictions of the shore, and the city where I lived—and I built a boat and did so. In its own way it was a liberating act.

The building of *First Boat* was also an imprisoning act in that Louis would never again be free from the compulsion to own a boat which he could from time to time go sailing in; and in response to this compulsion over the years he would buy and sell a whole array of small water craft, ranging from craft propelled by the winds to boats powered by outboard motors to larger ones propelled by considerably more powerful inboard motors.

Although his attraction to boats was first inspired by the traffic on the Ashley River, Rubin's passion for watercraft was predominantly the result of the many hours he spent as a boy on Charleston's Adger's Wharf. Long since disappeared, this wharf, located on the Cooper River in downtown Charleston, was available to Louis by "the slender umbilical cord of Charleston's Rutledge Avenue trolley," which would take him from his home "far uptown to the downtown city on the point of the peninsula" below which the Ashley and Cooper rivers converge in the sea.

Although boats of all kinds, from luxury cruise ships to tug boats, hold a fascination for him, Rubin still feels his strongest attachment to the kinds of boats that he saw berthed at Adger's Wharf. These included "shrimp trawlers, cargo launches that served the nearby sea island communities, commercial fishing boats, the harbor pilot boats, crab buy boats, and a variety of others." One would see also, at the south wharf, the three tugs of the White Stack Towboat Company, and a little upstream a boatyard with a marine railway and a machine shop. And not far beyond one would see the docks where the Clyde-Mallory passenger ships—which, bearing American Indian names like the *Shawnee*, the *Cherokee*, and the *Algonquin*—sailed between New York and the ports of the South Atlantic and the Gulf coasts. Though he never got to take a voyage in a Clyde-Mallory ship, Louis has a special attachment to the *Algonquin*, which he perpetuates in the name of the publishing house he founded. This attachment had developed when as a six-year-old boy he saw this ship moving one misty morning down the harbor channel on its return from New York with his father aboard and was greeted by a blinking lantern as the *Algonquin* slipped by, his father having tipped a deckhand to let him blink the lantern.

From the time he was old enough to get about on his own, Louis regarded

Adger's Wharf and its adjacent vicinity, including the dock of the ferryboat that linked Charleston and Sullivan's Island, as his "territory." But it was "Adger's Wharf itself that drew" him "like a magnet."

> On Saturday mornings I would linger there for hours at a time watching the proceedings, waiting for the tugboats to cast off their lines and go over to the Clyde Line dock to help the *Cherokee,* now bedecked with pennants, extricate itself and back out into the channel, then swing its stern upstream and proceed southward under its own power, very slowly at first, past Adger's Wharf and the High Battery until it turned eastward in the Ashley River channel and headed off to sea. Eventually the ship was no more than a long low shape in the water out beyond Fort Sumter, and was bound for New York or Jacksonville. By then it was getting toward late afternoon and time for me to walk up Broad Street to Meeting Street, to the post office. There I would board the Rutledge Avenue car that would take me all the way uptown to Sans Souci Street and home.

It would be years, Rubin says, before he "began to realize why Adger's Wharf had such significance" for him. Now he understands it was because the waterfront—its workboats: "its ships and cargo launches and tugboats and trawlers"—fused "two discreet realms of my experience: it was the stuff of literature and the imagination, and yet was *not* self-consciously picturesque or quaint but immediate and real and important to me." At the same time as the workboats carried out their daily tasks along the waterfront and the sea islands, they were operating in the waters "where the Civil War and the British attack on Charleston had taken place and the pirate ships had sailed." Thus "to be associated with a workboat was to unite two realms of existence." In his boyhood this was the only part of his experience that he "could identify as representing what I hope someday to attain: a place for grounding my imagination in actuality." Rubin refers to a grounding in the actuality that for poets and storytellers from ancient to modern to "postmodern" times has finally been the only actuality, memory: "When I come back to Charleston now I am a visitor, a tourist even. I have not lived there for almost half a century, and most of my friends and almost all of my family there are gone as well. Yet my imagination still inhabits the place as it was in the 1920s and 1930s and early 1940s, and what the intervening years have done is not to change the place that my imagination knows, but only the perspective from which I view it."

When at the age of sixty-five Rubin decided to abandon his practice of buying secondhand boats and build a boat he had himself designed "for purposes of pleasure and for going about on the water," he was, he says, contriving an emblem of the "transaction" of memory. Something of the depth and complexity of this emblematic transaction is revealed in his intriguing account of his adventures and misadventures with the secondhand boats in his life. These included most notably a twenty-eight-and-a-half-foot Triton sailboat, the *Virginius;* a cranky and rather ancient workboat with a small diesel engine and a bad transmission, the *Bill James;* a more spacious Chris-Craft cabin cruiser with twin two-hundred-horsepower Ford V-8 engines, which he proudly named the *Little Eva* in honor of his wife, and that early one morning, after he had berthed her in a marina overnight, he discovered with "only her cockpit protruding above the water"; "a lapstrake-hulled gasoline-powered wooden boat" with a temperamental Chrysler Crown engine that he had to replace at considerable expense; and a similar gasoline-powered wooden boat, the *Mary Simpson,* named for the wife of his friend, a prominent meteorologist and fellow lover of small craft, Robert Simpson. In spite of the more or less constant trouble his boats caused him, Louis always felt a reluctance to part with one, boats having "a way of insinuating themselves into one's affections and holding on for dear life."

It was inevitable, one judges, that Rubin's affection for boats would demand fulfillment in the building of one he could call wholly his own—a boat that would not only be a symbol of his long devotion to the art and craft of getting about on water in boats but a representation of the connection between this devotion and his deeper and more fundamental devotion to the art and craft of words and printing. Harking back to his childhood experience of building *First Boat,* and his varied experiences with all the second-hand craft he had bought in the interim between *First Boat* and the building of the *Algonquin,* Rubin envisioned the construction of this craft of his design as, in the deepest, most basic sense, the climax of the slow realization on his part that the experience of owning and operating boats was a symbolic act of the imagination—a symbol of the unfolding design of his life—in essence the experience of "approaching the world as a metaphor": "In the opening chapter of this book [*Small Craft Advisory*] I told of building a leaking, tippy skiff in order to go out upon the tidal marsh to the edge of the Ashley River, and I described it as a liberating act, an assertion of freedom. And indeed it was—and also an assertion of ambition. I remarked, too, that every other boat I have since owned and operated could be said to constitute an attempt to reproduce that early experience."

So it was that, watching the commemoration of the building and launching of the *Algonquin* at the "Great Book-and-Boat Celebration" held at DeeGee's Books and Gifts on the waterfront at Moorehead City, North Carolina, on May 26, 1990, Louis Rubin once again contemplated the meaning of boats in his life. Guests and participating authors included four younger writers who had come into increasing prominence after having first been published by Algonquin: Kaye Gibbons, Clyde Edgerton, Jill McCorkle, and Larry Brown. They had arrived at the dock of the "Sanitary Restaurant," the "oddly named" but oldest and most popular eatery on the Moorehead City waterfront aboard three boats: Louis's *Algonquin*, Bob Simpson's *Sylvia II*, and John McCallum's *Ruth* (McCallum was a friend who owned the Taylor Boat Works which had helped to keep Louis's boats in repair). Together these boats constituted "a nautical processional spanning some sixty years of traditional North Carolina wooden boatcraft." As he observed its unfolding, Louis reflected on the Book-and-Boat party as "the embodiment of so much of what" he "had set out to do": He "had taught and written about southern literature," he "had encouraged numerous young southerners to write more of that literature," and he had been able "to launch"—he uses the word deliberately, he says—"a group of them on their careers by editing and publishing their books."

In the concluding pages of *Small Craft Advisory* Rubin reflects further on the meaning of a career that had begun as he pursued what he had conceived to be the vocation he would follow all his life, that of newspaper reporter. His discovery that news reporting did not confirm his vision of vocation required fuller consideration than he could afford it in *Small Craft Advisory*. Ten years later he published a second volume of memoirs, *An Honorable Estate*, in which he sketches his short career in newspaper journalism, together with the reasons why he had given up a career two of his uncles had followed. It was a career that he had early on committed himself to follow, and he had never thought of abandoning it, until he began to realize that as a journalist he was lacking in "a certain quality of attitude" evident in the best of his journalistic colleagues. "Though very different as individuals," he says, they "had a kind of practicality of approach, one that in no way inhibited the full use of imagination or irony, but that gave authority and directness to all that they wrote." Instead, Louis Rubin says, he preferred to "deal with life at one remove, to keep language between myself and direct experience, more or less to approach the world as if it were a metaphor." This preference, he adds, afforded him the "kind of sympathetic identification" he needed to work with writing and writers. But it did not fit him "for the vocation that since childhood he had intended for himself."

Placed in the focus of its general historical context, Rubin's *My Father's People: A Family of Southern Jews* is a portrayal of a specific instance of the remarkable drama of the cultural assimilation of the large number of central and eastern European immigrants into American society in the last part of the nineteenth century. The assimilative process was seldom if ever easy, and not infrequently immigrants found that the fabled promise of a new life in America was an illusion. But however difficult it was to make the promise come true, more often than not the immigrants made a life in America that they believed was better than their life in the Old World.

This would seem to have been generally true even in the instance of numerous eastern European Jews; even in the case of the family of Hyman Levy Rubin, a Russian Jew who, born in East Prussia, came to New York in the 1880s at the age of seventeen and in 1886 or 1887 took a wife whose parents, born in Germany, had arrived in America before the Civil War. Louis says he does not know why not long after they were married Hyman and Fannie Rubin decided to leave New York City to take up residence in one of the chief spiritual bastions of the defeated Confederacy. It may have been because of a family connection his wife had in Charleston, where Hyman became associated with what was known as late as the 1930s as the "dry goods business"; there, in the next fourteen years he fathered eight children, seven of whom survived. But Hyman, it appears, was lacking in the business acumen needed to support his large family. The reason may have been that he had been displaced from the rabbinical tradition in his family, but this can only be a speculation, the history of the Rubins in their old home having largely been lost as a result of the tragic events in the history of the European Jews in the twentieth century. In any event, in the early 1900s when Hyman Rubin and Fannie Rubin both became ill, the financial situation of the family became so desperate that in 1902 the parents were forced to seek relief by placing three of their four sons—Dan, Manning, and Louis (the author's father)—in the Hebrew Orphans Home in Atlanta. The oldest son, Harry, at the age of twelve had already become "the family's breadwinner," and was to work all his life for a wholesale dry goods house. The Rubin boys had three sisters: Dora, the oldest child in the family and the last to die (at age 90 in the year 2000); Essie (Esther); and Ruthie. There was also a sister who died in early childhood. But, although he devotes one chapter to Dora and her career as a legal secretary, Louis Rubin's book is chiefly about his three uncles and his father, to whom he devotes a chapter each.

None of Hyman Rubin's sons had a formal education beyond the seventh grade, yet each in his own independent way did well in a forbidding world. Their independence is reflected in the fact that, although all of the Rubin boys were obviously endowed with a quite sufficient measure of mental ability, none of them, as one might expect, in view of the poverty in which they were reared, aggressively sought to fulfill the pattern of from rags to riches. Not even Harry, who, Louis says, in effect assumed the role of family patriarch. Harry rose from the job of stockboy in the dry goods business to a partnership in his firm, yet remained content with a relatively modest income. Having experienced the social humiliation of his family's poverty, he made the defining interest of his life not the acquirement of affluence but the acquirement and maintenance of "respectability." To this end he took the "local pieties for his own" and accepted the "ideals and values" of the Charleston gentry—not because as a Jew he expected or even wanted to be invited to join them but because he wanted to be favored by their "good opinions." To achieve this goal he cultivated a social conservatism that led him to assume "ideological and political stances" that were "exaggerated to the point of absurdity." As he grew older, Louis says in summing up his story, Uncle Harry "drew in his boundaries and constricted his sympathies" to such an extent that "he excluded the possibilities of joy." And thus "in a family chronicle that includes no small portion of blight," his story "is the saddest of all."

Like Harry, the three younger sons of Hyman Rubin all became doctrinaire southern conservatives, though they led lives less rigidly defined than Harry's by the need to seek the good opinions of the Charleston gentry. In fact, one of them, Uncle Dan ("with whom," Rubin says, "I was the closest"), broke away from Charleston to live in New York City and Hollywood and elsewhere. Dan's life was by choice a lonely one. He never married, acquired few possessions, and, save when he served in the army in the First World War (during which he was severely wounded), lived alone. His place of residence was one hotel room or another. Thinking the climate of the desert country would be good for him, he spent the last eighteen years of his life in a modest El Paso hotel.

Here he spent his time, as he had for many years, writing plays that were never produced. But the plays of this self-taught playwright—he served his self-directed apprenticeship to this art while working as a newspaper reporter—had in the 1920s and thirties been produced on Broadway, including *Devils,* a "morbidly realistic" play about the South (according to Brooks Atkinson in the *New York Times*), and a hit mystery drama called *Riddle Me This* that ran the whole of the

1932 Broadway season. When his plays suggested to Hollywood producers that Daniel Rubin might be a good man to write the scripts for the "talkies," he went to Hollywood on a long-term screenwriting contract with Paramount. At one point in his screenwriting career, Dan gave in to the Hollywood style and bought a Cadillac and drove it across the continent for a visit in Charleston. "The one instance I can recall of his ever affecting anything that might be thought of as ostentation," Louis comments. But by the late 1930s Dan had grown weary of Hollywood and left Tinseltown for good. His intention was to resume writing for the stage, and he did so for the rest of his life, though he never saw another play produced. Apparently the investments he had made in the good years were productive, and he was never in need. He had the satisfaction of doing the one thing he wanted to do, write plays, and that was enough.

Like Uncle Dan, Uncle Manning Rubin was a bachelor. Like Dan he also became a newspaperman. But unlike his brother, for whom journalism was a way of supporting himself while he pursued his aspiration to write for the stage, Manning never left the journalistic profession. Nor did he, like Dan, leave his native city. As a reporter, columnist (under the pseudonym "Strong Cigar," though he smoked cigarettes), and editor (he eventually attained the post of city editor of the *Charleston Evening Post*), Manning was a participant in the life of his community. But, Louis says, he was rather inexplicably isolated. "In a deeper, more complete, and perhaps more ultimate way than anyone else I have ever known, he was *alone*—more so even than Dan, for whom isolation was a deliberately willed condition."

Having sketched the portraits of his patriarchal uncle, his play-writing uncle, and his newspaperman uncle, Louis turns to the portrayal of the youngest of the Rubin boys, his father. Sent to the Atlanta Hebrew Orphanage when he was seven, Louis D. Rubin, Sr., remained there for three years. The experience does not seem to have been a terribly traumatic one, as it had been for Dan and Manning; indeed in later years Louis Rubin, Sr., remembered it with gratitude. Like his brothers, however, compelled by the necessity of his family's poverty, as soon as he completed his elementary education, he went to work in a hardware store. But before long he was energetically pursuing an interest in "the newfangled use of electricity," and by 1916 at the age of twenty-one he had established his own retail and contracting electrical business. After service as a technical sergeant in a signal unit of the Marines during the American participation in the First World War, he returned to a business enterprise that expanded rapidly as the possibilities of electricity expanded. Endlessly inventive in his merchandising techniques, he was on his way to becoming affluent, when a disabling illness struck him. Although he was never again to resume an active life, he was relieved of undue worry about his family's livelihood by the fact that he had providently taken out a substantial disability policy. The income from this investment was supplemented by the insurance benefits he enjoyed as an ex-serviceman. In the long years ahead he found various interests, including gardening, an activity that brought him some local fame in Charleston, and in enterprises undertaken by the American Legion post to which he belonged.

But he attained greater notice after the family moved to Richmond, Virginia, in 1942. Here he began to cultivate his lifelong interest in weather phenomena, especially in cloud formations. He pursued this interest with such avidity that he developed genuine confidence in his ability to forecast the weather; and with the publication of his booklet on *How to Forecast the Weather,* he became a respected amateur meteorologist, whose forecasts not only became known throughout the state of Virginia but attracted national attention when he entered the field of long-term forecasting with predictions based on the influence of volcanic eruptions on global weather. The spells of bad weather he forecast became known as "Rubin Days." Fifteen years or more after the death of Louis D. Rubin, Sr., his weather book was published by Louis D. Rubin, Jr.'s Algonquin Press. It still has a steady sale. Paying tribute to his father, the junior Louis Rubin says that "his life constituted a striking refusal to yield to adversity." With "a courage and resilience that overcame youthful poverty, the collapse of a hard-won business success and the abrupt loss of his health, partial paralysis, and a seemingly confined prospect for the future," he created "a totally new, highly imaginative career for himself."

What was true of his father, as Louis Rubin shows in *My Father's People,* was true for his brothers. Each in his way was courageous and imaginative in creating a life for himself in spite of adversity. How much, or how little, the fact of their Jewish identity marked their struggle with the circumstances of life the Rubin brothers confronted is suggested to some extent in the final chapter of Louis's memoir, a moving meditation on the subject of "Vocations." Although the opportunities they had were few, Louis concludes, they made the most of them to the best of their considerable ability. And they had advantages, too: "They were Jews, and they were Americans. These were enough."

In the final chapter of *My Father's People* the author remarks briefly on his relation to the heritage of a family that still had an attachment to the beliefs of the Reform Jewish faith. His remarks include the account of how as a boy in the 1930s he attended the Sabbath School of the reform congregation of K. K. Beth Elohim in downtown Charleston, and at the Saturday morning services in the temple next door was one of the boys who went up to the altar to help the Rabbi "remove The Torah from the ark and unroll it on the altar," so that the Rabbi could read from it; and then, after the Rabbi had completed the reading, how he had replaced the ornaments and bore the weight of the sacred scroll upright on his lap while the Rabbi "read the day's passage from the large bound volume containing the whole of the Old Testament."

Somehow one feels that in this recollection Louis Rubin suggests the influence on him of the intellectual, and, not less, spiritual ambition, still present in spite of the Holocaust, of a rabbinical tradition in the Rubin family. Did not the force of this implicit tradition assert its presence when Louis turned from the profession of journalism to that of scholar and critic? In doing so he responded to the phenomenon that, Hegel suggested, has marked the literary history of the West since the sixteenth century, that is to say, a secularization of the spiritual countered by a sacralization of the secular.

There is a haunting moment in *Small Craft Advisory* when Louis tells about how on a gray January day at the beginning of the year after the Great Book-and-Boat Celebration he found himself, for no easily discernible reason, driving alone the one hundred and fifty miles from Chapel Hill to the permanent berth of the *Algonquin* at Gillikin's Boat Basin on Peltier Creek in the Moorehead City area. Stepping aboard, he started the diesel engine, freed the mooring lines, and went for a brief run on the deserted waters of Bogue Sound. Then he returned the *Algonquin* to her berth and, securing the lines, went below into the cabin beginning to be warmed up by a small heater he had on board, lay down to rest for a bit, and fell asleep: "When I realized I had been asleep, I looked at my watch. I had napped for almost an hour. The cabin was now, if anything, too warm; it was necessary to turn down the thermostat on the heater. I looked outside through the port; all was winter gray. I lay down again, and enjoyed being warm and comfortable. It was as if the boat were a cocoon, or a return to the womb."

Rereading this passage in *Small Craft Advisory* the other day, and thinking about the story of his family Louis tells in *My Father's People*, I thought fancifully—perhaps not too fancifully—about the shaping form of memory we recognize in the greatest symbolic boat story: the one in Hebraic tradition about that massive wooden boat God told Noah to build—and how this boat did its work, becoming the womb from which Noah and his family, and a pair representing each species of the other creatures of the world, reemerged to re-create the world after God's visitation of His wrath on the sinful race of mankind in an all-destroying flood.

THE LAST AGRARIAN
Andrew Lytle

Andrew Lytle was not only the last of the Nashville, or Vanderbilt, Agrarians; he had the singular distinction of being the only Agrarian for whom the agricultural way of life was more than a metaphor. Indeed, although his attraction to farming early on became secondary to that of a literary career, he attempted to make the lesser attraction serve the stronger.

It was not a consistent attempt. When he received his B.A. degree from Vanderbilt in 1925, Lytle "bached" for a year with his father "in the two-room frame house, with a dog-run porch between the rooms," and helped run Cornsilk, the elder Lytle's two-thousand-acre farm near Guntersville, Alabama. But he soon found that the interest in a literary career that had been inspired by his exposure to the literary atmosphere of Vanderbilt during the days of the Fugitive poets—and in particular by his classes under Donald Davidson and John Crowe Ransom and his friendship with another undergraduate, Robert Penn Warren—demanded a chance for further definition. And, intrigued with the possibility of becoming a dramatist (as Warren was to be somewhat later), in 1926 Lytle became a student of George Pierce Baker at the noted 47 Workshop at Yale. He also became an apprentice actor. Eventually he had one play produced by Baker's Experimental Theatre, acted in several other plays Baker produced, and even made an appearance in a Broadway play. He continued an active interest in the theater until the summer of 1931, when he helped to form the Hampton Players at South Hampton on Long Island and had a leading role in a comedy called *The Immodest Violet*. But by then the allure of the New York stage had diminished. Together with his former mentors Ransom and Davidson, his friend of the Vanderbilt years, Warren, and a more recent friend, Allen Tate, he had become involved in a reappraisal of the significance of his native world that Tate hopefully called the "southern movement." Tate, who had graduated from Vanderbilt two years before Lytle, had inaugurated a long-lived close friendship with Lytle in 1927, when he invited the aspiring playwright and actor to visit him in New York City. Here Tate was trying to establish himself as a writer but was at the same time becoming more and more committed to a crusading vision of the American South as the last bastion against the spiritually devastating force of industrial capitalism. Heavily influenced by Tate's ideas and his militant attitude, but at the same time moved to seek his own vision of the meaning of the South, Lytle contributed "The Hind Tit" to the controversial Agrarian declaration of principles *I'll Take My Stand* in 1930. "The Hind Tit" was followed a year later by a biography of Nathan Bedford Forrest, the Confederate general from Alabama.

In contrast to the culture of the plantation world, Lytle, in both "The Hind Tit" and *Bedford Forrest and His Critter Company,* celebrated the virtues—and too the faults—of the culture of an agricultural society still vividly present when he was a child and still discernibly present when he began to write in the 1920s. Broadly speaking, this was the culture of the southern "backwoods," as Lytle called it, that large, varied, and complex frontier and semi-frontier world known to historians as the "Old Southwest." Heavily populated by nonslaveholding, independent yeoman farmer families descended from English, Scottish, and Irish immigrants, this subregion comprised much of the antebellum South beyond the Appalachians, including Tennessee, Alabama, Kentucky, Mississippi, Louisiana, and western Georgia. But Lytle's world, personal and literary, was more particular, consisting specifically of the part of the Old Southwest where he grew up and was to spend most of his days, roughly the area extending from Monteagle and Sewanee, Tennessee, on the north to Murfreesboro, Tennessee (where he was born), and Guntersville, Alabama, on the south.

It was essentially this small part of the backwoods South, both as it had been and as it was in his time, that, shortly after he had written the biography of Forrest, Lytle began to conceive as a subject for fictional representation. But, though "Old Scratch," his first, rather rudimentary work of fiction, appeared in the *Virginia Quarterly Review* in 1932, he was still largely preoccupied with the Agrarian cause; and for the next three years he turned his hand mostly to writing supportive essays and reviews, while in a related activity, he assisted in a legal battle involving the mortgage rights to Cornsilk, the place he called home and still helped to maintain. By 1935, however, when the Alabama Supreme Court ruled in favor of his father's right to Cornsilk, Lytle was actually devoting most of his time at Cornsilk to the writing of *The Long Night,* his first novel.

In a discerning retrospective essay on this work, Robert Penn Warren commented on the rich comprehension of life in "the deeper back country in the hills beyond the plantations" that Lytle had at his command by this time:

> He knew the language, every shade of its tone and phrase, every inflection, every hint of pain or poetry, the bawdiness, every expression of face. He knew the objects and practices of the old timers, and of the backcountry, how meat was dressed, how food was cooked, how meal was ground or hominy made, what people—men, women, or children—wore, how wool was carded, how shakes were split and whiskey run. He knew such things because he had the keenest of eyes, the shrewdest of ears, insatiable curiosity, and an elephantine memory; but most because he had a natural curiosity and simplicity of heart and could stop a stranger on the road or lounge on the steps of the most desolate crossroads store and in ten minutes be swapping crop-talk or tales with the local whittlers, in perfect ease and pleasure and with devoted attention.

But, as Warren understood, Lytle's "natural curiosity and simplicity of heart" were subject to the sensibility of a trained and ever attentive and demanding literary artist, a sensibility that leads Mark Lucas to say in *The Southern Vision of Andrew Lytle* that Lytle employed his knowledge of the backwoods culture with the sophistication of a novelist of manners. Yet, the critic indicates, the controlling sensibility we observe at work in Lytle's fiction is hardly that of the novelist of manners. It is the wider sensibility reflected in Lytle's recollection of the circumstances of the composition of *The Long Night*.

> I wrote most of *The Long Night* on a hill back of the house. I would strip to my shorts and carry my typewriter to its log, and there spend the day. The birds and small animals got accustomed to me, as if I were a stump. Once a snake, its head raised high in the air, chased a frog, but the frog made it up a tree as the snake struck the bark. He then crawled onto a pile of dead brush without shaking a leaf or making a sound. He turned and looked at me for a while. His eyes were too steady. I lost my nerve and killed him.

This account of how he wrote his first novel, one suspects, bears the stamp of poetic embellishment; and properly so, for Lytle meant it to suggest that as he wrote his dark story about Pleasant McIvor's obsession with revenge and its consequences he was quite consciously shaping the conception that would inform both the substance and the art of all his fiction, of all his writing for that matter. This is the idea that "for the Western mind" one myth underlies history, the myth of a Garden of Innocence into which a serpent intruded. Conceiving the Edenic myth of the origin of the knowledge of good and evil as governing the history of the Western world, or, to put this another way, as providing the mythic context of this history for the past two thousand years, Lytle—in "The Working Novelist and the Myth Making Process," "The State of Letters in a Time of Disorder," and elsewhere in his critical writings—developed a sweeping Christian interpretation of what happened to the art of letters (for that matter to all art) when Columbus made a "hole" in what Lytle idealistically imagined as the unified, noncommercial community of Christendom that had existed before the fifteenth century. Following upon the discovery of the New World, Lytle said, the westward movement of Europeans "not only shattered the narrow physical boundaries of Christendom, but, like all extension, weakened it by reducing a union composite of spiritual and temporal parts to the predominance of material ends." But in this extension, Lytle thought, the traditional community of Christendom survived to some significant degree in that part of the Americas that became the American South. In contrast, envisioning the impact of the European migration on that part of the Americas that became New England, Lytle conceived a quite different situation, one clearly discernible in the apocalyptic, and "satanic," theology of the Puritans, which was destructive of the sense of the good, of the God, in man and an exaltation of the "little man who plays God and aspires to conquer Heaven and earth." In the American South, on the other hand, where conditions made for "either a pastoral or an Agrarian society"—where "the images and references which the arts find to hand" were "to things natural and supernatural: to men, animals, plants, winds, water and fire, not indiscriminately used but always through their proper functions and necessities"—the sense of the God in man remained strong. Although the nonmaterialistic attitude southerners took toward the meaning of life did not, according to Lytle's myth of the South, at all free them from the propensity to evil innate in mankind, it gave them the capacity to recognize this propensity—to see it as inherent in mankind's participation in a drama of good and evil, the meaning of which must ultimately be referred to a mystery beyond the human understanding. This referral is writ large in the southern achievement in the literary art of Lytle's time, not only in the work of the Agrarians but in Faulkner, Caroline Gordon, Eudora

Welty, Flannery O'Connor, and Walker Percy, and others. In none of the southern storytellers and critics is it more acutely present (in his fiction by implication, not overt statement, his regard for the art of fiction prohibiting didacticism) than in the author of *The Long Night, A Name for Evil,* and *The Velvet Horn.*

But it is present not only in Lytle's writings; it is present in the way he lived his life, or aspired to lead it, as a writer whose vision of the meaning of human existence was based solidly on not only the necessity of recognizing its natural limitations but the equal necessity of recognizing that the context of the natural is the supernatural, that we live in a community of the living and the dead. Such a recognition is basically the motivating theme of Lytle's family chronicle (the story of the Lytles and the Nelsons, his mother's family), which bears the ironic title *A Wake for the Living.* Convinced that the recognition of our basic community dims and may be forgotten when the writer loses a direct association with the land, Lytle aspired to keep this connection. This became more difficult when he got married in 1938 and took on the responsibility for a wife and in time three daughters. Yet—following a year or two teaching at the University of the South and serving as the managing editor of the *Sewanee Review*—in the mid-1940s, with the hopeful intention of combining writing, raising turkeys, and growing tobacco, he moved to a 330-acre farm he had bought in Robertson County, Tennessee. Within a year he confessed to his close friend Allen Tate that he had grown doubtful about his decision. "I am getting up at three and four in the morning to get my writing done without interruption from the farm, which is a very hard thing to operate in these times. Ordinarily I would like it better, for I believe for me it is the simplest way to make a living and get any writing done. A university does not serve me. But now the difficulties are supreme. If I find they require heroism, I will sell the farm. I am no hero." Soon Lytle decided to do what Tate had done after failing to make a living as an independent man of letters, let the university serve his vocation by providing a stable source of income in exchange for his knowledge of writing skills. After filling a temporary position in the writing program at the University of Iowa in 1947–1948, he accepted the newly inaugurated position of lecturer in creative writing at the University of Florida, where he remained for twelve years. At the end of this time he returned to the University of the South to teach creative writing and edit the *Sewanee Review* for another twelve years. He began his second period at Sewanee with a symbolic gesture. He bought back the house he had sold in 1949 while he was at the University of Iowa. Located on what is known as the Sunday School Assembly Ground in Monteagle, a small town in close proximity to Sewanee, this dwelling, called the Log Cabin, had, before its sale, been in the Lytle family since his father had acquired it in 1907. Made of substantial pine logs, more spacious than a backwoods cabin ever was, yet reminiscent of the backwoods world, the Log Cabin seemed to those who knew Lytle, and no doubt to Lytle himself, to personify both the personal and literary character of its owner. He did leave the Log Cabin once, yielding one more time, after he retired from Sewanee in 1973, to the allure of farming. But not entirely. This time he tried to make a go of it on seventy-five acres in Kentucky while he held down a lectureship at the University of Kentucky. But nothing worked very well, and after a couple of years, he decided once again that he was no hero and came back to Monteagle. Here he might be seen in the spring and summer and on into the fall of the year in his broad-brimmed straw hat still satisfying his desire "to get his hands in the dirt and plant seed" by assiduously tending a bountiful vegetable garden. From time to time he entertained friends at memorable dinners featuring vegetables he picked from the garden and cooked immediately before they were served.

Life was not idyllic. His wife had been dead for several years, friends died, a beloved daughter died, and various health problems beset him, including severe difficulties with his eyesight. Meanwhile, he wrote a few more essays, among them a remarkable study of Flaubert published in the *Southern Review* in 1984; he assisted with the publication of *Southerners and Europeans: Essays in a Time of Disorder,* a collection of his literary essays, and *From Eden to Babylon,* a collection of his social and political essays; and from time to time he ventured away from Monteagle to read from his stories, lecture, or receive one of the several honors that came to him.

Whatever he did or whatever happened, Lytle remained convinced that the true artist, whether he fully knew it or not, had his being in the Christian community of the natural and the supernatural. The strength of this conviction no doubt seemed bizarre in a world that had become more completely materialistic in every respect, including its religion. But an understanding of Lytle depends on a willingness to accept his commitment to the traditional community of Christendom.

I thought about this when last December I received the news of Andrew's death at the age of ninety-three. I found myself going back to a letter he wrote to me in 1986, not long after the only journey abroad he made in his later life. It was a voyage to England with two friends, one a medical doctor, the other a priest. Shipboard life was not altogether to Andrew's liking, but an experience one night in a cottage in the English countryside made up for that. As he said, "The voyage was worth the ghost." The ghost had appeared one night when he and his companions were staying in a seventeenth-century cottage in the English countryside. Alone in a room he was sharing with the doctor, having gone to bed early, Andrew was awakened out of his sleep by a "blinding light." At the center of the light he saw a face bearing an expression of deep sorrow: "It was not looking at me but it was so alive it vibrated. . . . I sought its eyes and, frightened, looked away. I think I saw the abyss. I know, feel, it was another atmosphere penetrating the air it breathed." It was, Andrew adds, "not a still, cloudy ghost" but "stood out of a brightness, in vibrant life." He ended the description of his experience by saying he was "going to work on it." How much he may have done so I don't know, but when I had a visit with him some time later the ghost was still "vibrantly" alive in his memory. I have the fanciful notion now that Andrew did work on this ghost and, like the ghost of Major Brent in *A Name for Evil,* made it a part of that community of the living and the dead he had created in his art and thought.

EUDORA WELTY
The Outside of the Inside

The place is the comfortable, old-fashioned living room of the Tudor-style house across from Belhaven College on Pinehurst Street in Jackson, Mississippi. The time is an evening in the later 1970s, or perhaps the early eighties. We are a small group: my wife and I and another couple; and our hostess, Eudora Welty, who has lived in this house since the early 1920s. This was when her father, on the rise in the insurance business, had built it and moved his family from the house on Jackson's North Congress Street, where Eudora had been born in 1909. She lived most of her ninety-two years in the house on Pinehurst and did nearly all her writing there—in an upstairs room before a window that opened on the street, "her post of observation," as Walter Sullivan has termed it.[1]

On the evening I refer to, for some reason I can't now remember, I am recalling the time two or three years earlier when my wife and I were in San Francisco and saw what we took to be relics of the age of the "flower children" wandering here and there in the streets and parks. Eudora says that she has wondered what has happened to the flower children. We drift on in our conversation to other subjects. It is some time before I notice Eudora is no longer taking part in the talk. Later, when it is time for us to be taking our leave, she rouses and says in her soft, inimitable voice (Mississippian in tone and inflection, yet never, like Faulkner's, quite so distinctly so): "I wonder what has happened to them? I wonder what has happened to *all* of them?"

It takes me a moment to realize why Eudora had fallen silent some time back in the evening. She had become completely preoccupied with wondering about the fate of the youthful dissidents of the sixties. I wanted to find out what had gone on in her reverie about the flower children. But it was late and not a time to linger.

The fate of those who become lost in the world: what salvation is there for them? Is this not one way to sum up the subject of Eudora Welty's fiction? And if we do so, are we not in a larger sense summing up the subject of all her contemporaries—of all those who came into the world in the time before, during, or immediately after the First World War? And, for that matter, of all the European and American novelists who have come into the Euro-American world since it fell to pieces in August 1914 and everybody became lost in the ruins?

In his later years Robert Penn Warren increasingly felt that his writings were a personal response to this question. In my rereading of Eudora Welty's short stories and novels following her death in July 2001, I seem to have sensed more than I had before the subtle lyric quality not only of her fiction but of her small body of carefully crafted essays and reviews as well. That is to say, I seem to have felt more distinctly than before the autobiographical cast of her writings. I refer to the way in which she suggests a subtle struggle to define a sense of personal identity with the subject of being lost in the world. I have come to feel indeed that her stories and essays often turn on a paradoxical desire both to reveal and conceal this struggle. "I'm just a private person," she told an interviewer in 1986. Then added enigmatically: "But I tell my innermost secrets through my fiction. It's all there."[2]

Welty usually wrote about American southerners, the people she says she knew best, but she wrote a few memorable stories about people from elsewhere. I am thinking of "Music from Spain" but more particularly of "The Bride of the Innisfallen," and, more particularly still, of the haunting story she first published in the *New Yorker* in 1952 called "No Place for You, My Love."

In "The Bride of the Innisfallen" the chief character is identified only as an "American girl." She has come to England with her husband, but when the reader encounters her at the beginning of the story she is seated in a compartment of a train at the Paddington station waiting to leave for Fishguard, where the passengers will transfer to the *Innisfallen*, an overnight ferry to Cork, Ireland. After arriving in Cork, she walks about in the city for almost the whole of a rainy day in a strange state of joy. As evening comes on she shelters herself from the rain in the "warm doorway" of a pub, and hearing the voices coming from within, drops a telegram she has composed to send to her husband into a gushing street drain, and walks "without protection into the lovely room full of strangers." She has no idea what may happen to her in that room; nor, on the basis of the evidence presented in the story, does the reader. And on the same basis, one can say neither does the author of the story, human relationships in Welty's stories being at times comically, at times pathetically, at times tragically, but always mysteriously irresolute.[3]

In "No Place for You, My Love" there are two characters, a man and a woman, each, like the chief character in "The Bride of the Innisfallen," nameless; though, unlike the American girl who goes to Cork, they are pointedly described as nonsouthern Americans. The man is a "businessman" from Syracuse, New York; the "girl" (as the author refers to her) whom the man judges to be younger than he is, perhaps thirty-two, is from Toledo, Ohio. Strangers to each other, they meet in New Orleans on a heated Sunday afternoon in July. Each has come to Galatoire's with a group of southern friends. Mutual friends in the two parties see each other across the restaurant and the groups combine into one luncheon party. When the man from Syracuse meets the woman from Toledo, he thinks—himself "long married"—that here is a woman who is having an affair, "with a married man most likely." The girl from Toledo thinks, "It must stick out all over me. . . . People in love like me, I suppose, give away the short cuts to everybody's secrets." As the luncheon progresses the man and the girl—two outsiders, "two Northerners keeping each other company," though they say nothing about it to each other, experience the sense of having discovered a bond. Thus it is that after the luncheon, they find themselves, at the suggestion of the man, driving out of the city in his rented red Ford convertible to see what the world is like "south of New Orleans." In the "*degrading* heat," as the girl calls it, they drive down a concrete strip flanked by "raging insects" and cluttered with crayfish and terrapins, and eventually cross to the other side of the Mississippi River on a ferry crowded with people enjoying a Sunday outing (*Stories*, 465–68).

Among the several passengers who get out of their cars to walk about the deck is a boy with an alligator on a chain. "Both respectable and merciful, their hides," the woman thinks. "Deliver us all from the naked in heart." After they get off the ferry and resume their southward trek on the west side of the great meandering river, the man asks himself:

> Had she felt a wish for someone else to be riding with them? He thought it was more likely that she would wish for her husband if she had one (his wife's voice) than for the lover in whom he believed. Whatever people liked to think, situations (if not scenes) were usually three-way—there was somebody else always. The one who didn't—couldn't—understand the two made the formidable third. (*Stories*, 471)

As the man from Syracuse and the girl from Toledo drive into an even more intense heat than they have felt before, the pavement ceases and the road, flanked by fishermen's shacks, becomes one made of the shells of mollusks. They continue until they come to the little town named Venice at the end of land, where as darkness descends around them, they turn around, and shortly afterwards find a bar and restaurant, a "homey place," housed in a barnlike structure and run by the owner, bartender, and cook. Here at Baba's Place they order sandwiches and beer. Later, when they no longer sense the brief initial curiosity their presence has aroused in the local patrons, they join them on the dance floor and move to "a slow piece" emanating from the jukebox.

> Surely even those immune from the world, for the time being, need the touch of one another, or all is lost. Their arms encircling each other, their bodies circling the odorous, just-nailed-down floor, they were, at last, imperviousness in motion. They had found it, and had almost missed it: they had had to dance. They were what their separate hearts desired that day, for themselves and each other. (*Stories*, 478)

Later, "in the thickening heat," they dance to a lively song, while Baba joins "the mosquito-voiced singer" on the record in singing the chorus of "*Moi pas l'aimez ça.*" Finally, "bathed in sweat," they depart for the return to New Orleans. Once the man stops the car to clean the windshield of bugs; a little later he stops, puts his arm around his companion, and kisses her, "not knowing ever whether gently or harshly." His loss of the capacity to make this "distinction" brings him back to an awareness of the world they have come out of. "They had ridden down into a strange land together and they were getting safely back—by a slight margin, perhaps, but margin enough." But even as he mutters, "We're all right now," and lights a cigarette, "something that must have been with them all along suddenly, then, was not." It rises, "tall as panic," and cries out "like a human," and then drops back (*Stories,* 479–80).

The girl from Toledo and the man from Syracuse go back across the river to the east side, this time by "the bridge." (The Huey P. Long Bridge, completed in December 1935, three months after Long's assassination. This and other details, as well as the general atmospheric aura of the story, indicate its setting may be the later 1930s or the early 1940s.) Back in the city, the man finds the hotel where his companion is staying, and, apparently without having ever exchanged names, the two part, with a restrained handshake, on the sidewalk at the hotel entrance. Looking back, the man from Syracuse thinks he sees a man strolling across the lobby to meet the girl from Toledo.

Two or three years after writing her story about the strange journey two strangers take into a strange place, Welty wrote an essay that, although it bears an impersonal title, "Writing and Analyzing a Story," is largely a reflection on her personal—one is tempted to say deeply personal—experience in writing "No Place for You, My Love." The only essay in *The Eye of the Story* (the compilation of selected essays and reviews Welty published in 1978) in which she examines one of her own stories, it is prefaced by the remark that it is in actuality not so much a critical analysis as "a piece of hindsight from a working point of view." The author explains that shortly after she had completed a story called "No Place for You, My Love"—"a story, told in subjective terms, of a girl" who is "caught fast in the over-familiar, monotonous life of her small town, and immobilized further by a prolonged and hopeless love affair"—she made a summertime visit to New Orleans.

One day during her visit "an acquaintance" had invited her to take a drive through the country south of the city. When she returned home to Jackson she discovered that during her journey into "that once-submerged strange land of south from South," the story she had just written had come into her head "in an altogether new form." As a result she discarded the first version, and, though retaining the title, wrote "a new version from scratch" to accord with her realization that the image of the strange world she had just journeyed through had "stamped itself" on her imagination as the "very image" of the "predicament" she was seeking to portray in "No Place for You, My Love." Conceiving that the point of view she had employed in the first version of this story—the subjective view of the southern girl "sealed in her world, by nature and circumstance"—had worked to its "detriment," she "escaped" the mind of this girl altogether by divesting her of the "half-dozen familiars" she had around her and transforming her into a midwesterner. Then she "invented a single new character, a man whom I brought into the story *to be* a stranger." "I was to keep out of his mind too," Welty adds; and thereby "had double-locked the doors behind me."[4]

Escaping from the minds of her characters, Welty discovered, as she "wrote further into the story," that "something more real, more essential, than the characters were on their own was revealing itself." She had found the true point of view: "outside" the characters—"suspended, hung in the air between two people, fished alive from the surrounding scene":

> In effect, though the characters numbered only two, there had come to be a sort of third character along on the ride—the presence of a relationship between the two. It was what grew up between them meeting as strangers, went on the excursion with them, nodded back and forth from one to the other—listening, watching, persuading or denying them, enlarging

or diminishing them, forgetful sometimes of who they were or what they were doing here—in its domain—and helping or betraying them along. (*Eye*, 111–12)

In the course of their journey through the place that is the lower reaches of Louisiana, Welty observes, her characters come into touch with "something wilder" than an ordinary relationship "between well-disposed strangers," with something that responded to "the speed of the ride pitted against the danger of an easy or conventionally tempting sympathy." The "heat that in itself drives on the driver in the face of an inimical world" is "demoniac"—being at once "more ruthless and more tender, more pressing and acute than" the "automatic saving ironies and graces" (*Eye*, 113).

The defeat of the saving ironies is, to be sure, implicit in what Welty says is the subtle "plot" of the "little story," which is the "vain courting of imperviousness in the face of exposure."

> Deliver us all from the naked in heart, the girl thinks (this is what I kept of her). . . . Riding down together into strange country is danger, secretly poetic, and the characters, in attempting it as a mutual feat, admit nothing to each other except the wicked heat and its comical inconvenience. The only time they will yield or touch is while they are dancing in the crowd that to them is comically unlikely (hence insulating, nonconducting) or taking a kiss outside time. Nevertheless it happens that they go along aware, from moment to moment, as one: as my third character, the straining, hallucinatory eyes and ears, the roused up sentient being of that place. Exposure begins in intuition; and the intuition comes to its end in showing the heart that has expected, while it dreads, that exposure. (*Eye*, 113)

Welty sums up her intention in "No Place for You, My Love" as her desire "to make the story's inside outside, and then leave the shell behind" (Eye, 112–13). She had "no wish to sound mystical," she says, but, she admitted, if she could, she "did expect to sound mysterious now and then"; for she regarded her story as paradoxically "a circumstantial, realistic story in which the reality *was* mystery."

> The cry that rose up at the story's end was, I hope, unmistakably, the cry of that doomed relationship—personal, mortal, psychic—admitted in order

to be denied, a cry that the characters were first able (and prone) to listen to, and then able in part to ignore. The cry was authentic to my story: the end of a journey *can* set up a cry, the shallowest provocation to sympathy and love does hate to give up the ghost. A relationship of the most fleeting kind has the power inherent to loom like a genie—to become vocative at last, as it has already become present and taken up room; as it has spread as a destination however unlikely; as it has glimmered and rushed by in the dark and dust outside, showing occasional points of fire. Relationship *is* a pervading and changing mystery; it is not words that make it so in life, but words have to make it so in a story. Brutal or lovely, the mystery waits for people wherever they go, whatever extreme they run to. (*Eye*, 114)

In the original version of "No Place for You, My Love," Welty says, she had aspired to tell "a story of concealment, in terms of the hermetic and familiar," but she had somehow ended up with a story that concealed "what I had meant to show." Transformed into a story about a journey a girl from Toledo and a man from Syracuse take on Sunday afternoon into the coastal extremities of Louisiana, the new version of the story embodied what she wanted it to: the revelation of the mystery of the relationship between two human beings through the power of the "sentient being" of place (*Eye*, 113).

It is curious that in "Place in Fiction," published a year after the essay on the writing of "No Place for You, My Love," Welty seems bent on modifying the emphasis on the mystique of place in her self-interpretation of this story:

I think the sense of place is as essential to good and honest writing as a logical mind; surely they are somewhere related. It is by knowing where you stand that you grow able to judge where you are. Place absorbs our earliest notice and attention, it bestows on us our original awareness; and our critical powers spring up from the study of it and the growth of experience inside it. It perseveres in bringing us back to earth when we fly too high. It never really stops informing us, for it is forever astir, alive, changing, reflecting, like the mind of man itself. Sense of place gives equilibrium; extended, it is sense of direction too. Carried off we might be in spirit, and should be, when we are reading or writing something good; but it is the sense of place going with us still that is the ball of golden thread to carry us there and back and in every sense of the word to bring us home. (*Eye*, 128–29)

Yet the sense of place in "No Place for You, My Love" is distinctly otherwise. "Feeling" in her "story's grip," Welty says, it became "literally apparent—that in the country south of South secret and shadow are taken away . . . by the merciless light." She was "writing of a real place," she says, but doing so in order to write about her subject: "exposure to the shock of the world." Or, she might have said, exposure to the shock of the discovery that in "merciless reality" the world is a "place" in which the girl from Toledo and the man from Syracuse are forever lost (*Eye*, 112–13). Is not the austere, ultimate implication of the journey they take through the coastal parishes of Louisiana on a Sunday summer afternoon their momentary glimpse of the veiled truth that there was no place for them in the world they have come out of, or the world they have come to, or the world to which they must return?

Reviewing *The Bride of the Innisfallen* in the *Sewanee Review*, Louis D. Rubin was moved to comment that this work assures us that "a sensitive, discerning artist is steadily extending her range." As in all her work "a great deal goes on, much of it humorous, piquant, graceful," while "beneath the surface there is another dimension entirely."[5] This other dimension, it occurs to me, is marked by the underlying conflict—the animating "tension"—in Welty's stories between her sense of place and her sense of time.

Present from the beginning of her career as a storyteller, this revealed itself to Welty herself, one judges, only slowly, and she did not attempt to come to grips with it, at least in formal critical comment, until 1973, when she published "Some Thoughts on Time in Fiction" in the Eudora Welty issue of the *Mississippi Quarterly* in 1973. Since, at the request of the publication's editor, the late Peyton W. Williams, I was serving as the special editor of this issue, I was privileged to read this essay as soon as it arrived from the hands of the author; and, with a certain sense of shock, realized that in effect it constituted an important revision of Welty's essay "Place in Fiction," which since its publication in 1955 had acquired something like classic status among her readers as the key to the interpretation of her fiction.

"Some Notes on Time in Fiction" begins with the statement that time and place—"the two bases of reference upon which the novel, in seeking to come to grips with human experience, must depend for its validity"—may seem to the novelist to operate together, that is, until the novelist "comes to scrutinize them apart." This self-conscious act reveals that place, "the accessible one, the inhabited one," the one possessing a "blessed identity," has not a friend but an implacable enemy in time—"anonymous," bearing "the same face the world over," telling us "nothing about itself except by the signals that it is passing," never giving "anything away." The essay on time in fiction also implies, it seems to me, another, and more subtle, revisionary emphasis, not only in Welty's conception of the basis of fiction but of its form or forms. She had effectively begun her career with six notable short stories (including the classic tale the "Petrified Man") that Cleanth Brooks and Robert Penn Warren published in the first series of the *Southern Review,* and by the time the complete collection of her short stories came out in 1980, she had long since achieved the status of a master of this genre.

But, in her essay on time in fiction, Welty suggests that the form she most revered was not the short story but the novel, the literary form most deeply associated with the modern preoccupation with time. Indeed, she says that "the novel is Time's child." Welty's meditation on time—which, it may be said, resembles a prose poem even more than her meditation on place—depicts the modern novel as having its fundamental meaning in its metaphorical relation to the prime symbol of modernity, the mechanical clock. In making this observation, she refers to Mann and Proust: "Mann attacking the subjectivity of man's knowledge of time, and Proust, discovering a way to make time give back all it has taken, through turning life by way of the memory into art, left masterpieces that are clocks themselves, giant clocks stationed for always out in the world, sounding for us the high hours of our literature." But Welty makes it clear that she also regards Faulkner—whose work "is magnetized to the core of time"—as being among the makers of the giant clocks marking "the high hours of our literature." Perhaps, for her, to be sure, Faulkner is the most significant clock maker. In the all-important distinction she makes in "Time and Fiction" between fictional time and the "arbitrary, bullying power" clock time exerts on the life of daily reality, her appeal is primarily to Faulkner—who, asserting in *Light in August* that "memory believes before knowing remembers," has "crowded chronology out of the way many times to make way for memory and the life of the past."

> Remembering is so basic and vital a part of staying alive that it takes on the strength of an instinct of survival and acquires the power of an art.

Remembering is done through the blood, it is a bequeathment, it takes account of what happens before a man is born as if he were there taking part. It is a physical absorption through the living body, it is a spiritual heritage. It is also a life's work. (*Eye*, 165–71)

As with Faulkner, the exploration of the spiritual heritage of the southern culture of memory—of the comedy and the tragedy of the perpetuation of this culture—became Eudora Welty's life's work as an eminently self-conscious, completely dedicated artist. But there is a distinct difference between her vision of memory and Faulkner's. In creating the Yoknapatawpha stories Faulkner was always deeply conscious of the intimate presence in his vision of southern history—and its relation to modern history—of the American Civil War, and of the South as the place where much of this war had been fought. He was in particular eminently aware of the transfiguring effect of the war on his native place, and especially of its consequences as these were embodied in the lives of the people of the state of Mississippi, including the members of his own family and, not least, his own life.

In my experience of reading Faulkner, however, I did not realize for a rather long time the significance of the fact that, as a member of the southern literary generation that came into its own in the 1920s and early 1930s, he belonged to the last generation of southern writers who experienced the sense of a vital personal connection with the Civil War through the daily presence in their lives of people who had not only survived its battles but were living embodiments of the drama of surviving the long and bitter aftermath of "the defeat" and the Reconstruction. This realization did not fully come to me until—thinking about the meaning of Welty's long career in American letters—it occurred to me how little, in contrast to Faulkner's stories, the memory of the Civil War counts for in her stories; how essentially different from Faulkner's is her sense of her relation to the southern culture of memory.

She had been born into this culture in Jackson, Mississippi, in 1909, not far from the Old State Capitol. Here Mississippians had taken the fateful step of withdrawing from the Union; here, a hundred years later, in 1973, they had held an official celebration of Eudora Welty's career (a "Eudorafication" her friend Malcolm Cowley called it) and symbolically crowned her with the laurel wreath. Yet in Welty's case memory of the Civil War was not, as in Faulkner's case, a bequeathment of the blood. Welty understood perfectly what Quentin Compson means when he tells his Canadian friend Shreve on that frigid night in their Harvard dormitory room that to understand Quentin's attachment to the South he would have to have been born there: born like Quentin into the world of the flesh and blood survivors of "the defeat"; and, as their flesh and blood heirs, have had the experience of living the long death of the southern nation after the Civil War. Welty's family history cut her off from this experience. She was the daughter of Christian Welty, a Yankee born in Ohio, who in 1904 opportunistically came to the capital city of Mississippi, entered the insurance business, and left as his highly visible legacy the Lamar Life Insurance Building, still a dominant feature of the Jackson skyline. He was accompanied on his venture into the Deep South by his bride, Chestina, who came from West Virginia—a state formed in the midst of the Civil War by Unionists, some of them, like her mother's family, the Andrews, originally Virginians, who had exiled themselves from the slave South when they moved into the wild, mountainous world of western Virginia.[6]

But while she did not share directly in the Faulknerian experience, at once vexing and stimulating, of blood memory—of believing before knowing remembers—Welty had the advantage of being free of the Faulknerian burden of the invariable association of memory with the memory of the Civil War. Free, it seems to me—with a less agonizing effort than is evident in Faulkner's struggle to do the same thing in, say, *The Sound and the Fury*—not only to conceive of fiction as time's child but, in that "dark and painful novel," as Hermione Lee has called *The Optimist's Daughter*, to symbolize, in the story of Laurel Hand's return to Mt. Salus for her father's funeral, the reconciliation of place and its enemy, time.[7]

In *The Optimist's Daughter* time becomes a dimension of place and place a dimension of time. As, to be sure, it is not only in all her stories but also in the marvelously moving photographs in *One Time, One Place*, which may be taken to symbolize Welty's greatest achievement as a writer. This is, to paraphrase a haunting, retrospective statement in the introductory essay to *One Time, One Place*, coming "to terms" with her own "lifelong exposure to the world"—coming to terms, that is, with an artist's lifelong exposure to time and place.

Ironically, unless one saw them on exhibit in the Mississippi Department of Archives and History, or on occasion, in New York City and elsewhere, one had to wait another twenty years after the initial publication of Welty's photographs, until 1989, to see a published representation of Welty's photographs worthy of them—this in the 1989 University Press of Mississippi edition, with a fine introductory essay by Reynolds Price and a provocative interview with the photographer herself.

In the Mississippi edition one could finally appreciate the story Welty tells in the introductory essay to *One Time, One Place* about how early in her career as a writer she had discovered and confirmed the connection of place, time, and human relationships, when she had taken a seminal journey—traveling by automobile to all eighty-two counties in her native state. This had been in fulfillment of her official duties as a "junior grade" public relations agent of the Mississippi office of Roosevelt's Works Progress Administration during the years of the Great Depression. At night, in lonely country-town hotel rooms (cooled in summer by "loud electric fans"), she had written reports (for "county weeklies to publish if they found the space") about "newly opened farm-to-market roads" and new airfields "hacked out of cow pastures"; she had set down interviews with judges of juvenile courts, described putting up exhibits at county fairs, and written news stories about riding along on Bookmobile routes, "distributing books into open hands like the treasures they were."[8]

But Welty had had something else to think about at night in those country-town hotel rooms: the images of people and places she was making on film as she drove about in Mississippi; for, while she fulfilled the task of making a written record of what she did for the WPA with due diligence, the task that meant the most to her was the unofficial, self-assigned, largely private one of making a photographic record of life in 1930s Mississippi. Her work as an amateur photographer did not become generally known until 1971, when Random House published a selection of her pictures in *One Time, One Place,* subtitled "Mississippi in the Depression / A Snapshot Album." This volume, which one southern reviewer called "Miss Eudora's Picture Book," is introduced by an evocative essay, in which Welty explains that she took her pictures with a Kodak "one step more advanced than the Brownie" and developed them in the kitchen when she was back home in Jackson on weekends. To make enlargements she used a secondhand enlarger she got from the state highway department. "A better and less ignorant photographer would certainly have come up with better pictures, but not these pictures," she says; for he "could hardly have been as well positioned as I was, moving through the scene openly and yet invisibly because I was part of it, born into it, taken for granted" (*One Time,* 4).

Unfortunately the meaning of Eudora Welty's photographs as a revelation of a story-writer's search for the truth that is hidden in the outside of the inside is represented more clearly in her introduction to *One Time, One Place* than in their reproduction on rough paper in the Random House edition. Even so, one responds to the power Welty herself found in them.

> When a heroic face like that of the woman in the buttoned sweater—who I think must come first in this book—looks back at me from the picture, what I respond to now, just as I did the first time, is not the Depression, not the Black, not the South, not even the perennially sorry state of the whole world, but the story of her life in her face. And though I did not take these pictures to prove anything, I do think they most assuredly do show something—which is to make a far better claim for them. Her face to me is full of meaning more truthful and more terrible, and I think, more noble than any generalization about people could have prepared me for or could describe to me now. I learned from my own pictures, one by one, that we are the breakers of our own hearts. (*One Time*, 7)

Whether it exists between the photographer taking the picture and the woman in the sweater, or between the storyteller writing the story and the girl from Toledo and the man from Syracuse, there is the undying presence of the mystery of their relationship. But the shock of experiencing a vision of place and time that reveals the mystery of "the living relationship between what is going on and our selves" suggests a measure of salvation. "I learned quickly enough when to click the shutter, and what I was becoming aware of more slowly was a story-writer's truth: the thing to wait on, to reach there in time for, is the moment in which people reveal themselves. You have to be ready, in yourself; you have to know the moment when you see it" (*One Time*, 7–8). We break our own hearts in the pathos, and not less the comedy, of our indifference to this moment.

> We come to terms as well as we can with our lifelong exposure to the world, and we use whatever devices we may need to survive. But eventually, of course, our knowledge depends upon the living relationship between what we see going on and ourselves. If exposure is essential, still more is the reflection. Insight doesn't happen often on the click of the moment, like a lucky snapshot, but comes in its own time and more slowly and from nowhere but within. The sharpest recognition is surely

that charged with sympathy as well as with shock—it is a form of human vision. And that is of course a gift. We struggle through any pain or darkness in nothing but the hope that we may receive it, and through any term of work in the prayer to keep it. (*One Time,* 8)

From the moment she first clicked the shutter of a camera, Welty knew that, though her vocation was to make stories, not pictures, her wish, indeed her "continuing passion"—as so poignantly illustrated by her picture—no, her vision, of the woman in a sweater—"would be, not to point the finger in judgment but to part a curtain, that invisible shadow that falls between people, the veil of indifference to each other's presence, each other's wonder, each other's human plight" (*One Time,* 8). Or, we might say, employing the kind of abstraction Welty despised, to point the finger to each person's isolation under the conditions of modern history.

The subtle drama of seeing into the outside of the inside, or the inside of the outside—and depicting the terrifying yet exalting truth of the story of human relationships under the historical circumstances in which we live our lives: this in abstract terms is the sum and substance of the story of our relationships with each other as told by Eudora Welty. While we may seldom transcend the conditions of our existence—may almost never penetrate the veil of our imperviousness to others; indeed do all we can to keep the veil intact; and consequently are doomed to be the breakers of our own hearts—one may in some special moment glimpse in a Welty story what lies beyond the veil; and, whether the momentary vision is owing to the grace of God, or the grace of art, or both, become in that cruel, but precious, moment healers of our own hearts.

I remember another evening in Eudora's living room. It is crowded with guests attending a reception she is giving during the "Eudorafication" in 1973. I am talking to Walker Percy about the Pulitzer that has just been awarded to Eudora for *The Optimist's Daughter,* and Walker is remarking in a confidential voice, "You know, it is about Eudora herself." In that moment, I think, I glimpsed the complex irony implicit in Eudora Welty's creation of the fictional Laurel Hand, the optimist's daughter.

NOTES

1. Walter Sullivan, "Eudora Welty, 1909–2001," *Sewanee Review* 109 (September 2001): 482.

2. Quoted in Ann Waldron, *Eudora: A Writer's Life* (New York, 1998), 332.

3. Eudora Welty, *Collected Stories of Eudora Welty* (New York, 1980), 518. Subsequent parenthetical references to Welty's stories are to this edition.

4. Welty, *The Eye of the Story: Selected Essays and Reviews* (New York, 1978), 111. Subsequent citations are given in the text.

5. Louis Rubin, "Two Ladies of the South," *Sewanee Review* 63 (Autumn 1955): 671.

6. See Welty, *One Writer's Beginnings* (Cambridge, Mass., 1984), 52–58 .

7. Lee Hermione, "On Eudora Welty," *New York Review of Books* 67 (September 29, 2001): 32.

8. Welty, *One Time, One Place: Mississippi in the Depression: A Snapshot Album* (New York, 1971), 3. Subsequent citations are given in the text.

WALKER PERCY AND THE CLOSURE OF HISTORY IN THE SELF; OR, THE LONELINESS AT THE END OF A WORLD

> What is the task of the Christian novelist who mirrors in himself the society he sees around him—who otherwise would not be a novelist—whose only difference from his countrymen is that he has the vocation to be a novelist?
> —WALKER PERCY, "Notes for a Novel about the End of the World"

> One of the peculiar ironies of being a human self in the Cosmos: A stranger approaching you in the street will in a second's glance see you whole, size you up, place you in a way in which you cannot and never will, even though you have spent a lifetime with yourself, live in the Century of the Self, and therefore ought to know yourself best of all.
> —WALKER PERCY, *Lost in the Cosmos*

I knew Walker Percy personally for something like twenty years. In terms of the time I actually spent in his presence, or was in communication with him either by mail or phone, my friendship with him is not to be described as close. Yet, like several such friendships resulting from connections made in the course of editing and writing activities, it was somehow more than merely professional. To use an old-fashioned term, Walker and I had a literary friendship.

Yet it was somehow more than that; and Walker's death on May 10, 1990, proved to be a more painful experience than I had anticipated when I first learned of his terminal illness. In fact, save for the moments I spent writing a brief memorial for the fall 1990 *Southern Review*, I more or less tried to deny the event.

Six months after I had attended Walker's funeral mass at St. Joseph's Abbey in Covington, Louisiana (and had seen him laid to rest in the part of the Abbey cemetery reserved for members of the Benedictine Lay Confraternity), I made myself perform the symbolic task of transferring the Walker Percy file from the active section of the *Southern Review* correspondence files to the drawer bearing the stark label "Deceased." I put the file in its new alphabetical place between jackets bearing the names Norman Holmes Pearson and Katherine Anne Porter. At that moment I felt I had performed a conclusive act. But a few days later I found myself taking out the Percy file, sitting down with it, and—thoughtfully, meditatively you might say—rereading all the letters in it.

The experience proved to be less painful than I had feared. Eliciting not so much the sense of Walker's absence as his presence, it made me more aware of something I had felt all along in my acquaintance with Walker: the way in which his career represented a lengthy, highly self-conscious, lonely quest for a transforming vision of the meaning of his vocation to writing. In the following comments on this quest I hope memoir and interpretation find a degree of compatibility.

Written for the most part in his angular scrawling hand on his personal stationery (a small white sheet of medium-quality white paper imprinted with his name and post office box in Covington), Walker's letters to me were usually succinct. A few were hardly more than telegraphic notes, which reminded me of the hastily scrawled prescription the doctor hands you as you leave his office, and of course Walker was a physician. Although he had given up the practice of medicine before he really got started, he kept his membership in the American Medical Association current all his life—doing so, I think, in recognition of the fundamental connection between his medical and literary careers.

One emblem of this connection was Walker's practice of writing the initial drafts of his manuscripts in big, awkward spiral-ring blue books. Each book was identified on the inside cover as belonging to "Walker Percy, 1001 Bard Hall, College of Physicians and Surgeons, Columbia University, N.Y., N.Y." He had purchased these notebooks in such generous quantity in medical school days that he never used them up.

Another emblem of the connection between the physician and the writer in Walker's case was the standard hospital swivel bed-table he used for a writing desk. In fact, he did most of his writing while propped up in bed or on a couch. "I am lazy," he said. The bed-table, I take it, was emblematic of Walker's relation to medicine both as a patient and as a physician, signifying the association between his career as a writer and his periods of confinement in tubercular sanatoria. The first period was 1942–1944, when he was a patient at the Trudeau Sanatorium in Saranac Lake, New York. He went there after he contracted pulmonary tuberculosis while serving an internship in pathology at Bellevue, and although in recollection he tended to make light of his illness, it was serious. How serious became apparent when, a year after his release from Saranac, it was discovered that the disease had not yet been arrested. This time he went to Gaylord Farm Sanatorium in Connecticut, where he was assigned the same bed the young Eugene O'Neill had occupied when he had been a patient there in 1912.

Even though he was never again hospitalized for treatment as a tubercular patient, Walker's confinement at Saranac Lake and later at Gaylord Farm constituted the central experience in his life and the shaping force of his career as a writer. Perhaps it may be said the swivel bed-table signified a certain sense on the part of one who had been trained in medicine of being a lifelong "outpatient."

A third emblem of Walker Percy's literary career was the large, old-fashioned rolltop desk in his bedroom (which was also his work room). The desk had belonged to "Uncle Will" (in actuality a cousin), William Alexander Percy, the Mississippi planter, poet, and philosopher who had formally adopted Percy and his younger brothers and brought them into his home after the violent deaths of both their parents. (His father by suicide in 1929, his mother in a possibly suicidal automobile wreck in 1932.) Finding it difficult to read his own handwriting when it became cold, Walker told me once, he gave up the comfort of bed or couch every day to sit down at a manual typewriter (an Underwood, as I recall) located on Uncle Will's desk to transfer his handwriting into print while he could still read it.

Although the letters Walker and I exchanged are dated as far back as 1967, they were written mostly after the time in the early seventies when I first met him in person at a Sunday brunch at the Baton Rouge home of the writer and editor Martha Hall. To be honest, I was slow in picking up on Walker. I knew virtually nothing about him when he published *The Moviegoer* in 1961. I saw him in a brief appearance on the old NBC Today Show after this, his first novel, received the National Book Award, but I did not rush out to buy a copy. In fact, I did not read *The Moviegoer* until I discovered a year or two later that some of my students were onto Binx Bolling's uncertain "search" for the meaning of life in a world universally afflicted by the modern spiritual "malaise"; or, to refer to the line from Kierkegaard employed as the epigraph to *The Moviegoer,* by the "despair that does not know itself." I became curious about the student interest in a fictional being who, for all his cynicism, was not only a respectable middle-class citizen—an honorably discharged veteran of the Korean War, manager of a brokerage firm in New

Orleans, and a resident, not of the French Quarter but of Gentilly; who was, moreover, thirty-one years old, and therefore, according to the doctrine of the dissident young in the Vietnam era, just beyond the age when anyone could be trusted. At the same time I developed an interest in the creator of Binx Bolling, and in an incidental kind of way acquired a general impression of the facts of Percy's life.

He had graduated from the University of North Carolina in 1937 with a major in chemistry, and had subsequently entered the Columbia University College of Physicians and Surgeons. I had a rather vague impression that a few years after he was awarded his M.D. degree Percy had become a convert to Roman Catholicism; that at some point after his conversion he had given up the practice of medicine and made a kind of career for a few years as an obscure philosophical essayist, appearing in *Commonweal* and on occasion in such journals as *Philosophy and Phenomenological Research* and *New Scholasticism,* but, save for once in the *Sewanee Review* and once in the *Partisan Review,* not in places ordinarily seen by the literati. I also knew that Percy had pursued a self-directed apprenticeship to novel writing, and after writing and discarding more than one novelistic effort, had, at least twenty years late for a beginning novelist, emerged at the commencement of the revolutionary decade of the sixties as the forty-five-year-old author of an award-winning first novel.

These were facts about Walker Percy I was more or less aware of in 1965, when, twenty years after its first distinguished series had ceased publication, the second series of the *Southern Review* was inaugurated. At this point the minor editorial role I played in Walker's career as an editor of the *Review* began to bring me into a professional and, to some extent, a personal association with him. The initial motive in this association stemmed from my conviction that if the new series of the *Southern Review* was to have a legitimate "southern dimension," we must seek to determine what kind of writing was going on that might still be defined as "southern." By the time Percy's second novel, *The Last Gentleman,* was published in 1967, I was actively planning a special issue of the *Review* based on the theme "Writing in the South." In view of the way his second novel had confirmed Percy's status among serious reviewers as a significant new southern novelist (though he himself had reservations about being labeled a "southern writer"), a contribution from him for the "Writing in the South" issue seemed eminently desirable. Although he politely refused my invitation to send something, my hope of having Percy in the issue was not entirely foiled. I was fortunate enough to acquire one of the first substantial interviews with him. Conducted by the Baton Rouge writer and veteran newsman Carlton Cremeens, this added significantly, I recall, to the success of the issue for the spring quarter, 1968. Perhaps the interview also added to the increasing recognition of Walker Percy.

I may have done more toward this desirable end, however, through my editorial relation with the LSU Press. A year or so after the publication of the Percy interview I was asked by the editor of this press to comment on the publication possibilities of a revised doctoral dissertation entitled "The Sovereign Wayfarer: Walker Percy's Diagnosis of the Malaise." Written by Martin Luschei, a teacher at California Polytechnic University, this proved to be a detailed and illuminating study. But, like the editors at the LSU Press, I had an academic queasiness about publishing a whole book, no matter how good it might be, on a fifty-year-old novelist who, although he had some claim to prominence, had only two novels to his credit, hardly enough to establish what could be defined as a novelistic career. But when Percy's publisher announced the forthcoming appearance of *Love in the Ruins*, we thought for some reason that three novels would qualify Percy as a proper novelist, and Luschei was informed that if he would write another chapter dealing with Percy's new novel, his book would be accepted. He wrote a brilliant additional chapter, and *The Sovereign Wayfarer* was published. Still indispensable to the serious student of Percy, Luschei's pioneer study not only intensified and deepened the attention Percy already had on the American campus, where he was tending to become a cult figure, but helped to create a wider audience for him.

By the time *The Sovereign Wayfarer* appeared I knew Walker personally. Examining my correspondence with him from this time on, I have been interested to see that the file appears to suggest two things: one is that, while, as I have indicated, we hardly had a close personal friendship, we did in the latter days of the Vietnam era establish an acquaintanceship that reflected a certain intellectual and perhaps even spiritual rapport; two, although the correspondence (including, though not invariably, copies of my part of it) represents only fragmentary moments in Percy's career, it is yet full enough to suggest the drama of the last two decades of his literary life—the time, that is to say, when Percy published the bulk of his work: his third novel, *Love in the Ruins: The Adventures of a Bad Catholic at a Time Near the End of the World* (1971); the collection of essays entitled *The Message in the Bottle*, and brazenly subtitled *How Queer Man Is, How Queer Language Is, and What One Has to Do with the Other* (1975); the novels *Lancelot* (1977) and *The Second Coming*

(1980); a more or less unclassifiable work called *Lost in the Cosmos: The Last Self-Help Book* (1983); and, finally, a sixth novel, *The Thanatos Syndrome* (1987).

Whatever sense of mutuality there was between Walker and me had a good deal to do, our letters show, with our being of the same generation, having been born within two months of each other in 1916, Walker on May 28 of that second year of World War I, and I on July 18.

The close proximity of our birthdays made for some drollery on Walker's part. When I offered a congratulatory note on his sixty-ninth birthday, he replied, recalling that his closest friend Shelby Foote was born in November 1916: "Many thanks for your letter and the birthday greetings. The main point is that being older than you and Shelby, I'm entitled to a certain respect which I never seem to get." A year later when I sent Walker a note of congratulation on his seventieth birthday, he wrote back to say:

> I've got news for you. It's not all bad being in your 71st year. So you young fellows [a reference to Shelby and me] can relax.
> As a matter of fact, I feel it's a gift, a free ride. Nobody in my family ever lived so long. What it is is Early Times and clean living.[1]

But there was, I think, a more substantial basis for a certain generational concord between Walker and me than the coincidental proximity of our birthdays. What this might be slowly unfolded as I reread our letters. Evoking more than a reflective sadness, they educed—I don't know how to put it—the remembrance of a cultural atmosphere, a generational aura.

Our circumstances of birth, family, and rearing had been markedly disparate. To mention only one thing, there was a considerable difference between coming of age in Greenville, Mississippi, as a descendant of the Mississippi patriciate—an heir of the community of planters who had ruled the pre–Civil War plantation empire of the "Old Southwest"—and Jacksboro, Texas, a community dominated by farmers and ranchers, who in the 1850s had established themselves on the fringe of the westward expansion of the southern slave empire. During the Civil War the citizens of this world, the "new" Southwest, had been involved in fighting Indians and Yankees at the same time; indeed, only thirty-five years before I was born, had still been engaged, with the considerable assistance of the United States Army, in the bloody dispossession from their homeland of the last stubborn Comanches and Kiowas. Yet—as representatives of a heritage bequeathed by those who had fought and lost the War for Southern Independence and of those who had more immediately ratified the "reconstruction" of the South by fighting to "make the world safe for democracy" in the Great War of 1914–1918—Walker, Shelby, and I, having a bent toward the literary, shared a generational sense, or perhaps it may be put, a sense of participation in the drama of a generational sensibility. I don't know when Walker Percy began to have self-conscious intimations of his involvement in this drama, but it is interesting that apparently we both discovered Thomas Mann's *The Magic Mountain* in the mid-1930s. In its symbolic representation of the advanced state of the spiritual and intellectual illness of Western civilization, of which the First World War was the undeniable symptom, *The Magic Mountain* (published in German in 1924 and in an English version in 1927) has, like T. S. Eliot's poem *The Waste Land* (1922), become a major symbol of the modern age.

In my case I first read Mann's novel in the summer of 1934, after my freshman year in college. According to Shelby Foote's recollection, Walker first read it (he borrowed a copy from Shelby) a year later while he was a junior at the University of North Carolina. But Walker no doubt was a more precocious reader than I was. He remembered the experience of reading Dostoyevsky's *The Brothers Karamazov* during a summer vacation from high school in the early 1930s; I didn't have a go at *Crime and Punishment* until my freshman year in college. In any event, however dimly we grasped the deeper implications of Mann and Dostoyevsky, two southern youths of literary inclination were exposed at about the same moment to the "high culture" of Europe: to the density of the modern European literary mind and the crucial cultural dialectic that in the haunted moment between great wars from 1918 to 1939 produced a renascence in art and literature in western Europe. This renascent moment in Europe bore a close relation to what Malcolm Cowley called "a second flowering" of art and letters in the United States. The first had been centered in mid-nineteenth-century New England. Developing a half century beyond what has been called the bloodiest civil conflict in recorded history, the second renascent moment in American writing was a national phenomenon but assumed a distinctive regional quality in the writers of the American South.

What I am trying to get at, I think, is the relationship between Percy's quest for a career and the history of the first and second generations of twentieth-century southern writers. Growing up in the 1930s and 1940s, the second generation—the generation born in the years of the First World War in contrast to the generation born in the 1890s or early 1900s—was influenced in a primary way by the apocalyptic sensibility of the prior generation, whose members had either fought in the Great War or had come of age during the war years or in the aftermath of these years from 1918 to 1939. But the influence of the sensibility of the "Hemingway generation," or the "Faulkner generation," was not restricted to that of a chronological generation. There were older writers at the time of the Great War for whom this event became a major literary reference. There were even writers who had died before the summer of 1914—as well as those who, as in the case of Henry James, died in the midst of it, or, as in the case of Proust, died four years after the Armistice—who, because of their prescient anticipation of its mood, were participants in the drama of the age of the Great War. For plainly the generational sensibility of writers who came of age in the time of the 1914 war, or in the twenty years before it resumed in 1939—the generation of Joyce, Virginia Woolf, Hemingway, Fitzgerald, John Crowe Ransom, Allen Tate, William Faulkner, Robert Penn Warren, Caroline Gordon, and Eudora Welty—comprehended an awareness of Hardy, Yeats, Henry James, Proust, Valéry, Thomas Mann, Flaubert, Dostoyevsky, and Chekhov; and, to speak especially of the American South, of Edgar Allan Poe and Mark Twain. The sensibility of the writers of the period of the Great War and its aftermath also embraced any number of crucial philosophers and scientists—among these, Kierkegaard and Nietzsche as well as Einstein, Freud, and Jung. Taking into consideration all of the elements of its context, one may say that the sense of the literary vocation in post–World War I writers was informed by a dramatic tension between a vision of the possibility of the effective destruction of the institutions of Western civilization and a vision of a revitalizing "recovery of memory and history" that promised even at this late date a further fulfillment of the institutions of Western civilization through a restoration of the Classical-Judaic-Christian tradition. Seeking to envision the possibilities of the time, men of letters created a dialectical drama of possibilities, in which even those writers who were prophets of doom paradoxically became participants in a renascent surge in Western art and letters.

But for the generation that came of literary age in the late 1930s and early 1940s, the cultural energy of this productive tension snapped in 1939, when the twenty-year period of the "Armistice" ended with the German invasion of Poland and the British declaration of war against Germany. In the 1940s not only the renewal of global war but the decisive extension of the capacities of science and technology that accompanied the Second World War—the fatal extension that would bring it to a catastrophic end with the dropping of the first atomic bomb in 1945—made for a more drastic loss of confidence in the cultural power of art and letters than had occurred during and after the First World War. There were critics and scholars of the generation of 1916—of whom, I am, I suppose, a minor instance—still influenced by the idea of a restoration of the institutional sense of letters, but it had become obvious that the acceleration of the scientific-technological revolution during the Second World War had created a new age—a "postmodern age," as it would soon become known as—that would refuse accommodation to the older modes of literature and philosophy.

In the eighteenth century it was still possible for philosophers to consider "the whole of human knowledge, including science, to be their field," Stephen Hawking observes in *A Brief History of Time: From the Big Bang to Black Holes*; and they talked about big questions, like "Did the universe have a beginning?" But in the nineteenth century science had begun to assume a character that would become definitive in the twentieth: it began to be "too technical and mathematical for the philosophers, or anyone else except a few specialists" to understand. Pointing out that Wittgenstein, "the most famous philosopher of this century," came to the conclusion that "the sole remaining task for philosophy is the analysis of language," Hawking exclaims, "What a comedown from the great tradition of philosophy from Aristotle to Kant!"[2]

In his exploration of twentieth-century philosophy, Walker Percy attempted, in varying degrees, to come to terms with the thought of a whole panoply of modern philosophers, theologians, psychologists, and linguists, including—besides Nietzsche, Kierkegaard, Freud, and Jung—Jaspers, Heidegger, Wittgenstein, Gabriel Marcel, Jacques Maritain, Romano Guardini, and that singular American philosopher to whom Percy was greatly attracted, Charles Sanders Peirce. Even in the instances of Kierkegaard and Peirce—both of whom he studied with devotion—the precise extent to which Percy may have been influenced by modern thinkers is difficult to determine. But all of them—and others too, for his reading was wide—bear a relation to Percy's growing conviction that freeing philosophical, psychological, and/or religious language from its universal bondage to the analytical language of empirical science is only the initial step toward developing a language adequate for the expression of the intellectual and spiritual character of postmodernity.

Beginning with his first published philosophical essay in 1954, in which Percy both agreed and disagreed with the approach to language in Suzanne Langer's *Philosophy in a New Key*, the possibility of a liberating theory of language became increasingly important to him. Whether his preoccupation with this possibility enhanced or detracted from his sense of vocation to the novel may be a matter of opinion. However, one must always recognize that the simple yet profound, or profoundly simple, basis of Percy's work was not his acceptance of "the gift of faith" but his complex struggle to accept this gift; to come to terms with its meaning.

In spite of his often acknowledged debt to Kierkegaard, Percy did not suddenly make a Kierkegaardian "leap into the absurd." Accepting what he regarded as the evidence over a period of time of the presence of God's grace in his own individual life, Percy felt enabled, in "a post-Christian world dependent on the scientific methodology"—or, in more exact terms, in a world dependent on "pseudo-science" or "scientism" (there being nothing wrong with genuine science)—to make a deeply self-conscious commitment to "the Christian, specifically the Roman Catholic, version of history." Even though he did not wholly subscribe to Kierkegaard's notion of the leap into faith, Percy believed in the possibility that the self, any self, in quest of itself, in the act of refusing "to be abstracted like the scientific self," may, by the grace of God, become aware of "itself transparently before God," and in this mystical moment become "a fully incarnate being in the world."

In the most specific sense Percy's problem of vocation was related to the fact that in a society in which males of his class were expected to become doctors, lawyers, engineers, planters, or clergymen, he had given up the assurance of enlisting in the service of one of the honored professions for the pursuit of nothing more substantial than a vaguely formulated desire to be a writer, an occupation that at best had a dubious status in the eyes of his fellow citizens. But Percy faced a more forbidding problem than the social acceptance of his projected vocation. If he was to be a writer, what was he to write about, and how was he to write it? He had concluded that science imposes a limitation he could not accept. Declaring that "science can say everything about a man except what he is in himself," he had, if he had not rejected it altogether, distinctly modified the possibility of interpreting himself and the world by the Freudian concepts he had become familiar with, not only by reading Freud but by undergoing three years of strenuous psychiatric analysis. He had accepted Roman Catholic doctrine; but, since by the time of his conversion he was married, and happily so—his wife went through the process of confirmation with him—the possibility of emulating someone like Thomas Merton in a rigorous exercise of faith was not available to him. Though his becoming a lay member of the Benedictine Order in his later years may suggest that under different circumstances he might have committed himself to the religious vocation, Percy—in a world he envisioned as having lost both its metaphysical and its moral frames of reference—believed that the most direct possibility of defining his vocation would be through a layman's searching inquiry into philosophy and theology. The goal of his inquiry—to discover, and report on, what a man, or a woman, is in himself or herself—reflected the current modes of thinking and feeling generally grouped under the umbrella of "Christian existentialism" or "crisis theology." Since, according to an encyclical issued by Pope Pius XII in 1950, "crisis theology" violates the traditional doctrines of the faith that Percy had embraced upon his conversion, he had taken a path that offered major impediments to the perpetuation of his faith. Even though he feared more than once, I think, that his hold on faith might slip—a fear that reached its most troubling point in the 1970s, when he remarked to me (how seriously I don't know) that he was holding on to faith by the hardest effort—Percy never experienced a genuine loss of the basic belief he had accepted upon his conversion from "scientism to religion": that God had "entered history as a man, founded a Church, and will come again."[3]

Although he initially recorded the drama of his struggle with faith in essays, Percy was drawn early on to the notion of this struggle in fiction, apparently first glimpsing the definite possibility of becoming a novelist while at his last place of confinement as a tubercular patient, Gaylord Farm Sanatorium. Here, where Eugene O'Neill said he had been reborn when he discovered his vocation to the theater, Percy, reading Dostoyevsky's *Notes from Underground* and finding that "cultural criticism" and the "fictional characterization of a man in extremis" could be effectively joined, had the first distinct intimation that, having given up his vocation to medicine, he might be reborn as a novelist.[4] This idea became more substantial when later on, after he had begun writing for philosophical magazines, Percy, discovering contemporary French novels like Sartre's *Nausea* and Camus's *The Stranger,* had the "very exciting idea" that one might hold a certain belief and "communicate it . . . through a novel." In an essay written after he had become widely recognized as a novelist, "Notes for a Novel about the End of the World," he explained that, although as a Christian he had been concerned with the "scientific humanist" and his contribution to "the massive failure" of Christendom in the Western world, as a "Christian novelist" he understood that in the contemporary spiritual situation neither the polemics of "death-of-God theologians" nor the assertions of orthodox theologians about a "conflict between Christian doctrine and the scientific method" are important. What is important is "the *tertium quid* within which all such confrontations take place," the consciousness of the individual who, living at the end of the modern age, embodies the emergence of a "new" consciousness. One prominent version of this individual is the novelist, who "sees, or rather senses . . . a certain quality of the postmodern consciousness as he finds and incarnates" it in characters who represent what he sees in himself and in other people: "a new breed of person in whom the potential for catastrophe—and hope—has suddenly escalated."

> Everyone knows about the awesome new weapons. But what is less apparent is a comparable realignment of energies within the human psyche. The psychical forces presently released in the postmodern consciousness open unlimited possibilities for both destruction and liberation, for an absolute loneliness or a rediscovery of community and reconciliation.[5]

What then is the situation of the Christian novelist? Like most novelists, he writes in a form that, invented to serve as a mirror of modern society, has been subtly transformed since its invention in the eighteenth century to project, not the novel, but the novelist as the mirror of society. The Christian novelist, Percy implies, like the non-Christian novelist, "mirrors in himself the society he sees around him." "Otherwise [he] would not be a novelist, his only difference from his countrymen" being that, like all serious novelists, "he has the vocation to be a novelist." But the demands of this difference are considerable: not only has the Christian novelist inherited "a discredited Christendom," he has "inherited a defunct vocabulary." Conscious at once of his inextricable relation to the society around him and of his alienation from this society—the sense of alienation being all the greater because he must seek to communicate with his fellow citizens through the discovery of a vocabulary that will replace one now "defunct"—how can the Christian novelist fulfill his vocation? The answer is vividly ironic: "He does the only thing he can do. He appeals to James Joyce; or, speaking more precisely, to Joyce's Stephen Dedalus, who in *A Portrait of the Artist as a Young Man* "calls on every ounce of cunning, craft, and guile he can muster from the darker regions of his soul" (*Message*, 118). He appeals, that is, to a writer who had begun his career by announcing in an autobiographical novel that he had rejected not only the priesthood but the Church, and not only the Church but Christianity itself; who, in doing so, had not simply replaced the Christian priesthood with the concept of the priesthood of the secular artist but, dedicating himself in the most absolute way to the sovereign self of the literary artist, had declared the artist to be God. Although for the Christian novelist to call on Joyce is, Percy implies, to call on a representative of "the darker regions of the soul," the appeal is justified by Joyce's archetypal representative of the "secular-spiritual" literary artist, who dared to assume the power the contemporary novelist must assume, the power to create not only a new vocabulary but a new language. Like Joyce, he must use the language of "violence, shock, comedy, insult, the bizarre" as "the everyday tools of his trade." In view of the fact that the "wrong questions are being asked," and in worn-out language, it cannot be otherwise. For the Christian novelist, Percy indicates, the "proper question is not whether God has died . . . [or] whether the Good News is no longer relevant." The question is whether or not "it is possible that man is presently undergoing" such "a tempestuous restructuring of his consciousness" that he cannot "take account of the Good News."

> For what has happened is not merely the technological transformation of the world but something psychologically even more portentous. It is the absorption by the layman of the magical aura of science, whose credentials he accepts for all areas of reality. Thus in the lay culture of a scientific society nothing is easier than to fall prey to a kind of seduction which sunders one's very self from itself into an all-transforming "objective" consciousness and a consumer self with a list of "needs" to be satisfied. It is this monstrous bifurcation of man into angelic and bestial components against which the old theologies must be weighed before new theologies are erected. Such a man could not take account of God, the devil, and the angels if they were standing before him, because he has already peopled the universe with his own hierarchies. (*Message*, 113)

In response to this situation, Percy says, all serious novelists, even though the majority of them are non-Christian, write of "a man 'coming to himself' through some such catalyst as catastrophe or ordeal," and in doing so offer "obscure testimony to a gross disorder of consciousness and the need of recovering oneself as neither angel nor organism but as a wayfaring creature somewhere between." But the Christian novelist must respond to the crisis of disordered consciousness by more than "obscure testimony" to the "need of recovering oneself." He must seek a new vocabulary—a new stock of words, a new novelistic idiom—in which to express the significant forms of the Christian way of salvation. How, for example, can one "possibly write of baptism as an event of immense significance when baptism has come to be accepted as a minor tribal rite somewhat secondary in importance to taking the kids to see Santa at the department store"? Answering this question, Percy says, Flannery O'Connor accepted "as the tools of her trade" a vocabulary that in one novel "conveyed baptism . . . as a violent death by drowning," and in all her stories created "bizarre characters." For "the near blind," she said, the novelist must draw characters as "very large, simple caricatures" (*Message,* 118).

In his ironic appeal to Joyce it is perhaps significant that Percy speaks of the "darker regions of the soul" rather than "of the self." In Kierkegaard "soul" or "spirit" is conceived as the "ground of being" of the "authentic self." By "relating itself to its own self and by willing to be itself," Kierkegaard said, "the self is grounded transparently in the Power which posited it." But by a kind of post-Kierkegaardian mandate "soul" seems to have been replaced by "self" as the proper reference for the intrinsic, the authentic, identity of the person. Placed in the context of Percy's writings as a whole, the use of the term "soul" in "A Novel about the End of the World" may be taken to imply that the "soul" of the artist is identical with the "self" of the artist.

It was this, the Kierkegaardian concept of the self, that governed Percy's sense of what was at stake in his effort to define the vocation of the literary artist. In Kierkegaardian terms, it was an "either/or" situation. What was at issue was either the "liberation" of the self of the artist through a "rediscovery" of the community of faith that was created when God had entered history as a man and then transcended history in His resurrection from the grave; or else the "destruction" of the self of the artist through the recognition of its absolute isolation in history. Yet in spite of the emphasis he placed on the Christian novelist as artist, Percy would never be satisfied that in writing novels he had found a way to communicate what is essential if the capacity for belief is again to become a possibility. What is required is the development implied by the need to replace a defunct vocabulary, a theory of man that will replace the defunct theory of man "professed by the [present] age" by taking into account the "tempestuous restructuring of consciousness" that is occurring in this age (*Message,* 113).

This was how Percy had come to feel, I take it, when his long and ever growing concern with the meaning of language culminated in the audacious discovery that he himself possessed the capacity not only to be a novelist but to be a student of language, who might develop a theory of language that would contend with the theories of the leading professional theorists in the science of linguistic study. And more important than this, might indeed lead to a new theory of man based on the fact that—albeit denied by the scientists who spend years studying the "speech" of chimpanzees—man is the *only* creature who uses language.

In a kind of editorial comedy, I became an accidental agent of Percy's formal assumption of the mantle of language theorist. This happened as a result of my connection with the publication of "The Delta Factor," the only essay on linguistics, I believe, ever carried by the *Southern Review.* The comedy of the publication of this essay began in October 1973, when Walker wrote in response to one of my repeated solicitations of something for the *Southern Review:*

> Re *Southern Review:* you may be sure that if I do any criticism, belles-lettres or the consideration, you'll be the first to see it.
>
> I wish you were not limited to literature and criticism. I've been working for a long time on an obscure essay which I hope soon to finish and for which, I suddenly realize, there is no outlet or readership. It is about 40 pp. (c. 12,000 words) and is simply entitled "A Theory of Language" and is just about that: an anti-Chomsky, anti-Skinner, anti-Lévi-Strauss theory of the nature of language and especially the acquisition of language. It is quite condensed, unreadable and probably the most important piece I'll ever write. If you know anyone interested, I'd be obliged.

Intrigued by the possibility of publishing "the most important piece" Walker Percy "would ever write," and interpreting his equivocal note as a come-on, I ignored my editorial instinct to be wary about an ambivalent inquiry. I promptly wrote a note to Walker indicating that we would very much like to see "A Theory of Language" when it was completed. My note produced an equally prompt response:

I certainly will send this here essay when I finish it. Not that I think you can use it but (1) I'd be glad to have you look at it and (2) it gives me a reason to finish it. Perhaps you might someday do an issue of the extra-literary pursuits of literary folk: William Carlos Williams on pediatrics, what's-his-name the insurance executive poet on the insurance business [no doubt a reference to Wallace Stevens], Dickey on archery, Updike on golf etc.

At this point I began to worry a little that I had been so positive about the *Review*'s interest in an essay that, according to its author, represented an "extra-literary pursuit." After nearly five months had passed with no further word from Walker about his project, I began to admit to myself that I would be pleased *not* to hear anything more. Then one April morning there it was on my desk—"A Theory of Language" by Walker Percy—together with a covering letter. I picked up the letter first. In it Walker expressed an even more negative attitude toward the appropriateness of the essay for us than he had before: "O.K. you asked for it! I send it mainly to support my conviction that I don't see how the SR could use it, since it is mainly an attack on three schools of linguistic theory, mostly contra Chomsky, and this ain't exactly what your subscribers is paying their money for." But at the same time, Walker reaffirmed his conviction of the essay's significance that had so impressed me to begin with: "I do think it is the most important thing I've ever written, but it will be twenty years before anybody realizes it (current theorists must first perish from exhaustion)." I was further heartened when I looked at the first page of the essay and saw beneath the title, "A Theory of Language," one of those fascinating Percyian subtitles: "A Martian View of Linguistic Theory, Plus the Discovery That an Explanatory Theory Does Not Presently Exist, Plus the Offering of a Crude Explanatory Model on the Theory That Something Is Better Than Nothing." I took heart. It seemed possible that, employing an intriguing persona, the Martian space wanderer, Walker had written an erudite spoof that would be thoroughly available and entertaining to any reasonably sophisticated reader.

But I soon realized that what I had before me—a manuscript cluttered with linguistic equations and diagrams—was, as Walker had warned, not what our subscribers were paying to see. Yet, having allowed things to develop to this point, I felt that, although I had not commissioned the piece, I had in effect made a commitment to publish it. There was still some wiggle room. Walker, who had not yet made his final draft, had appended a postscript saying, "If you want to see the final version—o.k." I told Walker I would like to see this, and so delayed things a little longer. But not much. Upon my return to the magazine office two or three weeks later after a European trip, I found a revised manuscript waiting. It was accompanied by a letter (dated May 20, 1974).

> Herewith a more readable version of "A Theory of Language."
>
> I am glad you think you might be able to use it. One reason I want it in print as soon as possible is that I admit to being sufficiently seduced by the angelism-beastialism of scientists to want to get it in the public domain before being scooped. The vanity of theorists!
>
> Truthfully, I do believe it is a contribution and that it has, despite its crudities and naiveté, some value.

I am not sure at this remove quite how I first took this letter. Walker says of Kate in *The Moviegoer,* and again of Barrett in *The Last Gentleman,* that they "missed it." I think I had missed it; had missed, I mean, a major implication of what was before my eyes in the letter of transmittal. Reading it again several years later, I was impressed by the fact that Walker clearly implied his motive in his equivocal yet strangely persistent approach to me about "A Theory of Language." Maintaining the self-conscious evasiveness of his earlier communications—saying, even though he must have felt sure that I would publish his essay, "I am glad you think you might be able to use it"—he indicated that all along he had simply been moved by the desire to find a way into print, not an easy task for a linguist who was not only a maverick but a nonprofessional and therefore lacked the credentials for access to the standard periodicals in the field. In offering a decidedly more modest estimate of the value of his essay than he had earlier, was he not virtually confessing that his sensitivity to his probable rejection by professional linguists—that is to say, his vanity—had urged him to seek publication in a less than suitable periodical? I think by this time I was too concerned with the problem of doing what I had to do—that is, make a formal commitment to publish "A Theory of Language"—to appreciate, as I suspect Walker did, the ironic nuances of the little comedy we had got involved in. My response was flat as a pancake: I said that I was glad to find the revised manuscript when I returned, that it would appear in the January 1975 issue, and that there would be time to consult about any problems "that may occur in setting up the essay." I knew problems would occur. None of us in the office knew anything about the special language of linguistics. I was not even sure the printer could handle the typesetting. There was some comfort to be taken in the fact that Walker had agreed to be a part-time member of the LSU faculty during the 1974–1975 term and would be available to us in person when the proofs were ready to be checked.

But then suddenly the story of "A Theory of Language" took two more ironic twists. On September 20 Walker sent the manuscript of an essay he had never before mentioned. Entitled "The Delta Factor," its sudden appearance remained unexplained in the first part of an accompanying letter, in which Walker wrote that he had a "couple" of changes to make in the manuscript of "A Theory of Language." He thereupon listed no less than eleven revisions. All of these seemed tedious and one or two were more or less incomprehensible to me; so I was pleased that Walker said he could "easily make these changes by coming to your office." But then a total surprise.

> Finally, you're easily off the hook with this article if it [i.e., "A Theory of Language"] is beginning to look queerer and queerer for the SR. Present plans are for Farrar and Straus to publish it in Spring as part of a collection. (By the way if you do want to publish it in SR, will you grant permission for it to be used in the collection?) So if you don't want to use it, don't—I send you something even queerer, entitled:
> THE DELTA FACTOR
> or
> How I Discovered the Delta Factor Sitting at My Desk One Summer Day in Louisiana in the 1950s Thinking about an Event in the Life of Helen Keller on Another Summer Day in Alabama in 1887
> (It's another excursion into language, Delta being, not the Mississippi alluvium, but Greek delta, the triad.)

Reading "The Delta Factor," I discovered that I really was off the hook with a replacement essay that, anticipating the style and method of *Lost in the Cosmos*, is, in contrast to "A Theory of Language," mostly a nontechnical interpretation of the story of Helen Keller; and altogether an intriguing and entertaining presentation of the essential core of Percy's prophetic theory of language. As I gratefully accepted "The Delta Factor" in place of "A Theory of Language" I wondered, and I still wonder, why Walker had not before mentioned the possibility of the substitution. Was it because he considered "The Delta Factor" and "A Theory of Language" to be saying essentially the same thing? Or was it because now that he had a deal with his publisher to bring out a collection that would include "A Theory of Language" he could relax his anxiety about publishing what he considered to be the more important essay before somebody got the jump on him with a piece advancing a similar thesis? Or was it because he believed "The Delta Factor" to be the more important essay, in that it directly and forcefully reveals, not only in a professional but in a profoundly personal sense, how central his attempt to formulate a theory of language had become to his struggle to define his vocation?

"A Theory of Language" did of course appear before long in *The Message in the Bottle* as the concluding essay of this book, with "The Delta Factor" as the introductory essay. Thus a series of older pieces documenting Percy's lengthy interest in language and communication are neatly boxed in *The Message in the Bottle* by two pieces exuding a climactic sense of fascination with the subject. Altogether in this book, Percy says with genuine yet carefully calculated modesty, he is presenting "the meager fruit of twenty years' off-and-on thinking about the subject [of language], of coming at it from one direction, followed by failure and depression and giving up, followed by making up novels to raise my spirits, followed by a new try from a different direction or from an old direction but at a different level, followed by failure, followed by making up another novel, and so on" (*Message*, 10). Was Percy, who had by this time published three successful novels and was being hailed as a significant addition to the ranks of American novelists, saying that all along his vocation to the novel had been secondary to his true vocation as a theorist of language?

"What does a man do when he finds himself living after an age has ended and he can no longer understand himself because the theories of man of the former age no longer work and the theories of the new age are not yet known, for not even the name of the age is known, and so everything is upside down, people feeling bad when they should feel good, good when they should feel bad?" The answer is that he will "start afresh as if he were newly come into a new world, which in fact it is; start with what he knows for sure, look at the birds and beasts, and like a visitor from Mars newly landed on earth notice what is different about man." Becoming aware that "beasts can be understood as organisms living in environments which are good or bad" and to which they respond as they have evolved to respond, the visitor from Mars asks, "How is man to be understood if he feels bad in the best environment?"

> Where does one start with a theory of man if the theory of man as an organism in an environment doesn't work and all the attributes of man which were accepted in the old modern age are now called into question: his soul, mind, freedom, will, Godlikeness?
>
> There is only one place to start: the place where man's singularity is there for all to see and cannot be called into question, even in a new age in which everything is in dispute.
>
> That singularity is language.
>
> Why is it that men speak and animals don't?
>
> What does it entail to be a speaking creature, that is, a creature who names things and utters sentences about things which other similar creatures understand and misunderstand? (*Message*, 7–8)

"The Delta Factor" reaches a climax in Percy's reference to Helen Keller's remembrance of the radical event that occurred one Alabama summer morning in the eighth year of a blind, deaf, and speechless child. On this morning she went to the well-house with Miss Sullivan, where her teacher put one of Helen's hands under the water spout. As the cool water gushed into her hand, Miss Sullivan spelled the word *water* in her free hand. "Undoubtedly," Percy says, "there were three elements somehow involved in the event—Helen, the water, and the word *water*. But how? What was the base of the triangle? What is the nature of the mysterious event in which one perceives that *this* (stuff) '*is*' *water*? What is the natural phenomenon signified by the simplest yet most opaque of symbols, the little copula '*is*'"? Then, Percy says, the "breakthrough" came in the "sudden inkling that the triangle" is "absolutely irreducible," being "nothing less" than "the ultimate and elemental unit not only of language" but "the very condition of the awakening of human intelligence and consciousness" (*Message*, 40). Contemplating Helen Keller's *The Story of My Life*, Percy realized, he had come upon a story that distilled nothing less than the mystery of the primary event in the history of man: the discovery of the power to name and to make sentences. Possessing this power, the human being is not, as modern scientists say, just another, if perhaps superior, organism. Each human being is a unique being, a singular self, who through language has a unique relation not only to nature but to other human beings; and, not only to other human beings, but to God.

Yet, although Percy experienced an intense sense of exhilaration when he discovered what he called the "Delta phenomenon" (the Greek letter, he points out, signifies "irreducibility"), neither his essay "The Delta Factor" nor *The Message in the Bottle* as a whole actually represents a decisive breakthrough in his lengthy attempt to define his vocation. Although in conceiving of himself as a theorist of language he thought he had defined his true vocation, he had at the same time reached another crisis in his career. It was one he would never resolve.

In its inception Percy's search for the meaning of the self—for the meaning of his own existence as a creature of God—represented the random questing of the seeker who is described in the title essay of *The Message in the Bottle*. First published in 1958, this essay depicts the seeker as bearing a resemblance to the traditional Christian "pilgrim" or "wayfarer" but, in another metaphorical sense, as also bearing a resemblance (Percy calls on a Kierkegaardian image) to a "castaway" on a desert island. Describing this castaway as a "scientist," Percy says, "I use the word in the broadest possible sense to include philosophers and artists as well as the positive scientist." (Before the age of specialized literacies, we may remind ourselves, these designations were comprehended in one term, "man of letters.") If the castaway is sufficiently aware of his plight, he may receive knowledge, even knowledge *sub specie aeternitatis,* from a message contained in a bottle washed up on the beach. But if the castaway is dominated by pride in the "scientific" theory of man, he will get no "news" of his salvation, unless, that is, he does something no one else can do for him: recognize that he is a castaway. If and when he does so, he will be capable of reading the "'little advertisement,'" the "'*nota bene* on a page of universal history,'" the momentous yet simple news contained in the bottle: "'We have believed that in such and such a year God appeared among us in the humble figure of a servant, that he lived and taught in our community, and finally died'" (*Message,* 130, 148).

But in his reading of Kierkegaard, Percy puts more emphasis than does the Danish philosopher himself on a modification Kierkegaard made in his concept of how the castaway receives the message in the bottle. He cannot simply read it. He must "hear" it; and hear it from a messenger with very special qualifications: a messenger who not only has an apostolic "commission" to bring the news but has the capacity to perform his mission "in perfect sobriety and with good faith and perseverance to the point of martyrdom." And there is still something else: if the message is to be "the very news the castaway has been waiting for," it must tell the castaway not only "where he came from and who he is." It must tell him "what he must do" and inform him about "the means by which [he] may do what he must do." Only then will the castaway, "by the grace of God," be *enabled* to "believe" the messenger (*Message*, 147–49).

What are the implications of Percy's reading of Kierkegaard's depiction of the castaway who receives a message? How does Percy accommodate the radical existentialistic individualism to the hierarchical, authoritarian structure of Catholic doctrine and practice? What are "the means" by which the castaway "may do what he must do"? Is it enough for the castaway, in the manner of the fundamentalist, simply to believe, to have faith, in the good news that "God appeared in such and such a year," etc.? Or must he conform his belief in the news to the doctrine—the dogma—and practices of Roman Catholicism? And another question: did Percy, the novelist and philosopher, who accepted the Catholic version of the doctrine of the unique apostolic character of Christianity, yet believe himself to be in some sense a messenger bearing good news? What precisely is the relation between the "motive" of the existentialist commitment to the vocation of writing and Percy's commitment?

In its purest Kierkegaardian state, the quest to come to oneself discovers its meaning only in the experience of the personal enactment of the quest, which if it is successful will result in the uniquely personal experience of taking the "leap into faith." According to the logic of its inherent nature, the existential quest is corrupted when the seeker begins to speculate about its meaning, for then it is no longer experiential. In seeking to objectify his quest, the seeker becomes a theorist.

When Percy—dedicated to the refusal of the self to be abstracted—described himself in the letter to me about "A Theory of Language" as being "anti-Chomsky, anti-Skinner, anti-Lévi- Strauss," he made evident the conflict in his thought and emotion between his regard for the self's creation of its meaning through the enactment of an existential search for meaning and his "scientific" impulse to theorize about the meaning of the search. He had become a novelist, he said, so that he could do what Sartre and Camus do in their novels, incarnate ideas in concrete, or "existential," situations. But his success in doing this did not resolve his desire to formulate and set forth a prophetic theory of man that would repudiate the sociological and psychological—the "scientific"—theories of human behavior. Although, because of their author's scrupulous devotion to the art of their making, his novels effectually transcend this essentially programmatic desire—Percy, as he always said, left his novels open to interpretation by his readers—they are nonetheless integral expressions of the conflict of motives in his vocation to writing.

How this is so is evident in the close relationship between the author and the identity of the leading characters in his novels. In each story the consciousness of the chief character is the narrative or controlling consciousness; and, whether the story is told from the perspective of a first- or a third-person narrator, each of these characters, as Edward J. Dupuy has brilliantly shown, in one way or another incarnates Percy's own experience of the search for self-identity.[6]

But this is most evident of course in the novels controlled by a first-person narrator, as is strikingly illustrated in Linda Whitney Hobson's interview with Percy in 1981, in which he said:

> Scientists [as the context indicates, he is now thinking of scientists as specialized inquirers] are strange people, as are artists. What are artists up to? And what does it mean to be a scientist, being out of the world, playing God and arranging order in the world, and then, as Kierkegaard would say—or as Binx Bolling said as he was lying in a hotel room in Birmingham—what do you do when you develop a theory? Then how do you live the rest of the day?

Percy was referring specifically to a small but crucial scene in *The Moviegoer*, when Binx, lying on a bed in a hotel room in Birmingham, is reading a book he considers to be "fundamental," *The Chemistry of Life*. As he reads, Binx is moved to ask himself about the connection between theorizing and living. He comes to the conclusion that he will give up trying to dispose of the universe. In Kierkegaardian terms, he abandons a "vertical search"—a purposeful, directed search for meaning—in favor of a "horizontal search." Declaring that "what is important is what I shall find when I leave my room and wander in the neighborhood," he goes "about in the streets" looking, hoping something he sees or someone he encounters will reveal to him the meaning of his looking.

The reference for this scene in *The Moviegoer*, as Percy put it in the Hobson interview, is Kierkegaard's description of the man "who read Hegel, understood himself and the universe perfectly by noon," but then begins to feel "that though he had disposed of the universe" he had not truly disposed of himself. Feeling "left over," and stuck with "the problem of living out the rest of day," will Binx encounter a messenger in the streets who has authoritative news about the mystery of his existence? Or, like the castaway in "The Message in the Bottle," receive news that transcends cognitive knowledge, and, receiving it, "come to himself," know who he is and why he exists?[7]

Having found out what science has to say about the human creature—not only through his medical training as a pathologist (a training that had become intimately relevant to him when he became a tubercular patient) but through his deep involvement in psychotherapy as both patient and lay student—Percy himself had become intimately aware of the feeling of being "left over." Searching for the reason he felt alienated (not less from the world than from himself)—trying to find a way to live out the rest of the day—he sought to define his feeling of alienation in philosophical essays. But discovering that what he really was seeking was a way not simply to describe but to tell—and in a sense to enact (a novel always being an enactment as well as a telling)—the story of his experience of alienation, Percy turned to the possibility of employing the form of the philosophical novel.

To realize this possibility he had to learn how to write a novel, a task that involved the question, What do self-conscious literary artists do? He asked this question with reference to the prior question he had asked, What do scientists do?—particularly those concerned with human behavior, and more particularly, those concerned with the most fundamental aspect of human behavior, the ability human beings have developed to employ language. According to Jay Tolson in *Pilgrim in the Ruins*, when the head of the National Institute of Mental Health solicited Percy's assistance in a professional project involving the problem of communication by schizophrenics, he replied that he was "a novelist by trade and a theorist of behavior only by avocation," but, nonetheless, he accepted the assignment. Although Percy liked to think of himself as being by vocation a novelist, and hence an artist, he remained aware, acutely so I think, that he was not only a scientist who had become a philosopher and a philosopher who had become a novelist; he was something of all three. As a student of the science of language—as a theorist of language—he hoped to develop the art that a new age, a postmodern age, essentially required of the novelist: the art of telling stories that not only enact the experience of the self suffering from the twentieth-century "malaise" but suggest at least the possibility of a new, a postmodern, theory of man.

At the time he sent "A Theory of Language" to the *Southern Review* Percy believed that he had made the exciting discovery of how this possibility might be fulfilled. Nothing was more indicative of his confidence than his self-conscious apology to me about his desire to see his essay in "print as soon as possible." When he said he had been "sufficiently seduced by the angelism-beastialism of scientists to want to get in the public domain before being scooped," then added, "The vanity of theorists!" Percy was paraphrasing without acknowledgment an ironic comment by Dr. Thomas More, the central character and narrator in, at the time of his letter, his most recent novel, *Love in the Ruins*. Referring to an article he has written, Dr. More exclaims: "The vanity of scientists! My article, it is true, is an extremely important one. Perhaps even epochal in its significance."

Earlier when I had written to Walker to express my admiring interest in *Love in the Ruins*, I had mentioned in an incidental way that in the late 1890s my father had written a sentimental novel, a very bad one, about a young man and young woman who are trying to make a go of love and marriage in the ruined South of the Reconstruction era. My father had called his story *Love Amid the Shadows of War: A Story of the South*, but, misremembering the title, in my letter to Walker I called it "Love Amid the Ruins of War." Acknowledging my letter, Walker referred to my father's novel with a typical wry downplaying of his own novel: "*Love in the Ruins* is not very serious. The title seems to evoke all sorts of tangential responses from everybody (Browning responses, Waugh responses, and now your father's novel). Actually it represents a lack of talent for making up titles. The original title was How to Make Love in the Ruins, abandoned as being too close to Masters and Johnson."

But, as Percy knew of course, *Love in the Ruins* is a very serious novel. His first explicit effort to write something that would fulfill his own suggestion that "it may be useful to write a novel about the end of the world," it was also an attempt to fulfill an increasingly insistent desire on Percy's part to write a "big one," a novel of "epochal" significance. Bearing the stamp of his attraction to the mode of science fiction, *Love in the Ruins* is about a world not quite at its end but in terrible disarray. Bearing the subtitle *The Adventures of a Bad Catholic at a Time Near the End of the World*, the novel might well have been subtitled "The Confessions of a Bad Catholic at a Time Near the End of the World," centered as it is in the confessions of the "bad Catholic" Dr. Thomas More. A feckless alcoholic who is subject to spells of manic depression, More has nonetheless written a "possibly epochal article" about the state of the present-day world, especially as it is imaged by "the old violent beloved U.S.A." The subject of this as yet unpublished article is how the inhabitants of More's world may be saved—not from the explosion and accompanying fallout of an atomic bomb—but from something even worse: a fallout of mysterious "noxious particles" causing widespread psychic illness. In the grip of this illness Americans have turned "against each other: race against race, right against left, believer against heathen, San Francisco against Los Angeles, Chicago against Cicero." As a result "vines sprout in sections of New York City where not even Negroes will live," and "wolves have been seen in downtown Cleveland, like Rome during the Black Plague." Dr. More expects the final end will come when "an unprecedented fallout" of these particles occurs. Although this fallout, unlike that from an atomic explosion, will not "burn the skin and rot the marrow," it will have even more destructive consequences. It will "inflame and worsen the secret ills of the spirit and rive the very self from itself," so that "if a man is already prone to anger, he'll go mad with rage"; or "if he lives affrighted, he will quake with terror"; or "if he's already abstracted from himself, he'll be sundered from himself and roam the world like Ishmael." As the discoverer of this illness, More has named it for himself, "More's Syndrome."

But More has not only discovered and described this illness, he has invented a remedy. A symbol of the scientific commitment to a behavioristic theory of the nature of man—a theory that represents the most deadly of all sins, intellectual pride—More's remedy is a scientific device designed not simply to diagnose but to do nothing less than cure the psychological, political, and philosophical ills of man. He calls it a "Qualitative Quantitative Ontological Lapsometer," and describes it as "the first caliper of the soul and the first hope of bridging the dead chasm that has rent the soul of Western man since the famous philosopher Descartes ripped the body loose from mind and turned the very soul into a ghost that haunts it own house." The lapsometer will heal the Cartesian fissure by measuring the tension present in an individual consciousness between the tendency toward "angelism"—the use of the human intellect as though it were an angel's—and the necessity of living in the real world. This measurement will enable the physician to prescribe in an individual case the right dosage of heavy sodium, which More has discovered affects brain centers in different ways: "For example, Heavy Sodium radiation stimulates Brodmann Area 32, the center for abstractive activity or tendencies toward angelism, while Heavy Chloride stimulates the thalamus, which promotes adjustment to the environment, or as I call it without prejudice, beastialism." But, although he has diagnosed the cause of More's Syndrome, More still does not know how to correlate the symptoms of the disease and the therapeutic dosage to use in a given individual. Experimentation with the dosage—which he unwisely places in the hands of a Mephistophelean colleague named Art Immelman—has disastrous consequences.

Since the inventor of the lapsometer who tells the story in *Love in the Ruins* is a Catholic and a psychiatrist, and since Percy said that had he remained in medicine he likely would have become a psychiatrist, we seem to be justified in assuming that More is directly identifiable as a persona of Percy. In *Walker Percy: The Last Catholic Novelist,* Kieran Quinlan points to a significant observation by Percy in an interview he gave the same year *Love in the Ruins* (1971) was published:

> I guess we're all what we are. If you're a Marxist, you can't help but be affected by that orientation in your writing. And I'm a Roman Catholic, although many Roman Catholics don't understand how I could write the novels I do and be a Roman Catholic. Of course that's an interesting subject in itself. What is a Catholic novelist? All I can say is, as a writer you have a certain view of man, a certain view of the way it is, and even if you don't recognize it or even if you disavow such a view, you can't escape that view or lack of view. I think your writing is going to reflect this. I think my writings reflect a certain basic orientation toward, although they're not really controlled by, Catholic dogma. As I say, it's a view of man, that man is neither an organism controlled by his environment, nor a creature controlled by the forces of history as the Marxists would say, nor is he a detached, wholly objective, angelic being who views the world in a Godlike way and makes pronouncements only to himself or to an elite group of people. No, he's somewhere between the angels and the beasts. He's a strange creature whom both Thomas Aquinas and Marcel called *homo viator,* man the wayfarer, man the wanderer. So, to me, the Catholic view of man as pilgrim, in transit, in journey, is very compatible with the vocation of a novelist because a novelist is writing about man in transit, man as pilgrim. I think it would be a disadvantage, for example, to be a Freudian

and a novelist. I think a great many novels have been spoiled by Freudian preconceptions. Or behaviorist preconceptions. And I think most Marxist novels are bad. (*Conversations*, 63–64)

In this observation, Quinlan says, Percy implies that with the publication of *Love in the Ruins* he felt "firmly established" in his vocation as "a Catholic novelist."[8] But is this quite so? Does not this description obscure a singular motive in Percy's novel: his intensely *personal* sense of being himself a man in transit? Concerned not so much with "man" as with man specifically embodied in Walker Percy, Percy's third novel represents another stage in his attempt to deal with the lifelong problem of defining, not the vocation of the novelist as such, but his continuing dedication to self-fulfillment. Employing Dr. More as a first-person narrator in *Love in the Ruins,* Percy suggests a closer association between narrator and author than he does in either *The Moviegoer* or *The Last Gentleman*. And if we take More—a perplexed and wayward Catholic—to be a persona of Percy, we may be inclined to see that a story told by a physician and scientist, whose name echoes that of the famous Catholic martyr who wrote *Utopia*—who not so much lived in the historical moment when the secularization of the sacred became complete as lived this time—*Love in the Ruins* may be read as a direct expression of the spiritual anxiety experienced by its author. A committed Catholic literary artist, who is also a physician and a scientist, Dr. Percy makes his novel into a diagnostic investigation of what, ironically, he had presumably unreservedly subscribed to at the time of his conversion, the Roman Catholic dogma about the nature of man and God and the relation between man and God.

The story in *Love in the Ruins* centers, this is to say, in the diagnostician, not the diagnosis. At the end of his account of events that transpire in the course of the novel, even though More has had intimations that the remedy he has offered for More's Syndrome is itself an expression of the syndrome, he is still saying that "my lapsometer can save the world—if I can get it right." Yet More, who for years had not gone to mass, still less to confession, tells about attending a midnight Christmas mass, for which he made preparation by going to confession. Although under the ministration of Father Smith, a valiant, if weary, parish priest, who like More has suffered at times from schizophrenic tendencies, More does not bring himself to the point of saying he is sorry for his sins; he does confess to being ashamed of failing to show enough "ordinary kindness to people." Accepting "an envelope containing ashes and a sackcloth," he pulls the black burlap sackcloth over his sport coat, indicating that he has at least become receptive to a message of faith, hope, and love.

More's account of his return to the confessional and the mass is the climax of his story. But if we take More to be a figure of the novelist as Catholic literary artist, do we believe he truly represents the possibility of bringing science, philosophy, and art into a compatible relationship, thereby suggesting the possibility of the redemption, both of himself and his country, from "chronic angelism-beastialism"? Or do we harbor the doubt that the teller of the tale—who has earlier confessed to himself that he believes "in God and the whole business" but loves "women best, music and science next, whiskey next, God fourth, and fellowman hardly at all"—will finally succeed in overcoming the deadly syndrome he has diagnosed?

In his fourth novel, *Lancelot,* Percy's quest to define his vocation is enacted by a teller who spins a darker, more powerful story than Dr. Thomas More's. The teller in this case—a member of the Louisiana patriciate named Lancelot Andrewes Lamar, a handsome, liberal, alcoholic lawyer—is, in the most profound way, *in* the tale he tells.

In his earlier years a gridiron star at LSU and a Rhodes Scholar at Oxford, Lancelot owns a showplace River Road plantation mansion named Belle Isle. To avenge his honor, and in a way simply to relieve his boredom, Lancelot invokes his heritage as a member of a class that had in a not too distant past professed its allegiance to what Walker's Uncle Will—a disciple of Marcus Aurelius and the Stoic philosophy—called "the broad-sword tradition." Going back to the age of Ulysses, this tradition embraced a simple code of honor: "if somebody offends you, you kill them." The knight of "The Delta Factor" (who may be compared to Kierkegaard's "knight of faith" in *The Sickness unto Death*) and the knight of Belle Isle—significantly not a lapsed Catholic but a lapsed Episcopalian who has become a Stoic (of sorts at least)—share an underlying identity. Even as the knight of faith envisions the possibility of a renewal of communication between human beings in a world healed of the Cartesian wound, he holds aloft a magic blade that will slice as clean as a surgeon's scalpel; even as the champion of the ancient Stoa envisions the promise of a new moral "Reformation," he brandishes a broadsword dripping with the blood of his unfaithful wife and her whole rootless entourage.

Percy said he first tried to write the story of Lancelot Andrewes Lamar and his cataclysmic destruction of Belle Isle using two characters and two contrasting voices. One voice would be that of Lancelot, by formal profession of faith an Anglican, and in practice a Stoic; the other would be that of his close friend Percival, a practicing Christian. But the simple dialogic structure did not work. Pointing out that Lancelot and Percival are connected by "biographical resemblances . . . to Percy (and to various ancestral Percys)," Jay Tolson says that in *Lancelot* "Percy was in fact writing a kind of Jungian drama between a self and a counterself, the self, one might say, of the shadow." Lancelot, like Percy, "has worked for civil-rights causes, drinks more than is good for him, feels increasingly contemptuous of the modern age and increasingly purposeless in his own life." But Percival is most obviously linked to Percy by his name. Portrayed as having been born in a house named Northumberland, he is even given the same college nickname Percy's SAE brothers had given him, "Pussy." Yet, Tolson says, these biographical resemblances between Lancelot and Percival are "relatively trivial."

> The salient connection between them and Percy is their dramatization of his [Percy's] own internal conflict between despair and hope, selfishness and selflessness, contempt for the world and charity. Percy once explained that he could not give these opposing voices equal time in the way that Dostoyevsky had; the age would not tolerate such preaching. But he could transform the dialogue into a monologue, allow the side of darkness to talk itself out in one long-winded rant, and by subtlest hints imply a response. (Tolson, 403–4)

Does Percy succeed in suggesting a response? In *Lancelot*, he said, he "had in mind," as in all his novels, the problem he sets forth in *The Message in the Bottle*, "the wearing out of language and the creation of a new language" to replace the worn-out language. But, it would appear, in writing *Lancelot* he had the problem of language more intensely in mind than before. While he was writing *Lancelot*, he remarked in an interview that "people say words, and words have become as worn as poker chips, they don't mean anything."

> Particularly religious words: baptism, sin, God. Things get worn out, and there is always a problem of rediscovering them. As the Psalmist says, you have to sing a new song: I think that is one of the functions of the novel-

ist. Right now I am trying to write a novel in which a man finds himself in some sort of a cell—it's not clear whether it's a prison cell or sanitorium cell. He's there for several reasons—he's not quite sure, as a matter of fact, he's amnesic. But he's very much aware that the language is worn out. And in the next room there's a woman who's in a state of catatonia; she's also mute, she's retreated from language. So he conceives the idea of trying to communicate with her by knocking on the wall.

"So they're really in the process of inventing a language?" the interviewer asked. Percy replied:

They're in adjoining cells, and their windows let out onto the same scene, which is a very narrow slice of New Orleans, uptown New Orleans. It's a corner of the old Lafayette Cemetery, and a slice of the levee, and a slice of a movie theatre—but you can see a lot, you know. It's a triad. The point also is, the idea of restriction being good. . . . So this man is in this cell and he likes it there, because it's the purest kind of triadic situation—an "I" and a "thou," something to look at, and an opportunity to create a language, like Adam and Eve. (*Conversations*, 140–41)

In his growing perception of the complexity of his motives in writing *Lancelot*, we glimpse Percy's need to confess an increasing sense of crisis in his conception of his vocation as a Christian, and, more specifically, a Roman Catholic, novelist. As though in ironic obedience to Joyce's dictum that "the novelist is entitled to a degree of artifice and cunning," Percy not only suggests in *Lancelot* the connection between his authorial identity and the consciousness of his protagonist, he implies that, in accordance with the logic of the narrative perspective, Percival does not exist in the novel save as he comes to the reader through the words of Lancelot, Lancelot's relationship to Percival being revealed to the reader solely through the narrator's depiction of Lancelot's unofficial confessor.

A deeply disturbed, lapsed Christian—significantly not a lapsed Roman Catholic but a lapsed Protestant—Lancelot bears a strong underlying resemblance to Faulkner's Quentin Compson. A member of a society that consisted of far more Protestants (Presbyterians, Methodists, Baptists, and Episcopalians) than Catholics, Lancelot is in actuality a lapsed Calvinist, or a lapsed southern

Puritan (one is tempted to say a lapsed Stonewall Jackson), who has embraced a romantic Stoicism. Possessing the temperament of a literary artist, he is indeed essentially a quite degraded version of the poet and memoirist William Alexander Percy.

I still remember a small personal encounter I had with Percy about the meaning of *Lancelot*. The only time I ever felt that he was truly irritated with me, this occurred during a session of a National Endowment for the Humanities seminar for high school teachers of English I conducted at LSU in the summer of 1983. Though I don't think he wanted to do so, Walker had kindly accepted an invitation to drive over from Covington and spend an hour or so in informal conversation with my group. Composed of teachers from all around the country, it was an interesting one. There was some good conversation, and the time passed pleasantly during both the seminar session and the informal luncheon that followed. But during the discussion of *Lancelot* there was the moment when I remarked that a reader might find the conclusion of the novel to be uncertain and possibly ambiguous. I referred to the scene in which Lancelot tells about questioning Percival's reason for listening to his (Lancelot's) story:

> So you plan to take a little church in Alabama, Father, preach the gospel, turn bread into flesh, forgive the sins of Buick dealers, administer communion to suburban housewives?
> At last you're looking straight at me, but how strangely! Ah, all at once I understand you. I read you as instantly as I used to when we were so close. All of a sudden we understand each other perfectly, don't we?
> Tell me if I'm right or wrong.
> You know something you think I don't know, and you want to tell me but you hesitate.
> Yes.[9]

Walker did not respond directly to my quibble. He simply commented tersely that some people seemed to be incapable of grasping the meaning of the novel. Realizing that I had unexpectedly touched a raw nerve, I was taken back. Walker had reacted differently, I remembered, after reading the same assessment of Lancelot's situation in an essay I had published earlier. He had said in a letter: "No, there is no hope for Lancelot, at least not in the novel."

Why did the creator of Lancelot Andrewes Lamar now seem upset because, on the basis of the evidence offered in the novel, I continued to wonder if the fate of Lancelot is ambiguous? If there is no hope for Lancelot in the novel, where is there hope for him? Where else does he exist? Where else will Lancelot come to himself? I found a possible answer a year or so following the seminar session in Percy's explication of *Lancelot* in an interview with Zoltán Abádi-Nagy in the *Paris Review.*

> The entire novel is Lancelot's spiel to Percival. Percival does not *in the novel* reply in kind. At the end Lancelot asks him if he has anything to say. Percival merely says yes. Lancelot, presumably, will listen. It is precisely my perception of the aesthetic limitations of the novel form that this is all Percival can say, but the novelist is allowed to nourish the secret hope that the reader may remember that in the legend it was only Percival and Lancelot, of all the knights, who saw the grail.[10]

In the light of this interpretation of his intention in portraying the Lancelot-Percival relationship, it would seem that in my seminar remark Percy felt that in my ignorance of the grail story I had failed to fulfill the "secret hope" he nourished that the reader of *Lancelot* will grasp the allusion to the story of the holy grail. But if I had failed to do so, it was not owing to ignorance but to the fact that my recollection of the story and Percy's were at variance. In the generally accepted legend of the knights of the Round Table only three knights are portrayed as being sufficiently pure in heart to see the grail: Galahad, Percival, and Bors. Being impure of heart, Lancelot is granted only the merest glimpse.

Percy's misremembrance of the grail legend matters substantially, I think, resulting as it did in a confusion about the perspective from which *Lancelot* unfolds. According to aesthetic logic, all the reader can know about either Lancelot or Percival is what Lancelot himself tells. In seeming to press Percival to tell him something that he does not know but needs to know, does Lancelot indicate that Percival, the messenger with authority to give him a message, hesitates to do so because the messenger (Percival) knows that the intended recipient (Lancelot) is not ready to hear it? Or is Lancelot simply posing a rhetorical question, in which he indicates that he knows about Percival's plan to perpetuate the sacramental community of family and church in some obscure country town in Alabama, that, in other words, he already knows what Percival hesitates to tell him?

Jay Tolson cites a letter Percy wrote to Shelby Foote while he was at work on

Lancelot in which Percy said that he was considering having Lancelot begin his story with the famous initial line of the *Inferno:* "Now in the middle of this journey of our life, I came to myself in a dark wood" (Tolson, 363). That he did not begin Lancelot's story this way may possibly be explained by the fact that Percy did not want to repeat a device he had used at the beginning of *Love in the Ruins.* He did provide a Dantean context for *Lancelot,* however, with another epigraph from the *Divine Comedy:*

> He sank so low that all means
> for his salvation were gone,
> except showing him the lost people.
> For this I visited the region of the dead . . .

From the vision of Purgatory in the second book of the *Divine Comedy,* these lines are spoken by Virgil, who has just conducted the poet through the regions of hell to the lower slope of the mountain of Purgatory, from whence he will conduct him to the mountaintop—where he will yield his guidance to Beatrice for the indescribable journey beyond. As employed by Percy, the lines signal a degree of hope for Lancelot.

Yet at the end of the novel we may doubt that Lancelot has gone through a purgatorial experience, or that he has even reached this stage in the Dantean drama of damnation and salvation. Inaugurating his confessional account of "the adventures of a bad Catholic near the end of the world" in *Love in the Ruins,* Thomas More says: "Now in these dread days of the old violent beloved U.S.A. and of the Christ-forgetting, Christ-haunted world I came to myself in a grove of young pines and the question came to me, has it happened at last?" When he abandoned the idea of having Lancelot begin his story with a reference to the *Inferno,* Percy may have done so for a more subtle reason than repeating a device he had already used. *Love in the Ruins* is told by a protagonist who has the possibility of "coming to himself." Although he struggled against the realization, Percy knew, even as he struggled against knowing this, that in *Lancelot* he had created a story told by a protagonist who has little or perhaps no possibility of coming to himself.

And does not this indicate that the relation of Dante to *Lancelot* is more significant than the relation of Dante to *Love in the Ruins?* Living in political exile and writing in his native language an epic summation of the meaning of human existence as this had developed during the centuries of the rise of Christendom, Dante became the prime figure in the alienation of literary language from the universal language of this dominion, and in this sense he became the archetypal figure in the history of Western literature of the alienated artist. In enacting his role in the *Divine Comedy*, Dante prefigured countless images of the modern literary artist as heroic "outsider," including, six centuries later, Walker Percy's ironic image of himself in the guise of Lancelot Andrewes Lamar, who envisions a radical opportunity to create a new language by communicating with a catatonic woman in the cell next to his.

Believing more and more that he lived during the final stage of the dissolution of the world of Christendom—at the utter end of modernity, or, if you prefer, at the beginning of "postmodernity"—Percy was engaged much of his life in writing the drama of the ending of what he called "the old modern world." Sharing with all modern Western writers—Joyce, Pound, Eliot, Mann, Faulkner, et al.—the classical-Hebraic-Christian tradition, Percy was possessed by an epochal sense of the desolating historical loss of this tradition. But unlike Eliot in *The Waste Land,* or even Joyce in *Ulysses,* he did not share in the illusion of the possibility of the recovery of tradition through its expression in a language that essentially represented a revised version of the old one. "Shakespeare had it easy," he wrote to Shelby Foote in 1973. "He had the language, a new language busting out all around him, and he didn't have to make up stories; the stories were around him too." But the situation facing the contemporary—the postmodern—writer is truly radical (as Joyce had later indicated in *Finnegans Wake*). "We have to do it *all*, including the impossible or all but impossible: make up a language as you go along. All you have to do to be a good novelist is to be like God on the first day."

In creating his stories Faulkner says he "listened to the voices"—and, as we know, like Shakespeare, he listened to a variety of voices. Percy listened more selectively; and in *Lancelot* he gives the impression of having listened only to two voices: that of Lancelot and that of Lancelot's friend, Percival. Yet is not this impression misleading? Lancelot's monologue begins with his invitation to Percival: "Come into my cell. Make yourself at home." According to the logic of the authorial point of view thus established, the reader can know what Percival says only through Lancelot's report. Yet the author identifies himself not only with Lancelot but with Percival, suggesting that Percival bears a relation to the history of the Percy family and even to the author's personal history. Percy himself once referred to Percival—who upon his ordination to the priesthood had taken the name John, the prophet who wandered in the wilderness foretelling the coming of Jesus—as "the rather shadowy priest, kind of a mirror image of Lancelot" (*Conversations*, 281). And, we take it, Lancelot is a kind of mirror image of Walker Percy? According to the inner logic of the narrative point of view in *Lancelot*—a logic not entirely comprehended (or else deliberately ignored) by the author of the novel?—the reader encounters Percival, or Father John, only as Lancelot presents him. We may well take Lancelot's confession to a priest whom he conceives as his "mirror image" as representing a confession to, as Tolson puts it, a "counter-self." May we not, therefore, take *Lancelot* to be a representation of the inner drama of Percy's midlife crisis of vocation—a symbolic portrayal of the fearful task inherent in the intensively subjective obligation of the modern artist to authenticate his existence by depicting his only possible world, the world he mirrors in himself? If, in addition to the mirror images of Lancelot and Percival we add Father John, do we not have a three-dimensional image of Percy?

Such a conception of the inner drama of *Lancelot* is supported, I think, by the assignment Percy accepted from *Esquire* magazine in the same year the novel was published. This was to perform a literary stunt, an interview with himself. Essentially a coda to *Lancelot*, Percy's self-interview, entitled "Questions They Never Asked Me So He Asked Them Himself," is, as Tolson says, a tour de force, comparable to Kierkegaard's "ironic and unsettling" *Point of View for My Work as an Author*. It reveals "something that no interviewer had ever managed to reach, the persona of the artist"; and in his persona as artist Percy turns out to be "a much less sweet and agreeable figure" than he had heretofore appeared to be in the numerous interviews he had granted—"fiercer, more smart-ass, far more troubling, and in certain ways, more honest." The climax of the self-interview occurs when the author asks himself about the meaning of a painting that hangs over the fireplace in his living room. By Lyn Hill, an artist friend of Percy's, the painting depicts Percy, in his own words, as a "not attractive" fellow standing "cold-eyed and sardonic," "mean as a yard dog," in front of what resembles a "bombed out . . . place after the end of the world." This fellow seems, Percy says, to be asking the viewer of the picture: *"You and I know something, don't we? Or do we? . . . True, this is a strange world I'm in, but what about the world you're in? Have you noticed it lately? Are we on to something, you and I? Probably not."*

According to the author's interpretation, the figure in the portrait, comprising "a kind of composite of the protagonists of my novels, but most especially Lancelot," invites the viewer of the painting to "look at the apocalyptic world" behind him.

> Something is going on . . . The dead blasted tree is undergoing a transformation. Into—? Into what? A bound figure? Figures? A woman? Lovers? The no-man's-land barbed wire is not really a wire but a brier and it is blooming! A rose! Behind him there is a window of sorts, an opening out of his dark world onto a lovely seascape/skyscape. A new world! Yet he goes on looking straight at the viewer, challenging him: *Yes, I know about it, but do you? If you do, well and good. If you don't, there's no use in my telling you or turning around and pointing it out.* There's a limit to what writers can tell readers and artists can tell viewers. Perhaps he is Lancelot with the world and his life in ruins around him, but there is a prospect of a new world in the Shenandoah Valley. There was something wrong with the old world, the old things, the old way of seeing them. They were used up. They have to be seen anew. Here is a new sky, a new sea, a new rose . . .

At the end of the self-interview Percy (or Lancelot-Percival-Percy?) explains the meaning of the painting in "Kierkegaardian terms":

> I see the painting as depicting the very beginning of the Kierkegaardian stages of life—which can apply to an individual, people, an age. It is the dawn of the aesthetic stage, the emergence of life from death, of light from darkness, the first utterance of words between people. The desert is just beginning to flower and there is the possibility that there may be survivors after the catastrophe. He, somewhat sardonic and smart-assed as usual, knows it but does not want to give the secret away too easily. So he keeps his own counsel, except for the faintest glimmer in his eye—of risibility, even hope?—which says to the viewer: *I doubt if you know what's going on, but then again you just might. Do you?*
> Do you understand?
> *No.*

Like the portentous "Yes" at the end of *Lancelot*, the portentous "No" is left hanging in the air at the end of Percy's self-interview.

About the time he completed the first draft of *Lancelot*, something over a year before the novel was published, Percy acknowledged my imposition on him of still another venture in literary interpretation. But this time he startled me by responding as though in reading what I had written something had happened to him comparable to what always happened to me when I read him, something more than a mere transfer of energy from the page to the eye. The piece I had sent him is called "Faulkner and the Legend of the Artist." I had put some extra sweat into composing it. Focused on Quentin Compson (in *The Sound and the Fury* and *Absalom, Absalom!*) as a symbol of the literary artist, my reflections on this theme show, I suppose, a rather strong Freudian bias in that I see Quentin's symbolic meaning as an artist as inextricably tied to his relationship with the rebellious and doomed Caddy. In this relationship, I argue, "the response of sexuality to the forces of history" is evident in the way in which Quentin reveals how in trying to save Caddy, "the frail doomed vessel" of his family's honor, he "yields his vain, self-created myth of himself as savior to implacable historical imperatives" and dies a suicide. Concerning my interpretation of Quentin, Walker wrote:

> Last night I read "Faulkner and the Legend of the Artist" with growing excitement. You can only understand my feeling if you get around to reading my most recent fictional effusion *Lancelot,* i.e., the incapacity of the post-modern consciousness to deal with sexuality. I hadn't thought of it in such explicit terms, however—and am grateful for your analysis.

I was intrigued, and of course flattered, to see that my effort to deal with Quentin's motives struck Walker as the formulation of a "major theme" in a new novel I had not yet seen—as a matter of fact, knew nothing about at the time I wrote the Faulkner essay. I was even more intrigued when I read *Lancelot* and found that in my exploration of sexuality in Faulkner I had indeed anticipated the theme that is graphically expressed when Lancelot tells Percival about his quest for "a true sin."

> Look across the street. Do you see that girl's Volkswagen's bumper sticker: Make Love Not War. That is certainly the motto of the age. Is anything wrong with it?
> Yes. Could it be possible that since the greatest good is to be found in love, so is the greatest evil. Evil, sin, if it exists, must be incommensurate

with everything else. Didn't one of your saints say that the entire universe in all its goodness is not worth the cost of a single sin? Sin is incommensurate, right? There is only one kind of behavior which is incommensurate with anything whatever, in both its infinite good and its infinite evil. That is sexual behavior. The orgasm is the only earthly infinity. Therefore it is either an infinite good or an infinite evil.

My quest is for a true sin—was there such a thing? Sexual sin was the unholy grail I sought. (*Lancelot*, 139–40)

There was another comment in Walker's letter about the coincidental relation of my Faulkner study to *Lancelot* that struck me forcibly when I did read the novel. I refer to the concluding sentence of his letter: "Having turned 60, I feel like 20—only in the sense of making a beginning in the task you speak of, the endless task of creating oneself and a world from the poor makings of the bloody, 'rootless ego.'" It was a little puzzling. For one thing, Walker's birthday had occurred six months before he wrote to me. For another, in referring to the dark and desperate "task of creating oneself and a world from . . . the bloody, 'rootless ego,'" Walker made a more explicit connection between my interpretation of Quentin as a persona of Faulkner the artist and his own feeling about his authorial relation to his Lancelot Lamar than I had made.

What had happened to the writer who in "The Delta Factor" had likened himself to Kierkegaard's "knight of faith" in *Fear and Trembling*; what had befallen the writer who, having discovered the triadic breakthrough, had dedicated himself to blazing "trails . . . into the dark forest," his "only tool the Delta blade of the symbolic breakthrough, Helen's magic Excalibur which she found in Alabama water"? Even in the joyful moment of writing "The Delta Factor," when he had assumed the role of the knight of faith and declared his allegiance to the exquisite blade of Excalibur, Percy, it would appear, had been haunted by the fearful awareness of a counterallegiance to the bloody broadsword brandished by the "ruthless, bloody ego."

Six years after the publication of *Lancelot* one of Percy's interviewers referred to John Gardner's criticism of the novel for its failure to make a conclusive moral statement. Percy commented:

He [Gardner] thinks that art should be edifying, and that's not bad—edifying in the best sense. But I would agree with Kierkegaard there; he would say that art functions at the aesthetic level. Let's face it. We're limited. The most we could hope to do as artists, and that's what a writer is or what he hopes to be, is to point out certain home truths. Faulkner said it too. He called it "the motions of the human heart"—to say how it is, how it is to be alive and how we find ourselves and what's there. Kierkegaard said himself—he said, "I'm not an apostle." In the aesthetic phase you can talk about how it is to be on an island, see how it is in a certain time and a certain place in a certain culture, even a Christian culture, but what you can't do is speak with the authority of an apostle. That's what Kierkegaard would say. He said himself, " I do not have the authority to tell you that God came into history and that therefore you should believe in Him." Now that's not for me to say. That's not for the novelist to say. The novelist can say how it is for a man in a certain state whether he's Christian or non-Christian or whatever—sinful, always sinful. But Gardner, I think, is confusing the aesthetic and the religious stage, at least in my mind. Maybe he can do it, but I can't. That's why the main criticism of my novels is that they all end indecisively, which is very deliberate. They'd be in big trouble if they ended decisively. (*Conversations*, 279–80)

Tailoring his characters to conform to the conventional, unexamined expectations of his reader, Percy said, a novelist fails to afford the reader the instructive opportunity to "recognize the outsider in himself, and to identify with the alienated values" of his characters. The novelist must aim "to design" a novel so that "it will cross the reader's mind to question the, quote, 'normal culture,' and to value his own state of disorientation." But if he is to effect such a design—if the novelist is to bring the reader to the realization that his own condition is like that of the spiritually disoriented characters in a fiction—he must first recognize his own state of spiritual disarray. The novelist's success in doing this, to speak in terms other than Percy's, depends on his capacity to distinguish between the role of the artist and the role of the priest.

In the post-Reformation, post-Enlightenment West, Percy says, following Kierkegaard, there occurred a movement from an aesthetic to an ethical to a religious stage. In "Questions They Never Asked Me," Percy envisions "the emergence of life from death, of light from darkness, and the first utterance of words between people" after the catastrophic end of the present world. But he does not envision the rebirth of life in the new aesthetic stage as being a self-contained phenomenon. It is continuous with the emergence of the ethical and religious stages. Percy, in other words, interprets Kierkegaard's idea of the aesthetic stage in relation to Hegel's conception of the sacralization of the secular that attends the secularization of arts and learning in the declining age of Christendom, when society fell off in its ethical and religious character; when, with the loss of the sustaining vision of genuine faith, aesthetic interpretation tended to become self-gratifying compensation for this loss, and so became "aesthetic damnation."

Percy had registered his sensitivity to the Kierkegaardian schema in his protagonists in *The Moviegoer, The Last Gentleman,* and *Love in the Ruins:* Binx Bolling, Will Barrett, and Thomas More. The motives of this trio may be explained by the author's depiction of their intersubjective relationships with other characters, but the narrator of *Lancelot* implies the dire possibility that his "aesthetic damnation" is inherent in such relationships (*Conversations* 113–14).

In *Lancelot* there are only two characters, and one (Percival) is the creation of the other (Lancelot). Lest he subvert the aesthetic integrity of this relationship, Percy could not allow Percival to speak save through Lancelot's report of what Percival says. In a *Paris Review* interview Percy would have it that at some time in the future under the influence of his old friend Percival—once a "bad" Catholic and now a priest—will experience the grace of God. Yet Percival, the priest, the messenger, the one who has the authority to bring the good news, is, Percy says, a "mirror image" of Lancelot, a moral monster, who has confessed to a calculated and horrendous murder, for which he suffers no sense of remorse. Does Lancelot's relation to Percival imply that ironically Percival is a repressed image of Lancelot's forlorn desire to be a knight in shining armor?

Ernest Hemingway said, "A writer should be of as great probity and honesty as a priest of God," identifying the artist as a priest whose vocation is to serve as the messenger of the sacred truth of Art. Joyce went further when he had Stephen Dedalus describe the artist as the supreme outsider: Having attained the ultimate "aesthetic distance" from his work—reposing above it, paring his fingernails—the Joycean artist is God.

"One of us is wrong," Lancelot declares to Percival. "It will be your way or it will be my way." Percival, according to Lancelot, says "*Yes,*" and that is all (*Lancelot,* 257). Is Lancelot saying that he knows that it will either be Percival's way, the way of the duly appointed messenger of the Judaic-Christian God; or Lancelot's way, the way of the secular artist as the self-appointed messenger of Art, which is to say, the way of the unrestrained, ruthless ego of the secular artist, the way of "aesthetic damnation"?

May we not take Lancelot-Percival-Percy to be the embodiment of a submerged, indeterminate tension evident in all of Percy's novels between the Christian novelist as secular-spiritual artist and the Christian novelist as secular-spiritual priest? Are we left to draw the conclusion that Lancelot's monologue represents an ironic confession by a highly self-conscious Christian novelist, who knows that, in his very rejection of the sacralized role of the twentieth-century novelist, he indubitably assumes this role? Is Lancelot's monologue a confession of the monstrous sin he recognized in his own struggle with the ruthless, bloody ego of the artist: the desire—Percy was taken with Allen Tate's use of the term "angelism" to describe it—to assume the role of God, or of God's avenging angel?

One of the fundamentally illuminating facets of the story of Percy's search for vocation is his relationship with his lifelong friend Shelby Foote. Percy apparently made no definite commitment to writing until 1948, when after settling in the Vieux Carré of New Orleans with his bride, Mary Bernice Townsend ("Bunt"), he, together with Bunt, was confirmed in the Catholic faith. Meanwhile, Shelby—his own commitment to the novelistic vocation never in doubt from his high school days on—had served a largely self-directed and self-disciplined but strenuous literary apprenticeship, which included close attention to the great modern novelists—Dostoyevsky, James, Joyce, Mann, and, most notably, Proust—"always Proust, who may just be the top knocker of them all aside from Shakespeare." Proust's "subject is a great one," he said to Percy, "the discovery of a hidden vocation. Art hunted him down like the hound of heaven and found him in the end." Now, indelibly marked by the tenets of "High Modernism," Foote was on the verge of a novelistic career that would soon be inaugurated by the publication of four novels in four successive years. All of these attracted attention, and at least one, a story about the Civil War called *Shiloh* (1952), won high praise.

Buoyed by his success, Foote felt fully qualified to counsel Percy as he began a belated effort to make himself into a novelist. The central theme of his counsel was the warning that art and religion must not be mixed. In 1946 when Percy first mentioned to Foote that he was thinking about becoming a Roman Catholic, Foote had warned his friend this could only mean he was now "in full intellectual retreat." Learning of his confirmation in the Church, Shelby told Walker, who had by this time begun tentative work on a never-to-be-published apprentice novel called "The Charterhouse," that at the very outset of his career as a novelist he had virtually destroyed "the possibility of becoming one of the great ones." No "good practicing Catholic can ever be a great artist," Foote said. "Art is by definition a product of doubt; it has to be pursued."

> I didnt think God would be hard on writers [Foote observed further in this letter of November 19, 1949]. We are the outriders for the saints; we go beyond (where they wont go) and tell them what we've found. If we burn for that, we'll take pride in our burning, our pain; the triumph wont be God's.
>
> All your dogma contradicts Proust's dictum: "Respect the natural movement of your thoughts." That is the secret of originality; it's so seldom done. And dont say it's simply Rousseau all over again—Proust is about as far removed from Rousseau as you are. . . .
>
> Of course with you it was simple. You rejected art. But how about those like myself, for whom rejection of art would be a rejection of life. You think God put us here as he put the devils? You think he gave us man's form and man's soul, and then merely the choice between two things, sin or suicide? I say again, the triumph wont be God's, not even by God's own standards.

At the end of his letter Foote softened his eloquent judgment of his friend's literary motives. A "little fret," he said, "brought on by anxiety" about one of his own novels in progress. But Foote meant what he had said and continued to admonish Percy over the years, at times severely, for in effect rejecting the pursuit of art in favor of the pursuit of God. Although his attitude toward his friend's writing became more complex, and more understanding, as time went on, Foote felt Percy harbored the wrong-headed notion that "the novelist is some kind of exalted pamphleteer," who thinks that fiction is simply a more attractive way than the essay to offer instruction about the moral and spiritual plight of modern man. Admitting that he admired "the Catholic religion for its unwillingness to compromise and its essentially realistic outlook," Foote nonetheless advised Percy that ever since *The Divine Comedy* the distinctive value of Catholicism had been undercut by "Catholic intellectuals," adding with self-conscious pomposity, "Thou shalt have no other gods before you, is a dictum of art, and whoever departs from this [citing contemporary novelist Graham Greene whom Foote disliked and Percy admired] is penalized to the degree of his departure." Yet it would never be too late, Foote advised his friend, for art to find him, and as time went on he was encouraged by any evidence of the grace of art he saw working on Percy. Finally he was rewarded by the news from Percy—who by this time had written all but one of his novels—that he had undertaken a reading of *Remembrance of Things Past*. Greeting this announcement with delight (in a letter to Percy dated March 3, 1984) Foote told Percy that he himself had read the whole of *Remembrance of Things Past* eight times, urging Percy not to "be put off by any foolish notion" that the massive work seems "loose" or "undisciplined." On the contrary, it "enlarges life," while being "altogether the tightest, best-constructed and most disciplined novel I ever read. You'll think so too, if you stay with it, and most of all if you'll reread it as soon as that first reading has had time to sink in."

In the same 1977 letter to me in which Percy refers to the dominance of the ruthless ego, he made another observation of considerable significance. In my essay on Faulkner I had quoted a seemingly incidental but striking remark by the author: "Ishmael is the witness in *Moby-Dick* as I am Quentin in *The Sound and the Fury*." Ignoring the contextual meaning of Faulkner's statement in my essay, Walker expressed his gratitude for my calling his attention to it. "Your taking seriously W. F.'s dictum 'I am Quentin' serves to remind me," he said, "that there is such a community as lonely artists—so lonely that one often forgets and needs to be reminded." I was not precisely sure what he was talking about, although obviously Walker was envisaging a sense of community he felt with the Faulkner who in his feeling of isolation as an artist had identified himself with his fictional creation, Quentin Compson III; and as Melville, according to Faulkner, seventy-five years before the creation of Quentin, had identified himself with Ishmael, his fictional narrator.

Was Percy saying: As Faulkner is Quentin in *The Sound and the Fury* and *Absalom, Absalom!* I am Lancelot in *Lancelot*? Percy's response to such a question would have been no. The most explicit identification he seems to have made between himself and one of his characters is with Binx Bolling, who, he said, "is Quentin Compson who didn't kill himself." Characters in southern fiction are usually looking back, but Percy explains,

> my character [Binx] is looking in the other direction; he's not looking back. And that's why I have always felt more akin to Faulkner's Quentin Comp-

son than to anybody else in his fiction because he's trying to get away from it. He is sick of time, because time means the past and history. So he tears the hands off his watch. He's wandering around this godforsaken Boston suburb, and the last place he wants to go is back to Mississippi, to time and history.... So, I suppose, I would like to think of starting with the Quentin Compson who *didn't* commit suicide. Suicide is easy. Keeping Quentin Compson alive is something else. In a way Binx Bolling is Quentin Compson who didn't commit suicide. (*Conversations*, 299–300)

Percy would seem to have imagined a Quentin his creator could not have imagined—a Quentin who in some improbable way, refusing instead of seeking his doom, loosed the implacable bonds of history and found his way into a world where he had been before, that of ordinary Wednesday afternoons. But Percy also imagined Lancelot Andrewes Lamar, and felt a certain identity with this doom-seeking southerner, who failed so spectacularly in his attempted apocalyptic suicide.

It is of some significance, I would think, that around the time Walker read my take on Faulkner, he wrote "Community," a loose poetic comment about how consoling it had been for him to find "a community of like-minded people outside the environment of the family." He referred to his participation in the luncheon meetings of a varying group of visual artists and writers who, calling themselves "The Sons and Daughters of the Apocalypse," for several years met weekly at Bechac's, a well-known restaurant in Mandeville. I quote the final lines.

> Now comes the artist to his life's surprise—
> A fond abstract middle-aged public man he....
> [Who] trafficked in loneliness, little brother, cell-mate
> And friend to him, and even turned to good use,
> A commodity, a good businessman selling solitariness
> Like GM selling Chevrolets or Burns furniture....
>
> Now comes the surprise—...
> But what a surprise!
> Twenty years of solitariness and success at solitariness,
> Solitary with his family like the Swiss family on their island
> Then all at once community.

Community? What friends out there in the world?
Yes.

The final word in the poem, it may be, is an ironic echo of the final word in *Lancelot*, the novel Percy was completing in its first draft at the time he wrote the poem.

"For a writer to reenter the world he has written about is no small feat" (*Lost*, 144). It is not the least irony of his career that Percy found an alleviation of his loneliness in contemplating, and in a sense sharing in, what he termed in his arresting essay on Melville the "ineffable sociability" sometimes shared by writers. Having transcended the world through their art and unable to accomplish the feat of reentry, there is the possibility that, like a Hawthorne or a Melville, they can find solace in their community with others in the same plight. If we can say that Quentin and Ishmael are symbols of the literary artist as "world-historical neurotics" (to adapt a term from Peter Gay I have more than once appealed to in other places), we lend credence to the supposition that in conceiving the relationship between Lancelot Andrewes Lamar and Percival, Percy had imagined a symbolic communion of world-historical literary aliens; and that in depicting their relationship Percy had, like Faulkner in contemplating his relationship with Ishmael and Melville, found a measure of comfort.

Yet, it would seem, in no truly reassuring sense. Faulkner, like Proust, assumed (as Proust's disciple and Walker's closest friend Shelby Foote assumed) that worthy modern, or postmodern, literary artists, however withdrawn they may appear to be as individuals, are members of the cosmopolitan republic of letters that came into being with the end of the Republic of Christ, and was in fact often seen as an opposing republic. Unlike Foote, a self-consciously committed Christian writer like Percy felt no easy rapport with this secular community. There is, one senses, a certain pathos in Percy's seeking on the one hand to discover community with other writers while on the other seeking community in an association with the Benedictine Order.

We may speculate with some assurance that Percy marked a second, more decisive climax in his career when, ten years after he had published "The Antimony of the Scientific Method," he referred to his career in "Notes for a Novel about the End of the World" as being not that of a modern Christian artist but a *postmodern* Christian artist. The significance of "Notes for a Novel about the End of the World" is enhanced when we read it in the light of a letter Patrick Samway quotes from Percy's fellow convert to Catholicism, Caroline Gordon, who in 1951, having just read the manuscript of "The Charterhouse," wrote to Percy: "You have an enormous—an incalculable advantage—over most people writing today; you know what it is all about.... When one is writing out of the Protestant *mystique*, which is what everybody who isn't a Catholic is doing—even the Communists, I think—one has the responsibility of setting up a new heaven and a new earth as one goes." It is different with a Catholic, who "knows that God has already created the universe and that his job is to find his proper place in it."[11] But Percy, like the Protestant Kierkegaard, obviously never accepted such a comfortable view of what it is all about and was constantly drawn toward the possibility of an apocalyptic ending of modern history followed by the apocalyptic beginning of a postmodern history.

Whether or not Percy completed even a first reading of Proust I don't know, but Proustian devotion to art could not have suggested to a writer with Percy's sense of the vocation a way to find his "proper place" in the universe. Envisioning the modes of human existence, Kierkegaard had recognized what happened to the literary artist in the modern cultural situation when the clear distinction between the secular and the sacred was lost in the sacralization of the secular. If the literary artist felt committed to religious tradition, he experienced a troubling tension between obedience to the declining sacramental authority vested in the priesthood of the Church and the loss of authority represented by the notion of "a secular-spiritual" priesthood of art, although Percy's career is a muted version of this tension in comparison to that offered by the careers of Joyce and Eliot.

Ralph Wood has said that Percy's novels constitute a "comedy of redemption." Looking back over Walker's career, I am inclined to think that *Lancelot* is the key work in this comedy. Like Eliot's *The Waste Land*, it is a confessional monologue, a deeply personal emanation from the crisis of vocation experienced by the modern writer who feels himself in the grip of the sense of apocalyptic alienation from the society about him. This sense permeates Percy's first four novels and reaches climactic expression in *Lancelot*. But unlike the resolution of Eliot's struggle for spiritual identity set forth in his climactic poem *The Waste Land*, the resolution of Percy's struggle for spiritual identity is uncertain, even enigmatic.

Some readers believe that Percy made an effective resolution of the crisis in his fifth novel, *The Second Coming*. Percy himself wanted to believe this, declaring that for *The Second Coming* he would make "only one small, single modest claim": it is the "first unalienated novel since *War and Peace*."

During a visit Charles East and I had with Walker in his home in Covington a few months after the publication of *Lancelot*, I had been silently debating whether or not to ask if he had plans for another novel, when he suddenly began to talk about having begun a story based on an actual incident. This was the unexpected appearance at his door in Covington one day of an old UNC fraternity brother, who one ordinary Sunday morning in North Carolina had suddenly become amnesiac and had come to himself several hundred miles later in the Greyhound Bus terminal in New Orleans. In spite of his confusion, he remembered that Walker lived across Lake Pontchartrain in Covington, and he was able to make his way to Walker's door in search of help. *The Second Coming* appeared three years later. In this story, a middle-aged Will Barrett, having survived the crisis of identity described in *The Last Gentleman,* has become a respectable golf-playing, upper-middle-class citizen. His temporary amnesia is the symptom of a second crisis, this of midlife despair. Becoming "a good Southern Episcopal Jacob—the Jacob who wanted God to show Himself, who wrestled with Him for an answer," Will again survives.

But in depicting Will Barrett's wrestling match with God in *The Second Coming* did Walker Percy resolve his own indeterminate wrestling match with God as depicted in *Lancelot*? One difficulty with *The Second Coming* is that the reader may have considerable trouble believing that Percy is convinced that in his love for Allie Will Barrett truly represents a transcendent as opposed to a sentimental resolution of his sense of despair. One may feel, on the contrary, that in *The Second Coming* Percy undercuts the depth and complexity of the search described in his prior novels for a saving sense of the literary vocation in a post-Christian world.

Percy's complex sense of the writer's alienation is reflected not only in his response to the vocation of the writer symbolized by Kierkegaard, but by his attention to the literary vocation symbolized by Nietzsche, to whom Percy appeals in the book that followed *The Second Coming*. According to the jacket blurb, a "provocative, funny, infuriating, and engaging" book that "may not change your life . . . but will probably blow your mind," *Lost in the Cosmos: The Last Self-Help Book* is usually labeled as nonfiction. It may be more accurately described as an elaborate "nonfictional-fictional" monologue, in which the author, assuming the role of "you," addresses demanding, at times inquisitorial questions—not only to you the reader but to the questioner, or the author himself—about "the peculiar status of the self, your self, and other selves" and "what to do with your self" and other selves "in these the last years of the twentieth century." The book flaunts a Nietzschean epigraph: "We are unknown, we knowers, to ourselves. . . . Of necessity we remain strangers to ourselves . . . each of us holds good to all eternity the motto, 'Each is the farthest away from himself'—as far as ourselves are concerned we are not knowers." After the first edition of *Lost in the Cosmos* was published, the author softened its stark epigraph by adding a supplemental one, St. Augustine's prayer, "God, give us the power to know ourselves." If invoking Augustine's plea alleviates the informing situation in *Lost in the Cosmos*—the plight of the self of the artist *in extremis* as embodied in the postmodern writer—it does so through invoking the saving power of "a semiotics of the self." Indeed Percy intended for *Lost in the Cosmos* specifically to suggest that the "scientific theory" of semiotics offers the means of the salvation of the dying secular-spiritual self.

Even before the publication of *The Message in the Bottle* (1975), the notion of eventually writing the book every writer dreams of writing, his "big one," had got a strong hold on Percy. The big one would not be the fabled "Great American Novel." (Percy had not even published a novel when he began to talk about the big one.) This would be a work primarily inspired by the theoretical approach to the understanding of language developed by various language theorists, including the one Percy was most attracted to, Charles Sanders Peirce. A brilliant, eccentric American philosopher-scientist, in the 1880s Peirce had advanced a theory of human communication based on the conception that it is achieved through the triadic interaction of sign, referent, and interpreter. He had named the science he founded on this theory "semeiotics" (Peirce preferred this spelling of the term). Based on semiotics, Percy's "big one" would be a major philosophical work devoted to the establishment of a theory that would definitively dispose of the Cartesian dilemma about man's knowledge of his own existence by expounding the proposition that "a theory of language is a theory of man." In the course of its exposition, the "Peirce-Percy theory" would provide an "anthropological model of man based on a semiotical model." Demonstrating that man, so far as it is known, is the only "sign-using creature" in the universe, the Peirce-Percy theory would become the basis of a revolutionary study of "self and consciousness as derivatives of the sign-function." In its total implications, Percy predicted, the work he envisioned would be nothing less than a "new" *Novum Organum* (*Conversations*, 178).

As time went on Percy's success as a novelist and his relative unsuccess as a semiotician did nothing to alter his determination to make his big one a treatise on semiotics. In this respect Patrick Samway's biographical account of Percy's continuous pursuit of linguistic theorizing is particularly illuminating in its description of Percy's friendship with a leading student of Peirce, Kenneth Laine Ketner. Yet, although Samway argues that in the years when Percy was writing *Love in the Ruins, Lancelot, The Second Coming,* and *The Thanatos Syndrome,* Peirce became a relatively greater influence on the shaping of his philosophical *ars poetica* than Kierkegaard, he tends to slight somewhat the significance of *Lost in the Cosmos,* the book most directly related to Percy's interest in semiotics. I am thinking of Samway's inattention to a 1981 interview in which Percy first announced (so far as I know) that he had in progress a singularly audacious work on language he was going to call *Novum Organum.* In contrast to contemporary technology—"which understands the interaction between things and things, and things and organisms, but . . . has nothing whatever to say about what it means to be a human being, to find oneself in human predicaments"—this work, Percy told the interviewer, would advance the tenets of a radically "new science" based on "the semiotics of the self."

Percy wasn't joking, though what came forth is considerably less grand than a "new" *Novum Organum.* A more or less unclassifiable nonfiction-fiction, *Lost in the Cosmos* presents itself as an elaborate, sophisticated spoof of the conventional self-help book. In a deeper sense it is a provocative parody of Carl Sagan's best-selling "splendid picture book, *Cosmos,*" which, as Samway says, is in its way another popular self-help book. But Percy regarded his treatment of Sagan as more than parody; as being but one aspect of a book that altogether is a more significant "short history of the Cosmos" than Sagan's. And if he had not fully succeeded in accomplishing his goal in writing *Lost in the Cosmos,* Percy thought that he had succeeded in setting forth the basis of a not only post-Christian but post-Baconian reconceptualization of the nature and meaning of man.

Advancing "a semiotic theory of the self," which holds that man is the sole "alien creature, as far as we know, in the entire Cosmos," Percy observes in sum that while the self of the scientist ignores its alienation in the universe and the self of the sculptor-artist or painter-artist merely recognizes it, the "writer-artist" not only truly apprehends the self's singularly alienated condition but comprehends that the self of the writer-artist is the ultimate representation of the self's alienation, not only from the world (the earth) but from the cosmos. While at the commencement of the Baconian age Shakespeare could still think of human existence as a drama enacted by individual human beings enacting their divinely assigned roles on the stage of the world—and five centuries later he himself might still appeal to the image of man enacting the role of the pilgrim on this stage—Percy knew that this image is hardly congruent with the actuality of the modern self's situation. Seeking to define its role, the modern self wanders about alone on a cosmic stage of inconceivable dimensions.

Percy proclaims a breakthrough in his effort to apprehend the place of the individual self on the cosmic stage in the section he considered to be the heart of *Lost in the Cosmos*. An "intermezzo of some forty pages," this is a primer on the semiotics of the self, or an "elementary semiotical grounding of self." "If I am remembered for anything a hundred years from now," Percy declares, "it will probably be for this."

> The thesis is radical and the evidence is there. The thesis is nothing less than a semiotical account of the emergence of man in all his contrarieties from the collision of atoms in the Cosmos and the interaction of organisms—something that evolutionists have failed to do and the religionists have copped out on by placing it all on God, a sure enough *deus ex machina*. (*Conversations*, 285)

Percy seems to have taken little or no comfort in the advantage of the Catholic writer envisioned by Caroline Gordon. How could he, when, as he says in "Notes for a Novel about the End of the World," the "psychical forces . . . released in the postmodern consciousness open unlimited possibilities for both destruction and liberation, for an absolute loneliness or a rediscovery of community and reconciliation"? The question for Percy was whether to accept his absolute loneliness or to engage in a struggle to rediscover the possibility of his participation in "community and reconciliation."

In his first three novels and in *The Message in the Bottle* Percy had conceived of beginning the search for community and reconciliation by representing "a man in a very concrete place and time" *coming to himself* in somewhat the same sense as "Robinson Crusoe came to himself on his island after his shipwreck" by responding to his sense of "wonder and curiosity." Percy had returned to this conception in *The Second Coming*. But by the time he published *Lost in the Cosmos*—a work that may well strike us as an even stranger mélange than *Either/Or*, being about "The Strange Case of the Self, your Self, the Ghost which Haunts the Cosmos; or

How you can survive in the Cosmos about which you know more and more while knowing less and less about your self, this despite 10,000 self-help books, 100,000 psycho-therapists and 100 million fundamentalist Christians"—Percy's sense of his alienation had become more extreme. He presents the question of "why it is that of all the billions and billions of strange objects in the Cosmos—novas, quasars, pulsars, black holes—you are beyond doubt the strangest." We see—and feel—Percy's sense of his personal embodiment of alienation in various ways but in no way more pointedly than in the contrast he draws between the artist as writer and the artist as painter or sculptor.

> The painter and the sculptor are the Catholics of art, the writer is the Protestant. The former have the sacramentals, the concrete intermediaries between themselves and creation—the paint, the brushes, the fruit, the bowl, the table, the model, the mountain, the handling and muscling of clay. The writer is the Protestant. He works alone in a room as bare as a Quaker meeting house and with nothing between him and his art but a Scripto pencil, like God's finger touching Adam. It is harder on the nerves.[12]

This startling metaphor of the writer as Protestant may be said to describe not only Percy's struggle to apprehend his personal situation, but the situation of all novelists and poets in the post-Christian—and we may add "post-Judaic"—world.

In his role as prophet in *Lost in the Cosmos,* Percy, speaking specifically of the "post-religious, technological society" as it exists in his own immediate time, says that the self either thinks of itself as immanent—as the consumer of the techniques, goods, and services of society—or else, appealing to the "available modes of transcendence" in his society, speaks of the self as "a member of the transcending community of science and art." Standing at a "peak period of scientific transcendence" in "a posture of objectivity" confronting a universe regarded as "a series of specimens or exemplars, and interactions, energy exchanges, and secondary causes," the "self as scientist" becomes the "prince and sovereign of the age," or, like Einstein, "the secular saint of the age" (*Lost,* 113–15).

In opposition to the conception of the scientist in the postreligious age as sovereign or saint, the prophet Percy projects a vision of the secular artist as a savior figure that is more extreme than Joyce's visionary portrait of the writer as artist.

But unlike Joyce's depiction, Percy's portrait is edged with irony, in that, although like Joyce, Percy envisions the transitory nature of the artist's transcendence, unlike Joyce he emphasizes his radical loneliness in an apartness so complete that, once he puts down his pen and seeks to return to the world he has transcended, the world of ordinary Wednesday afternoons, he discovers that to do so requires nothing less than an "assault" on the left cortex of the brain—which, citing John Carew Eccles, Percy says is the locus of consciousness. Yet the artist's

> work, if he is any good, comes from listening to his right brain, locus of the unconscious knowledge of the fit and form of things. So, unlike the artist who can fool and cajole his right brain and get it going by messing around in paints and clay and stone, the natural playground of the dreaming child self, there sits the poor writer, rigid as a stick, pencil poised, with no choice but to wait in fear and trembling until the spark jumps the commissure. (*Lost*, 147–48)

As strongly as Percy was attracted to the possibility of believing in a community that "is not the elect community of science, but the community of the artist and all who share his predicament . . . and understand his signs," he was uncertain whether his inquiries into the semiotics of the self supported this possibility or rebuked it. The chief sign the modern writer seeks, one that will authenticate his existence as a self in the age of science, Percy observes, may be undiscoverable even to the most skillful semiotician, who, as he must, becomes aware that "from the moment the signifying self [whether of the scientist or artist] turned inward and became conscious of itself trouble began as the sparks flew up."

> The fateful flaw of human semiotics is this: that of all the objects in the entire Cosmos which the sign-user can apprehend through the conjoining of signifier and signified (word uttered and thing beheld) there is one which forever escapes his comprehension—and that is the sign-user himself.
>
> Semiotically the self is literally unspeakable to itself. One cannot speak or hear a word which signifies oneself, as one can speak or hear a word signifying anything else, e.g. *apple, Canada, 7-Up.*
>
> The self of the sign-user can never be grasped, because once the self locates itself at the dead center of the world, there is no signified to which

a signifier can be joined to make a sign. The self has no sign of itself. No signifier applies. All signifiers apply equally. . . .

The signified of the self is semiotically loose and caroms around the Cosmos like an unguided missile. (*Lost*, 106–7)

Basically *Lost in the Cosmos* is a treatise on the pathology of self-consciousness—of the self's consciousness of itself—in the twentieth century. The self, searching for a sign of itself, attempts to understand itself as a "semiotic entity" or a "spiritual entity." Failing to find such a sign, the frustrated self, whether the self of the artist or the scientist, having nothing else to seek, seeks its own autonomy. Thereupon, encountering "the expanding nought" of "the self it seeks," the seeking self becomes subject to "demoniac possession." For although it may be "overtly committed to peace and love," the self "secretly" desires war and nourishes its "hatred of all other selves and perhaps of its own self most of all." Protestants, Catholics, Jews may all be obnoxious, but "none is as murderous as the autonomous self who, believing in nothing, can fall prey to ideology and kill millions of people—unwanted people, old people, sick people, useless people, unborn people, enemies of the state—and do so reasonably, without passion, even decently, certainly without the least obnoxiousness." In its fury over its "expanding" nothingness, the autonomous self, seeking its own death, may provoke a third world war; and, even if it somehow survives this cataclysm, will, in its continuing hatred of the deprivation of its meaning, seek its own extinction (*Lost*, 157, 192).

In short, in depicting the autonomous self, Percy develops the ultimate implication of the Nietzschean portrayal of the "death of God": For the past five or six centuries the autonomous self has conveyed the news of the death of God by living it, the death of God and the death of the self as spirit (or soul) being, not sequential, but simultaneous historical events. Present in Percy's writings from the beginning, his understanding—or, intuitive perception—of the Nietzschean implication becomes more explicit in *Lost in the Cosmos*, which, whatever else it may be deemed to be, is a disturbing meditation on the final phase of the death of God in the Century of the Self.

By the later 1960s Percy had come to entertain the possibility that finding his place in the created universe might have become well-nigh impossible for the postmodern novelist, even for one who subscribes deeply to the Catholic faith, unless he turns from his former task of "constructing a plot and creating a cast of characters from a world familiar to everybody" and sets forth "with a stranger [the stranger being himself] in a strange land where the signposts are enigmatic but which he sets out to explore nevertheless." To have any hope of success in his mission, the novelist must be not only accomplished in his craft; more importantly he must be able to distinguish between the often enigmatic signs in this strange land, some indicating old ways of thinking and feeling, others seeming to point the way to the discovery of a new heaven and a new earth.

But in his conflicted vision in *Lost in the Cosmos,* Percy, without explicit recognition of what he is doing, also in effect transforms his older vision of the artist-writer as wayfarer, or pilgrim, into a vision of the artist-writer as a savior figure: "the suffering servant of the age," who, through "his use of signs"—his semiotic skills—is able to identify and name, and in this sense, save the self from its predicaments in the twentieth century. This vision conveys the implication that when he is regarded as speaking not merely "to a small community of fellow artists but to the world of men who understand him," the literary artist becomes potentially "rescuer and savior" not only of other literary artists but of all his "fellow sufferers," of all, that is to say, postmodern humanity (*Lost,* 119).

One thinks of such symbols of the deification of the artist figure as Baudelaire on his knees in prayer to his mother and to Edgar Allan Poe, but extravagant gestures like these were inspired not so much from the desire to create a literary god to worship as from the impulse to discover a sense of a salvational community in the intersubjectivity of literary selves—the impulse to escape from, to paraphrase a remark by Percy, the terror of the twentieth-century disease of loneliness.

One thinks too of the secular Jewish intellectual Lionel Trilling, who was also much concerned with the ratification of the reality of the individual's existence. Trilling asked, "Why did Freud bring his intellectual life to its climax" with the "dark doctrine" espoused in *Civilization and Its Discontents* of the traumatic relationship between the self and civilization? What was his "motive in pressing upon us the ineluctability of the pain and frustration of human existence"? This question, Trilling points out, is one Nietzsche says "should guide our dealings with any systematic thinker." Freud wanted "us to look below the structure of rational formulation to discover the *will* that is hidden beneath," Trilling says; and to that question he proposed the answer that Freud, "insisting upon the essential immitigability of the human condition as determined by the nature of mind, had the intention of sustaining the authenticity of human existence that formerly had been ratified by God." Freud's purpose, Trilling says, calling on a Marxian insight, was "to keep all things from becoming 'weightless.'" In sum, according to Trilling:

"From religion as it vanished Freud was intent upon rescuing one element, the imperative actuality which religion attributed to life."

Do Percy's first two novels more nearly succeed in creating the sense of the imperative actuality of religion than the other four he wrote? Or, more nearly, do they create the sense of an imperative that is truly *lost*?

"In spite of all the emphasis on interpersonal relations, and how to get along with people, love better, and all the self-help books," Percy said in an interview with Jo Gulledge in 1984, "the fact is that people are, by and large, probably lonelier than ever."

> And one of the best things that ever happens in my novels is when the loneliness is bridged. There's a quote in the beginning of *The Last Gentleman* that talks about the end of the modern world—how the world will be stripped bare of all the old togetherness, even of love. But as it is and lonely as it is, it's going to be *honest, clean,* no bullshit, and there will actually be a possibility of one lonely person encountering another one, *really* encountering another one and perhaps even God in a way that hasn't been possible before, even in a culture which sets every value on togetherness, groups, and relationships. And that, to go back to what we were talking about earlier, is where *Lost in the Cosmos* ends up. (*Conversations*, 308)

But, although we may in some sense call *Lost in the Cosmos*, if not a novel, at least novelistic in character, this is not quite where Percy the novelist ended up. *Lost in the Cosmos* actually ends with a sentimental science-fiction fantasy about the possible cosmic intersubjectivity—the cosmic togetherness—of space aliens and earthlings. The implied intention of Percy's work is (1) to tell the story, not only in his novels but in his essays, of the secular-spiritual self's fall into inauthenticity because of the wearing out of the language in which it had been embodied for five centuries or so; and (2) to prophesy the coming of a theory of language that would provide the basis of a transcendent—a cosmic—spiritual community of modern or postmodern human selves, who, acting as individual selves, would bear testimony to the solution of the most troubling of all modern and postmodern imperatives: how to certify the authenticity of the existence of the individual human self.

If we consider *Lost in the Cosmos* rather than *The Second Coming* as the true sequel to *Lancelot*, we may interpret Percy's last novel, *The Thanatos Syndrome*, as, properly speaking, the sequel to *Lost in the Cosmos;* and as at once the most tightly constructed—the most "artistic"—of Percy's novels. Altogether, moreover—in its representation of the fate of the self of the secular-spiritual literary artist in the age of science and technology—we may interpret his final novel as at once the darkest and most hopeful of Percy's novels.

In *The Thanatos Syndrome* the narrator and chief character is the same Dr. Thomas More we have met in *Love in the Ruins*, save that he is older and on parole from the Louisiana State Penitentiary, where, following his involvement in the events described in *Love in the Ruins*, he has served two years on a drug conviction. More has decided to leave New Orleans and take up his life again in his native world, the Feliciana parishes. (Percy explains that, combining the parishes of East and West Feliciana and otherwise "scrambling" Louisiana geography in *The Thanatos Syndrome*, he refers to the world named by the Spanish, "a strip of pleasant pineland running from the Mississippi River to the Perdido.") A "curious region of a curious state"—"never quite Creole or French or Anglo-Saxon or Catholic or Baptist"—Feliciana "has served over the years as a refuge for all manner of malcontents." Here the malcontent More finds himself once again in the company of another malcontent, the alcoholic priest who also appears prominently in *Love in the Ruins*, Father Rinaldo Smith. More's account of the further career of Father Smith and his own relation to Father Smith's story is, to be sure, the moral and spiritual center of *The Thanatos Syndrome*.

But the chief events in More's story center in his discovery that the development of odd, at times sinister, behavioral patterns in the citizens of Feliciana is the result, for the most part unwittingly, of their daily ingestion of heavy sodium. This is contained in a water supply that has been drugged by the leading citizens of Feliciana as a way of promoting social harmony and happiness. The climax of More's investigation of the source of the heavy sodium occurs when he discovers that, under the influence of the drug, the teachers and administrators of the elite private school housed at Belle Ame, an antebellum plantation mansion of surpassing beauty, have converted it into an unspeakably obscene nest of pedophiles. Chief among those responsible for this is Dr. John van Dorn, the "Renaissance Man," who is the primary advocate of the therapeutic use of heavy sodium in Feliciana.

Father Smith seems to have no knowledge of the situation at Belle Ame, but

More's account of what is happening there is integrally related to his account of the confession Father Smith makes—not to a superior in the ecclesiastical order but to More, a paroled convict. The confession consists of Smith's story of his relation to the Holocaust, or, more exactly, of his retrospective interpretation of the meaning of this relation. When he was a young man of college age in the 1930s, Smith tells More, he went on a vacation trip with his father to the German university town of Tübingen, where he was introduced to his father's cousin, Dr. Hans Jäger, an eminent psychiatrist on the faculty of the University of Tübingen. Dr. Jäger gave him a copy of a book then being much discussed by German intellectuals, *The Release of the Destruction of Life Devoid of Value*. Smith also became friends with a younger cousin, Helmut Jäger, who, having just finished a period in the Hitler Jugend, had been admitted to the Junkerschule for training as a member of the Nazi SS. Helmut was already wearing "his field cap with the death's-head and his lightning-bolt shoulder patch," Father Smith recalls, when, at the end of his visit in Tübingen, he accepted a gift from Helmut: a small bayonet inscribed with the motto *Blut und Ehre*.

"So what? you seem to say," Father Smith says to More. "A valuable souvenir, the sort of Nazi artifact any G.I., any collector would be glad to have." But, he adds, "that is not my confession."

> This is my confession. If I had been German, not American, I would have joined him. . . . I would have gone to the Junkerschule, sworn the solemn oath of the Teutonic knights at Marienberg, and joined the Schutzstaffel. Listen. Do you hear me? *I would have joined him.*

He would have joined his friend Helmut, Father Smith confesses, in the slaughter of the only people with whom God has chosen to make a covenant, the only people in human history, as he puts it, who cannot "be subsumed." *The Thanatos Syndrome* reaches its moral and spiritual climax in Father Smith's recollection of a conversation he had several years later, when he returned to Germany as a lieutenant in an American army corps engaged in the liberation of the "death camps." During this time he encountered a nurse at a Nazi hospital which had served one of the camps. Smith finds out from the nurse that Dr. Jäger had been assigned to "the children's division" of this hospital. From time to time, she tells Smith, she had seen the eminent and kindly child psychiatrist enter a special room in the hospital to administer lethal doses of gas to Jewish children.

Regarded in a certain way, Percy would seem to suggest, the Holocaust was an aesthetic imperative of the Nazi passion for order; an imperative that found its ultimate culmination in the terror of the experiments by Nazi scientists carried out on other human beings, including children, whom they deemed to belong to an inferior branch of homo sapiens. In *The Thanatos Syndrome* More's account of pedophilia in Feliciana—in effect an account of the murder of traumatized schoolchildren in Audubon's happy land—is a devastatingly ironic reflection on the historical continuity of a "scientific" desire for order so compelling that a brilliant, humane, even "tender-hearted" scientist like Van Dorn becomes the leader of a conspiracy to achieve harmonious social order through the alteration by chemical means of the minds of his fellow citizens and their children. This in the same society that only a few years earlier had gone all out to destroy the Nazi power and in the name of the democratic brotherhood of man.

In this situation, Dr. Thomas More transcends his psychiatric role as analyst of the intersubjectivity of human selves. The psychiatrist who invented the lapsometer in *Love in the Ruins* emerges as a quietly heroic representative of the moral order of secularized "clerks" that had destroyed the "seamless" order of the medieval ecclesiastical community. In his encounter with a disturbed priest, who is haunted by the memory of his friendship with a German youth who had become a member of Hitler's SS, More identifies himself with Father Smith by, in a role reversal, becoming his confessor and the means of his salvation. I refer to the scene in which More restores order to the Mass when Father Smith falters in his attempt to conduct it. I would also refer to the concluding scene of the novel, when Dr. More encounters a patient who, recovered from her unwitting ingestion of heavy sodium, wants to talk to him again about a dream she has had "about being in the cellar of my grandmother's farmhouse in Vermont and the smell of winter apples and the stranger coming."

> "Do you know who the stranger is?" [Mickey LaFaye, the patient, asks Dr. More.]
>
> "Who do you think he is?"
>
> "I think the stranger is part of myself."
>
> "I see."
>
> "I am trying to tell myself something. I mean a part of me I don't really know, yet the deepest part of me, is trying to—"
>
> "Yes?"

"Could I talk about it?"

"Yes."

She falls silent, but her eyes are softer, livelier, are searching mine as if I were the mirror of her very self.

As if I were the very mirror of her very self. In his realization that the subtle transaction between analyst and patient has become a spiritual—in the scholastic sense a "real"—encounter between two lonely selves (and perhaps between these selves and God), does More come to himself as a self existing transparently before God? As usual with Percy, asking the question is more important than answering it.

My last written communication with Walker Percy was in the summer and early fall of 1988. The letters of that time carry me back to the initial essay in the present collection, "Eric Voegelin and the Story of the Clerks," which was originally written as a contribution to a 1987 symposium on Voegelin. I knew that Percy had expressed an interest in Voegelin's monumental *Order and History,* and I had intended to send him a copy of my piece right after the symposium was held. But I failed to get around to it until the following year. Meanwhile, Walker had published *The Thanatos Syndrome* and had accepted the invitation to deliver the 1987 Jefferson Lecture of the National Humanities Foundation. By then he was undergoing treatment for cancer of the prostate.

In a note accompanying my Voegelin essay I explained that, though I had been interested in Voegelin for years, this represented my only attempt "to deal at all extensively" with him. In attempting to locate Voegelin "in the tradition of the 'clerks,'" I said, "I am aware that Allen Tate is in this tradition: and I dare say that you are too—in the tradition of the good clerks, not the bad ones." Walker replied on August 21, 1988, to say that he had received the piece on Voegelin but had postponed reading it until he had recovered sufficiently from "a bout with fever." He added that he was "flattered to be called a clerk like Allen Tate." Two weeks later Walker wrote to say that, having been "laid up with one damn thing after another," he was going into the Ochsner Clinic for "more tests"; nonetheless he had "started reading 'Eric Voegelin and the Story of the Clerks,'" and was "getting a big kick out of it." He promised "more later when I finish it—maybe sitting in Ochsner's waiting room." I didn't receive this note until my wife and I had returned from a vacation trip to France and had written Walker a note about our experience. Shortly afterward a final note about the Voegelin piece arrived.

Sept. 24, 1988
Dear Lewis,

Sounds like you and Mimi had a very good French outing. One of the things of which I'm ashamed—and for which my Uncle Will would never forgive me if he knew—is that I have never seen Paris. Maybe we'll make it yet.

I am most excited by "Eric Voegelin and the Story of the Clerks"—even if I didn't understand all of it, e.g. metaxy, metastatic expectations (I know what a metastatic cancer is), noetic theophany—but that is not your fault, but V's and mine. What is exciting is the possible deep contradiction in his work. Which is to say, as I understand it, that on the one hand he seemed to take account of the incursion of God into history in his volume *Israel and History,* and on the other to shoot it down in his attack on Paul in *The Ecumenic Age.* Many thanks for sharing.

I have been tolerably well, but still annoyed by a low-grade fever, which they can't track down. I'm thinking of throwing away the thermometer (which, like Hans Castorp) I came to know as the "trouble stick."
Cordially,

But Walker was not about to throw away the trouble stick. Ever since he had read *The Magic Mountain,* a key work of one of the greatest exemplars of the novelist as modern "clerk," he had continued to take not only his own moral and spiritual temperature but the moral and spiritual temperature of his time. He was doing so, for instance, in the scene in *The Thanatos Syndrome* when Percy's persona in the novel, Dr. Thomas More, while serving his prison sentence for drug abuse, is reading a "new" history of the Battle of the Somme. In this battle, and the concurrent Battle of Verdun during the First World War, he reflects, two million young men had been slaughtered "toward no discernible end," adding, "As Dr. Freud might have said, the age of thanatos had begun."

In one of his later and most moving essays, "The Diagnostic Novel: On the Uses of Modern Fiction," Walker compares his own experience in dropping out of the profession of medicine and becoming a writer to that of another young tubercular physician, Anton Chekhov, who, though never a novelist, in creating his plays and short stories, like Percy, assumed the role of the writer as cultural pathologist. But the relation Percy felt to Chekhov was not as close as that he felt to Thomas Mann. Although none of the fiction he published is plainly imitative of Mann's most famous work, it is not surprising (as Gary M. Ciuba demonstrates in analytical detail in *Walker Percy: Books of Revelations*) that "The Grammercy Winner" (one of the two unpublished apprentice novels Walker wrote and the only one to be preserved) is a direct imitation of *The Magic Mountain*. Although the fiction that follows "The Grammercy Winner" is more sophisticated than this apprentice effort, all of it reflects the great German novelist's ambitious attempt in the story of Hans Castorp to incarnate in the novel an epochal sense of the bereft human self trying to live its life in a "rotten century," in which the "whole culture" is in "terrible trouble."

Kierkegaard, John Updike says, lives as a "man incarnated in his works," which is to say that Kierkegaard lived as a man who incarnated in his life and writings the nineteenth-century versions of the crisis of self-alienation that has marked each century since the age of Marlowe and Shakespeare. Walker Percy lived as a writer who incarnated in his life and writings the crisis of the identity of the secular-spiritual self as this crisis expressed itself after Kierkegaard, becoming the shaping force of an Age of the Self, which is concurrently an Age of Thanatos.

The "psychodrama" of Percy's incarnation of his historical time is recorded, not only in the writings for which he is largely known, his six novels, but, more explicitly, in the series of essays and meditations on language in *The Message in the Bottle,* in *Lost in the Cosmos* (which he said is an imitation of Kierkegaard's *Either/Or*), and in his final published work, "The Fateful Rift: The San Andreas Fault in the Modern Mind," the embellished title Percy gave the published version of the Jefferson lecture of 1988.

If he had lived long enough, would Percy have succeeded in propounding a theory of self and language that ensured, at least to his own satisfaction, the authenticity of a self which had so far failed to discover an authentic sign of itself? Save, that is, in a few striking instances: "There have existed, so I have heard," Percy said, "a few writers even in this day and age who have become themselves transparently before God and managed to live intact though difficult lives, e.g., Simone Weil, Martin Buber, Dietrich Bonhoeffer." And, he added, "some have even outdone Kierkegaard and seen both creation and art as the Chartres sculptor did, as both dense and mysterious, gratuitous, anagogic, and sacramental, e.g., Flannery O'Connor" (*Lost*, 157).

Walker Percy apparently never believed, or hoped to believe, that he himself belonged to the company he described.

His quest to resolve the conflict between his yearning for transcendent powers of vision in the Century of the Self (or the century of Thanatos) is exemplified in his novels and essays, which, as has been said of T. S. Eliot's poems and essays, bear the character of "confessional monologues." As such they probe the situation of a Catholic novelist who, a convert from Protestantism, was, one may suggest, in the deepest sense ironically engaged, not in creating stories and the people in them, but, under the conditions imposed by an "absolute loneliness," in trying to transcend an imperative Protestant austerity, which impelled him to seek a direct encounter not only with himself but with God. And in this encounter, with God's help, to create a whole, an authentic, self out of "the poor makings of the bloody, ruthless ego."

NOTES

1. The correspondence between Percy and Simpson can be found in the Lewis P. Simpson Papers, Hill Memorial Library, LSU.

2. Stephen Hawking, *A Brief History of Time: From the Big Bang to Black Holes* (New York: Bantam Books, 1990), 174–75.

3. "An Interview with Zoltán Abádi-Nagy," in *Walker Percy: Signposts in a Strange Land,* ed. Patrick Samway (New York: Farrar, Straus, and Giroux, 1991), 388.

4. Jay Tolson, *Pilgrim in the Ruins: A Life of Walker Percy* (New York: Simon and Schuster, 1991), 183. Subsequent citations are given in the text.

5. Walker Percy, *The Message in the Bottle* (New York: Farrar, Straus, and Giroux, 1975), 112. Subsequent citations are given in the text.

6. See Edward J. Dupuy, *Autobiography in Walker Percy: Repetition, Recovery, and Redemption* (Baton Rouge: Louisiana State University Press, 1996).

7. Lewis A. Lawson and Victor A. Kramer, eds., *Conversations with Walker Percy* (Jackson: University Press of Mississippi, 1985), 222.

8. See Kieran Quinlan, *Walker Percy: The Last Catholic Novelist* (Baton Rouge: Louisiana State University Press, 1996).

9. Percy, *Lancelot* (New York: Farrar, Straus, and Giroux, 1977), 256.

10. Abádi-Nagy interview, 386.

11. Patrick Samway, *Walker Percy: A Life* (New York: Farrar, Straus, and Giroux, 1997), 161.

12. Percy, *Lost in the Cosmos* (New York: Farrar, Straus, and Giroux, 1983), 147.

ACKNOWLEDGMENTS

The following essays originally appeared, sometimes in somewhat different form, in these publications:

"Eric Voegelin and the Story of the Clerks," in *Eric Voegelin's Significance for the Modern Mind*, ed. Ellis Sandoz (Baton Rouge: Louisiana State University Press, 1991), 71–110.

"The Betrayal of the Clerks in American Context: Benjamin Franklin and Thomas Jefferson," as "Jefferson and the Crisis of the American University," *Virginia Quarterly Review* 76 (2000): 388–402.

"Days of Faith: Malcolm Cowley and the Legend of the Fellow Travelers," as "Cowley's Odyssey: Literature and Faith in the Thirties," *Sewanee Review* 89 (1981): 520–39.

"The Poet and the Father: Robert Penn Warren and the Redemption of Thomas Jefferson," as "The Poet and the Father: Robert Penn Warren and Thomas Jefferson," *Sewanee Review* 104 (1996): 46–69.

"Lionel Trilling and Allen Tate: The Agency of Terror," *Partisan Review* 54 (1987): 18–35; first presented as a lecture at the University of Southwestern Louisiana on April 24, 1986, in honor of Professor Milton H. Rickels on the occasion of his retirement from the English faculty, under the auspices of the Flora M. Levy Endowment of the University.

"Diana Trilling: A Poetic of Cultural Politics," as "Imagining Our Time: The Vocation of Diana Trilling," in *Explorations: The Twentieth Century* 10 (2004): 1–31.

"A Charleston Jew and the Shaping Form of Memory: Louis D. Rubin, Jr.," as "Louis D. Rubin: A Charleston Jew, Boat-building, and the Shaping Form of Memory," *Southern Review*, n.s. 38 (2002): 712–22.

"The Last Agrarian: Andrew Lytle," *Southern Review*, n.s. 32 (1996): 390–402.

"Eudora Welty: The Outside of the Inside," as "The Outside of the Inside: The Vision of Time and Place in Eudora Welty," in *Place in American Fiction: Excursions and Explorations*, ed. H. L. Weatherby and George Core (Columbia: University of Missouri Press, 2004), 119–32. By permission of the University of Missouri Press. Copyright © 2004 by the Curators of the University of Missouri.

INDEX

A la recherche du temps perdu/Remembrance of Things Past (Proust), 74, 75, 230
Abádi-Nagy, Zoltán, 219
Abelard, Peter, 41
Absalom, Absalom! (Faulkner), 106, 224
Academy of Pennsylvania, 43
Adams, John, 42, 50
The Advancement of Learning (Bacon), 105
"Afterthought" to Being Here, 98–99
The Age of Reason (Sartre), 137
Agrarians, 110, 165–71
Albee, Edward, 139
Alexander, Shana, 146
Algonquin Press, 153, 158, 162
Alien and Sedition Acts, 50
All the King's Men (Warren), xiii, 90, 98, 102, 108n9, 108–9n18
American Philosophical Society, 42, 43
American Revolution, 42, 44, 61, 65, 82, 143
Anamnesis (Voegelin), 26, 31–36
"Anatomy of the World" (Donne), 37, 105, 120
And I Worked at the Writer's Trade (Cowley), 58, 64, 70–71
Anthologists, 45
Anti-communism, 129–33, 143–44. See also Communism
Anti-Semitism, 114–15. See also Jews
"The Antimony of the Scientific Method" (Percy), 232
Antiwar protests, 140–41
Arendt, Hannah, 29–30, 31
Areopagitica (Milton), 45
Aristophanes, 20
Aristotle, 20, 25, 26, 195

Armies of the Night (Mailer), 140–41
Arnold, Matthew, 111, 115, 120, 134, 137
"Art and Neurosis" (L. Trilling), 121
At Heaven's Gate (Warren), 90
Atkinson, Brooks, 160
The Auden Generation (Hynes), 131
Auden, W. H., 29, 34
Augustine, St., ix, 21, 24, 33, 235
Austen, Jane, 124–25, 126, 127
"Autobiographical Memoir" (Voegelin), 11–12

Bacon, Sir Francis, 29, 90, 105
Bacon, Roger, 7
Bak, Hans, 57
Baker, George Pierce, 165
Bakunin, Mikhail, 18
Baudelaire, Charles-Pierre, 57, 63, 120, 241
Bayle, Pierre, 27–28
"Bearded Oaks" (Warren), 106
Bedford Forrest and His Critter Company (Lytle), 166
The Beginning of the Journey (D. Trilling), 71–72, 128, 131–35, 137
Being Here (Warren), 98–99, 100
Bellow, Saul, 115, 121
Benda, Julien: on clerks, 6–10, 12, 13, 26–28, 34, 51, 150; as man of letters, 9–10; Voegelin and writings by, x, 2–3, 10–11
—works: *La fin de l'éternel*, 8–9; *La trahison des clercs*, x, 2–3, 6–8, 10, 26, 38n2, 51
Bentham, Jeremy, 18
Beyond Culture (L. Trilling), 110, 124
Bishop, John Peale, 60, 61, 111
Blackmur, R. P., 120

Blotner, Joseph, 108n9
Blue Juanita (Cowley), 57
Boats and boating, 153–58, 163–64
Bonhoeffer, Dietrich, 248
Bossuet, Jacques-Bénigne, 15
The Brazen Face of History (Simpson), 41
The Bride of the Innisfallen (Welty), 173, 179
A Brief History of Time (Hawking), 195
British Royal Academy, 42
Broch, Hermann, 3, 5–6, 34
Brooks, Cleanth, 98, 180
Brother to Dragons (Warren): and Book of Job, 88–89, 102; comparison of first and second versions of, 91–97, 103–4; and Dante's *Divina Commedia*, 102–3, 108–9n18; demonic nature of the self in, 103–5; end of, 102–3, 104, 108n17; and historical facts of murder by Jefferson's nephews, xii, 83–86, 89, 99, 100, 101, 105, 107n4; human condition in, 103, 109n19; irony in, 103, 104; Jefferson in, xii, 86, 88–89, 91–100, 103–5; Meriwether Lewis in, 86, 95–97, 100, 101, 108n13; and Minotaur myth, 95; myth versus fact in, 85–87; publication and editions of, 83; R.P.W. in, 86, 88, 92–98, 100–104; R.P.W.'s father in, 86, 97–98; second version (1979) of, 83–84, 89, 93–98, 99, 104, 108n13, 108n17; setting of, 99; theme of redemption in, 104–5; theme of self–identity in, 95; Warren's attitude toward generic form of, 87–88
The Brothers Karamazov (Dostoyevsky), 193
Brown, Larry, 158
Buber, Martin, 248
Buckminster, Rev. Joseph Stevens, 45–46
Buffon, Georges-Louis Leclerc de, 7
"Burnt Norton" (Eliot), 153
Burt, John, 107n3
Butler, Nicholas Murray, 114

Camus, Albert, 3, 34, 197, 208
"The Cannons of Kronburg" (Voegelin), 35–36

Canterbury Tales (Chaucer), 1
Carlyle, Thomas, 19, 28, 115, 118, 120
Cash, W. J., x
Catholicism: Foote on, 228–30; and Caroline Gordon, 233, 237; and Percy, xiv, 190, 196–97, 199, 208, 213–14, 228–29, 232, 240, 249; and Tate, 30, 126
Chambers, Whitaker, 132
Charleston, S.C., 153–64
"The Charterhouse" (Percy), 229, 233
Chateaubriand, François-Auguste-René de, 7
Chaucer, Geoffrey, 1
Chekhov, Anton, 194, 247
Church and State (Coleridge), 2
Cicero, 21
The Circus in the Cemetery (Simpson), xiii
Ciuba, Gary M., 248
Civil War, 82–83, 99, 181–82, 192–93, 228
Civilization and Its Discontents (Freud), 241
Claremont Essays (D. Trilling), 135, 137–38, 139, 148, 150
Clark, William Bedford, 107n3
"A Clean, Well-Lighted Place" (Hemingway), 78
Clerks: Abelard as, 41; Benda on, 6–10, 12, 13, 26–28, 34, 51, 150; Broch on, 5–6; in Chaucer's *Canterbury Tales*, 1; Coleridge's term *clerisy*, 2; and Crowley, 65; meaning of, 1; Tate on, 30, 31; Valéry on Hamlet as, 3–5; Voegelin on, 12–27, 31–38, 246. *See also* specific authors
"The Cloud Castle" (Voegelin), 35
Coleridge, Samuel Taylor, 2, 120
College of William and Mary, 47
Columbia University, 11, 112, 114–15, 140–42, 190
Common Sense philosophy, 11
Commons, John R., 12
Commonweal, 190
Communism: anti-anti-Communism, 143–44; and anti-communism, 129–33, 143–44; and Cowley, 56–79, 112; as religion, 66–67, 70; and D. Trilling, 71–72, 112, 129, 131, 132,

133, 144; and L. Trilling, 71–72, 110, 111, 112, 114, 131; in U.S. during Great Depression, 56–79, 130–32, 144; and Wilson, 64, 70–71
"Communism and Christianity" (Cowley), 79n1
"Community" (Percy), 231–32
Comte, Auguste, 18–19, 22, 23–24
"The Concrete Consciousness" (Voegelin), 26–27
Condorcet, Marquis de, 65
Conrad, Joseph, 89–90, 91
Contemporary Jewish Record, 115
Copernicus, 120
Cosmos (Sagan), 236
Coughlin, Father, 55
Cowley, Malcolm: and Communism, 56–79, 112; death of, 58; family background of, 60–61; and Great Depression, xii, 55–79; on Hemingway, 73–74, 76, 78; as man of letters, 57; as moral historian, xiv; *New Republic* essay-reviews by, 57, 63–64, 67; on New York City, 67–68; on Proust, 74; resignation of, from League of American Writers, 72; on Revolution of the Word, 62–63, 65–66; self-portrait of, 60–61; Simpson's personal recollections of, 77–79; as speaker at literary conferences, 74–75, 77–78; and Welty, 181; writings by, 57–58; at Yaddo, 72
—works: *And I Worked at the Writer's Trade*, 58, 64, 70–71; *Blue Juanita*, 57; "Communism and Christianity," 79n1; *The Dream of the Golden Mountains*, 55–70, 72–73, 76–77; *Exile's Return*, 57–58, 63, 64, 65, 76, 77; *A Many-Windowed House*, 57; *A Second Flowering*, 58, 75–76, 193; *Think Back on Us*, 57
Crane, Hart, 65, 75, 78
Cremeens, Carlton, 191
Crèvecoeur, St. John de, 61
Crime and Punishment (Dostoyevsky), 104, 193
"The Crisis of Mind" (Valéry), 3–5
Crosby, Harry, 77

Cuomo, Mario, 146

Daily Worker, 72
D'Alembert, Jean Le Rond, 18
Dante: as clerk, 7; Foote on, 229; and Percy, 220–21; and Warren, 88, 102–3, 108n9, 108–9n18
—work: *Divina Commedia*, 88, 102, 108n9, 108–9n18, 220–21, 229
Davidson, Donald, 165
Declaration of Independence, 50, 82–83, 87, 89, 90–91, 93, 94, 98, 99–100, 104, 107n6
Dehon, Theodore, 45
"The Delta Factor" (Percy), 201–7, 225
Democracy of letters, 44, 51–52
Dennie, Joseph, 44–45
Depression, economic. See Great Depression
Descartes, René, 7
Devils, 160
"The Diagnostic Novel" (Percy), 247–48
Dickens, Charles, 116, 124
Dickinson, Emily, 118–20
Dillon, George, 63
Divina Commedia (Dante), 88, 102, 108n9, 108–9n18, 220–21, 229
Dogood Papers, 43
Donne, John, 37, 105, 120–21, 123
Dos Passos, John, 78
Dostoyevsky, Fyodor, 62, 194, 228; *The Brothers Karamazov*, 193; *Crime and Punishment*, 104, 193; *Notes from the Underground*, 197
Dr. Faustus, 90
The Dream of the Golden Mountains (Cowley), 55–70, 72–73, 76–77
Dreiser, Theodore, 59
Dreyfus case, 6
Dryden, John, 120
The Dunciad (Pope), 44
Dupuy, Edward J., 209

East, Charles, 234
Eccles, John Carew, 239

The Ecumenic Age (Voegelin), 14, 22–26, 247
Edgerton, Clyde, 158
Education. *See* Universities
Einstein, Albert, 194, 238
Either/Or (Kierkegaard), 237, 248
Eliot, George, 19, 28, 115
Eliot, T. S.: as clerk, 34, 65; compared with Benda, 9; compared with Percy, 233; and liberal-progressivism, 116; and pathos of effort to reimagine meaning of tension, 121; as poet-critic, 120; symbolic interpretation of Middle Ages by, 30; L. Trilling on, 125; writings of, as confessional monologues, 249
—works: "Burnt Norton," 153; *The Waste Land*, 31, 75, 221, 233
Ellison, Ralph, 86
Emerson, Ralph Waldo, 58, 75
Enarrationes in Psalmos (Augustine), 33
Engels, Friedrich, 18, 65
Esquire magazine, 222–23, 226–27
"Eternal Being in Time" (Voegelin), 31–34
Eusebius, 21
Exile's Return (Cowley), 57–58, 63, 64, 65, 76, 77
The Eye of the Story (Welty), 176–81

The Fable of the Southern Writer (Simpson), ix
Fadiman, Clifton, 112
"The Fateful Rift" (Percy), 248
The Fathers (Tate), 111
Faulkner, William: and Civil War, 181–82; and classical-Hebraic-Christian tradition, 221; compared with Welty, 181–82; and Cowley, 76, 78; critical sensitivity of, 120; generational sensibility of, 194; good and evil in works of, 168; on historical past, 86, 181; on listening to voices, 221; and literary life, 34, 40; and Republic of Letters, 232; Simpson on, 224–25, 230–31; voice tone and inflection of, 172; Welty on, 180

—works: *Absalom, Absalom!*, 106, 224; *Light in August*, 180; *The Sound and the Fury*, 106, 182, 224, 230–31
"Faulkner and the Legend of the Artist" (Simpson), 224–25
Fear and Trembling (Kierkegaard), 225
The Federalist, 50
Federalists, 44–47
La fin de l'éternel (Benda), 8–9
Finnegans Wake (Joyce), 221
Fitzgerald, F. Scott, 73, 76, 78, 194
Flaubert, Gustave, 62, 73, 120, 124, 170, 194
Flowers of Evil (Baudelaire), 63
Foote, Shelby, 192, 193, 219–21, 228–30
Forrest, Nathan Bedford, 166
Franklin, Benjamin, xi, 42–44, 65
Franklin, James, 43
French Academy, 42
French Revolution, 42, 44, 46–47, 65
French Symbolists, 62, 63
Freud, Sigmund, 103, 114, 126, 148, 194, 196, 241–42
From Eden to Babylon (Lytle), 170
From Enlightenment to Revolution (Voegelin), 13, 14–19
Fugitive poets, 165
Fussell, Paul, 135

Galilei, Galileo, 7, 29, 120
Gangsterism, 54–55
Gardner, John, 225–26
Gay, Peter, 232
Gibbons, Kaye, 158
Gide, André, 116, 125
Gordon, Caroline, 168, 194, 233, 237
Grail legend, 219
"The Grammercy Winner" (Percy), 248
Grapes of Wrath (Steinbeck), 67
Great Depression: Communism in U.S. during, 56–79, 130–32, 144; Cowley on writers during, xii, 55–64; Simpson's memories

of, xii, 53–56; Simpson's uncle during, xii, 53–56
Green, Graham, 230
Grimshaw, James "Bo," 106, 107n3
Guardini, Romano, 195
Gulledge, Jo, 242
Guthrie, Ramon, 75

Hall, Martha, 189
Hamilton, Alexander, 42
Hamlet, 4–5, 37
Hamlet (Shakespeare), 119
Hardy, Thomas, 194
Harris, Jean, 128–29, 144–51
Harvard University, 11, 43, 44, 45, 48, 106, 139–40
Havard, William C., 13
Hawking, Stephen, 195
Hawthorne, Nathaniel, 58, 123, 232
Hayden, Tom, 141–42
Hegel, G. W. F., 18, 22, 23–24, 126
Heidegger, Martin, 12, 137, 195
Hellman, Lillian, 143
Helvétius, Claude-Adrien, 18
Hemingway, Ernest: Cowley on, 73–74, 76, 78; critical sensitivity of, 120; death of, 113; generational sensibility of, 194; and literary life, 34, 40; readers of, 77; L. Trilling on, 111, 112–13, 115; on writer as priest, 28, 227
—works: "A Clean, Well-Lighted Place," 78; *The Old Man and the Sea*, 113
Hill, Lyn, 222–23
"The Hind Tit" (Lytle), 166
Hitler, Adolf, 3, 19, 37, 62, 70. *See also* Nazism
Hobson, Fred, ix–xv
Hobson, Linda Whitney, 209–10
Hollander, John, 106
Holocaust, 244–45
An Honorable Estate (Rubin), xiv, 153, 158
Hook, Sydney, 72, 112
Howe, Irving, 152n1

Howells, William Dean, 124
Hulme, T. E., 9
The Human Condition (Arendt), 29–30
Huygens, Christiaan, 7
Hynes, Samuel, 131

I Thought of Daisy (Wilson), 136
I'll Take My Stand, 110, 166
Israel and History (Voegelin), 247

James, Henry: British citizenship of, xi; as clerk, 34; death of, 194; in Europe, xi, 62, 74; and Foote, 228; as poet-critic, 120; L. Trilling on, 124; and writing vocation, 73
Jaspers, Karl, 195
Jefferson, Thomas: death of, 94; and Declaration of Independence, 82–83, 87, 89, 90–91, 93, 94, 98, 99–100, 104; education of, 47; as founder of Republic, xii, 83; and Louisiana Territory, 96; and Meriwether Lewis's suicide, 96–97; nephews of, and murder, xii, 83–86, 89, 99, 100, 101, 105; and redemptive role of America, 61, 65; and Republic of Letters, 47–52; and Republic of the United States, 42; significance of, 105–6; tombstone for, 94; and University of Virginia, xi, 47–51, 94; in Warren's *Brother to Dragons*, xii, 86, 88–89, 91–100, 103–5
Jefferson Memorial, xii, 81, 107n1
Jews: Rubin family as, 153, 159–64; L. Trilling as, 113, 114–15; D. Trilling as, 152n1
Joachim of Flora, 16, 19, 21–22, 28
Job, Book of, 88–89, 102
John of the Cross, St., 66
John Reed Club, 56
Johnson, Samuel, 29, 42, 120
Jonson, Ben, 120
Joyce, James: on artifice and cunning used by novelist, 217; as clerk, 34; compared with Benda, 9; compared with Percy, 233; Cowley on, 62; critical sensitivity of, 120;

Joyce, James *(continued)*
    and Foote, 228; generational sensibility of, 194; and liberal-progressivism, 116; and literary artist as godhead of literary art, 65; L. Trilling on, 125; and writing vocation, 73
—works: *Finnegans Wake,* 221; *Portrait of the Artist as a Young Man,* 31, 198–99, 227, 238–39; *Ulysses,* 31, 75, 221
Judt, Tony, 152n2
Jung, Carl, 194, 216

Kafka, Franz, 9, 37, 116
Kant, Immanuel, 195
Das Kapital (Marx), 69
Karl Marx (Mehring), 63–64
Keats, John, 124
Keller, Helen, 206
Kennedy, John F., 138
Kennedy, Robert, 141–42
Kenyon College, 110
Kenyon School of Letters, 110
Kepler, Johannes, 7, 120
Ketner, Kenneth Laine, 236
Kierkegaard, Søren: and Percy, 194, 195, 200, 207–8, 222–27, 233–34, 236, 248; Updike on, 248
—works: *Either/Or,* 237, 248; *Fear and Trembling,* 225; *Point of View for My Work,* 222; *The Sickness unto Death,* 215
Korean War, 99
Korean War Memorial, 107n1

Lamartine, Alphonse, 7
Lancelot (Percy), 191, 215–28, 230, 232, 233, 234, 236, 243
Langer, Suzanne, 196
Language, 201–7, 210–11, 216–17, 221, 235–42, 248
The Last Gentleman (Percy), 190, 203, 214, 227, 234
Lawrence, D. H., 116, 125, 127
Le Sueur, Meridel, 66–67

League of American Writers, 72
Lee, Hermione, 182
Left Front magazine, 56
Leibniz, Gottfried, 7
Lenin, V. I., 19, 69
Leninism, 70
Letters from an American Farmer (Crèvecoeur), 61
Lewis, Charles, 84
Lewis, Isham, 84–85, 89, 95–96, 100
Lewis, Letitia, 84
Lewis, Lilburne, 84–86, 89, 95–96, 100, 101, 108n13
Lewis, Lucy Jefferson, 84, 85
Lewis, Meriwether, 86, 95–97, 100, 101, 108n13
Lewis, Randolph, 84
Lewis and Clark Expedition, 96
"Liberal Anti-Communism Revisited" (D. Trilling), 143–44
The Liberal Imagination (L. Trilling), 110, 116, 118
Light in August (Faulkner), 180
Lincoln, Abraham, xii, 83
Lincoln Memorial, 81, 107n1
Literacy, 44–46
Locke, John, 50
Long, Huey, 108n9, 175
The Long Night (Lytle), 166–69
Lost in the Cosmos (Percy), xiv, 187, 192, 204, 232, 234–42, 248
Louis XIV, 28
Louisiana State University (LSU), 1–3, 13, 218
Louisiana State University Press, 14, 191
Louisiana Territory, 96
Love in the Ruins (Percy), 191, 211–15, 220, 227, 236, 243
Lucas, Mark, 167
Luschei, Martin, 191
Lytle, Andrew, ix, 165–71

Madison, James, 48–50
The Magic Mountain (Mann), 193, 247, 248
Maier, Pauline, 107n6
Mailer, Norman, 121, 139, 140–42

INDEX   259

Maistre, Joseph-Marie de, 7
Malamud, Bernard, 115, 121
Mallarmé, Stéphane, 73
The Man of Letters in the Modern World (Tate), 30, 124, 125–26
Mann, Thomas: and classical-Hebraic-Christian tradition, 221; as clerk, 34; compared with Benda, 9; and Foote, 228; and generational sensibility, 194; and liberal-progressivism, 116; and Percy, 193, 247–48; Welty on, 180; and writing vocation, 7
—work: *The Magic Mountain*, 193, 247, 248
Mansfield Park (Austen), 124–25
A Many-Windowed House (Cowley), 57
Marcel, Gabriel, 195, 213
Maritain, Jacques, 195
Marlowe, Christopher, 90, 105, 119, 248
Marshall, Margaret, 133, 134
Marx, Karl, 18, 19, 22, 24, 63–65, 114
Marxism, 65, 69, 70, 71, 75, 143, 213–14. *See also* Communism
Matthew Arnold (L. Trilling), 111, 134, 137
Maximum Security Ward (Guthrie), 75
McCallum, John, 158
McCarthy, Joseph, 128, 132
McCorkle, Jill, 158
McKnight, Stephen A., 38n1
"The Meaning of a Literary Idea" (L. Trilling), 123
Mehring, Franz, 63–64
Melville, Herman, 58, 230, 232
Memoirs of Hecate County (Wilson), 136, 151–52
Men of letters, 2, 9–10, 42, 207. *See also* Republic of Letters; and specific authors
Merrill, Boynton, Jr., 107n4
Merton, Thomas, 197
The Message in the Bottle (Percy), 191, 199, 205–8, 210, 216, 235, 237, 248
Methodist Church, 53
Meye, Eduard, 12
Michelet, Jules, 7
Michener, James, 128

The Middle of the Journey (L. Trilling), 116, 118
Mill, John Stuart, 19, 115, 116
Millay, Edna St. Vincent, 63
Milton, John, 45, 126
Mind and the American Civil War (Simpson), ix
Mind in the Modern World (L. Trilling), 110
Minotaur myth, 95
Mississippi Quarterly, 179
MLA. *See* Modern Language Association (MLA)
Modern Language Association (MLA), 74–75
Montaigne, Michel de, 7
Montesquieu, Baron de La Brède et de, 7
Montgomery, Marion, 1
Monthly Anthology and Boston Review, 45–46
Moody Bible Institute, 53
More, Sir Thomas, 214
The Moviegoer (Percy), 189–90, 209–10, 214, 230–31
Mrs. Harris: The Murder of the Scarsdale Diet Doctor (D. Trilling), 128–29, 144–51
Murder: of slaves by Jefferson's nephews, xii, 85, 99, 100, 101, 105; of Tarnower by Jean Harris, 128–29, 144–51
"Music from Spain" (Welty), 173
Mussolini, Benito, 62
My Father's People (Rubin), 153, 159–63
Myers, F. W. H., 19, 28, 115

A Name for Evil (Lytle), 169, 171
Napoleon, 42
Nation, 133–35
National Archives, 81–82
National Committee for the Defense of Political Prisoners, 131
National Endowment for the Humanities, 52, 218
National Humanities Foundation, 246
National Institute of Mental Health, 210
National Science Foundation, 52
Nausea (Sartre), 197
Nazism, 131, 144, 244–45. *See also* Hitler, Adolf
New England Courant, 43

The New Leader, 71
New Masses, 66–67, 72
New Republic, 57, 63–64, 67, 71
New Scholasticism, 190
The New Science of Politics (Voegelin), 19–22
New York City, 67–69
New Yorker, 173
Newman, Cardinal, 116
Newsweek, 128–33, 146
Newton, Sir Isaac, 7
Niemeyer, Gerhart, 13
Nietzsche, Friedrich, 24, 194, 234, 240, 241
Night Rider (Warren), 90
"No Place for You, My Love" (Welty), 173–79
Nostromo (Conrad), 89–90
"Notes for a Novel about the End of the World" (Percy), 187, 197–201, 232–33, 237
Notes from the Underground (Dostoyevsky), 197

O'Connor, Flannery, 169, 200, 248
"Ode to the Confederate Dead" (Tate), 30
The Old Man and the Sea (Hemingway), 113
"Old Scratch" (Lytle), 166
Olney, James, x
On the Form of the American Mind (Voegelin), 11
"On the Steps of Low Library" (D. Trilling), 140–44
One Time, One Place (Welty), 182–85
O'Neill, Eugene, 197
The Opposing Self (L. Trilling), 110, 123, 124–26
The Optimist's Daughter (Welty), 182, 185
Order and History (Voegelin), xi, 13, 14, 22, 36, 246
Orwell, George, 124

Paris Review, 219
Partisan Review, 111, 143, 190
Pascal, Blaise, 7, 23
Paul, St., ix, xi, 23, 24, 25, 26
Pearson, Norman Holmes, 187
Peirce, Charles Sanders, 195, 235, 236
Pentagon antiwar march, 140–42

Percy, Walker: birthday of, 192, 225; and Catholicism, xiv, 190, 196–97, 199, 208, 213–14, 228–29, 232, 240, 249; on Christian novelist, 197–201, 227–28, 232–33; as clerk, 246; correspondence of, 187–90, 191, 192, 247; and Dante, 220–21; death of, xiii, 187; desk of, 189; *Esquire* self-interview by, 222–23, 226–27; family background of, 192; and Foote, 192, 193, 219–21, 228–30; Gardner on, 225–26; good and evil in works by, 169; honors and awards for, 189; illnesses of, 188–89, 197, 210, 246, 247; and Kierkegaard, 194, 195, 200, 207–8, 222–27, 233–34, 236, 248; and language, 201–7, 210–11, 216–17, 221, 235–36, 248; Luschei's study of, 191; and Mann, 193, 247–48; marriage of, 196–97, 228; medical training of, 188, 190, 210, 247; painting of, 222–23; and parents' deaths, 189; and Peirce, 195, 235, 236; philosophical essays by, 190, 195–96; and semiotics, 235–41; and Simpson, xiii–xiv, 185, 187–92, 218–19, 234; and Simpson's article on Faulkner, 224–25, 230–31; and Simpson's article on Voegelin, 246–47; and Sons and Daughters of the Apocalypse group, 231–32; and *Southern Review*, xiii, 187–88, 190–91; university education of, 190, 193; on Welty, 185; on writer as Protestant, 238; and writing initial drafts of manuscripts, 188; writings by, xiv, 191–92, 233, 248–49
—works: "The Antimony of the Scientific Method," 232; "The Charterhouse," 229, 233; "Community," 231–32; "The Delta Factor," 201–7, 225; "The Diagnostic Novel," 247–48; "The Fateful Rift," 248; "The Grammercy Winner," 248; *Lancelot*, 191, 215–28, 230, 232, 233, 234, 236, 243; *The Last Gentleman*, 190, 203, 214, 227, 234; *Lost in the Cosmos*, xiv, 187, 192, 204, 232, 234–42, 248; *Love in the Ruins*, 191, 211–15, 220, 227, 236, 243; *The Message in*

the Bottle, 191, 199, 205–8, 210, 216, 235, 237, 248; *The Moviegoer*, 189–90, 209–10, 214, 230–31; "Notes for a Novel about the End of the World," 187, 197–201, 232–33, 237; "Questions They Never Asked Me So He Asked Them Himself," 222, 226–27; *The Second Coming*, 191–92, 234, 236, 237, 242; *The Thanatos Syndrome*, 192, 236, 243–46, 247; "A Theory of Language," 201–5, 208, 211
Percy, William Alexander, 189, 218
Petrarch, ix, 7, 26, 28
"Petrified Man" (Welty), 180
Philosophes, 42, 98
Philosophy and Phenomenological Research, 190
Philosophy in a New Key (Langer), 196
Photography: by Eudora Welty, 182–85
Pilgrim in the Ruins (Tolson), 210
"Pioneers! O Pioneers!" (Whitman), 139
Piper, Henry Dan, 57
Pius XII, Pope, 197
"Place in Fiction" (Welty), 178–79
Plato, 7, 20, 22–23, 25, 26, 37
Poe, Edgar Allan, 120, 123, 194, 241
Point of View for My Work (Kierkegaard), 222
Pope, Alexander, 44, 120
Porter, Katherine Anne, 187
The Portfolio, 44
Portrait of the Artist as a Young Man (Joyce), 31, 198–99, 227, 238–39
Postmodern age, 40, 195, 210–11, 221, 224, 232–33, 240–41
Pound, Ezra, 65, 221
Printing, 44
"The Profession of Letters in the South" (Tate), 119
Profumo affair, 150
Proust, Marcel: as clerk, 34; compared with Benda, 9; Cowley on, 74; death of, 194; Foote on, 228, 229, 230, 232; Guthrie's teaching of, 75; and liberal-progressivism, 116; and Percy, 230, 233; on respect for natural movement of thoughts, 229; L. Trilling on, 125; and Voegelin, 3; Welty on, 180; and writing vocation, 73
—work: *Remembrance of Things Past*, 74, 75, 230
Puritans, 45, 120

"Questions They Never Asked Me So He Asked Them Himself" (Percy), 222, 226–27
Quinlan, Kieran, 213–14

Rabelais, François, 7
Racine, Jean, 7
Radcliffe College, 139–40
Random House, 183
Ransom, John Crowe, 110–11, 165, 194
Reactionary Essays on Poetry and Ideas (Tate), 118–20
Read, Herbert, 1
Religion: communism as, 66–67, 70; Cowley on Christianity, 79n1; and death of God, 240; Foote on mixing art and religion, 228–29; and Lytle, 168; Methodist Church, 53; and Percy, xiv, 190, 196–201, 208; Percy on Christian novelist, 197–201, 227–28, 232–33; Percy on writer as Protestant, 238; Simpson's uncle as minister, 53–56. *See also* Catholicism
Remembrance of Things Past (Proust), 74, 75, 230
Renan, Ernest, 7
The Republic (Plato), 20
Republic of Letters: and American republic, 2, 42–52; Buckminster on, 45–46; decline of, in nineteenth and twentieth centuries, 51; democracy of letters versus, 44, 51; and Faulkner, 232; and Franklin, 42–44; historical development of, in Europe, xi, 10, 27–30, 41–42; and Jefferson, 47–52; and University of Virginia, 51. *See also* Men of letters; and specific authors
Reviewing the Forties (D. Trilling), 135–37
Revolution of the Word, 62–63, 65–66
"Revolution of the Word" manifesto, 65–66

Richard III (Shakespeare), 119
Riddle Me This, 160–61
Rousseau, Jean-Jacques, 7, 229
Rubin, Dan, 159–61
Rubin, Dora, 159
Rubin, Essie (Esther), 159
Rubin, Fannie, 153, 159
Rubin, Harry, 159–60
Rubin, Hyman Levy, 153, 159
Rubin, Louis, ix, xiv, 153–64, 179; *An Honorable Estate*, xiv, 153, 158; *My Father's People*, 153, 159–63; *Small Craft Advisory*, xiv, 153, 157, 158, 163
Rubin, Louis, Sr., 159, 161–62
Rubin, Manning, 159, 161
Rubin, Ruthie, 159
Russian Revolution, 70, 131. *See also* Communism; Soviet Union

Sagan, Carl, 236
Samway, Patrick, 233, 236
Sandoz, Ellis, 11, 12
Santayana, George, 11
Sartre, Jean-Paul, 3, 137, 152n2, 197, 208
Schlesinger, Arthur M., Jr., 128
Scoundrel Time (Hellman), 143
SDS, 142
The Second Coming (Percy), 191–92, 234, 236, 237, 242
A Second Flowering (Cowley), 58, 75–76, 193
Semiotics, 235–41
Sewanee Review, 169, 190
Shakespeare, William: and crisis of self-alienation, 248; Foote on, 228; Hamlet as character of, 4–5, 37; intellect and self-will in, 90, 105; language of, 221; on marriage of true minds, 118; Percy on, 221; and view of human condition, 236–37
—works: *Hamlet*, 119; *Richard III*, 119
Shaw, George Bernard, 116
Shelley, Percy Bysshe, 120
Shiloh (Foote), 228
The Sickness unto Death (Kierkegaard), 215

Sidney, Sir Philip, 50
Simpson, Bob, 158
Simpson, Lewis: birthday of, 192; childhood of, xiii; and Cowley, 77–79; death of, ix; education of, xv, 1–2, 77, 193; family background of, 192–93; father of, 211; on Faulkner, 224–25, 230–31; at Louisiana State University, 1–3; and LSU Press, 191; and Lytle, 170–71; and Mann's *The Magic Mountain*, 193; marriage of, xv; and Percy, xiii–xiv, 185, 187–92, 201–7, 218–29, 234, 246–47; Ph.D dissertation of, 2; poetry by, xiii; retirement of, ix, 40; and *Southern Review*, ix, xiii, 40–41, 187–88, 190–91, 201–7; and Tate, ix, 110; and L. Trilling's writings, 110; uncle of, during Great Depression, xii, 53–56; and vocation of writing, xv; and Voegelin, x, 1–3; on Voegelin, 1–39, 246–47; and Warren, ix, xii–xiii; in Washington, D.C., xii, 81–82; and Welty, ix, 172, 185; writings by, ix–x, xiii
—works: *The Brazen Face of History*, 41; *The Circus in the Cemetery*, xiii; *The Fable of the Southern Writer*, ix; "Faulkner and the Legend of the Artist," 224–25; *Mind and the American Civil War*, ix; "Thomas Hole," xiii
Simpson, Mimi, xv, 172, 246
Sincerity and Authenticity (L. Trilling), 110, 123–24, 126
Singer, Israel Joshua, 115
Slaves: murder of, xii, 85, 99, 100, 101, 105
The Sleepwalkers (Broch), 5
Small Craft Advisory (Rubin), xiv, 153, 157, 158, 163
Small, William, 47
Socrates, 36, 37
"Some Thoughts on Time in Fiction" (Welty), 179–81
Sons and Daughters of the Apocalypse group, 231–32
Sophia, 36
The Sound and the Fury (Faulkner), 106, 182, 224, 230–31

Southern Review: and Brooks, 180; first series of, 180; Lytle's essay on Flaubert in, 170; Percy interview in, 190–91; Percy's article on language in, 201–7, 211; Percy's file at, xiii, 187–88; second series of, 190; and Simpson, ix, xiii, 40–41, 187–88, 190–91, 201–7; and Warren, xii, 180; Welty's stories published in, 180; Wheeler's essay on Simpson in, xv; "Writing in the South" issue of, 190–91
Southerners and Europeans, 170
The Sovereign Wayfarer (Luschei), 191
Soviet Union, 70, 129–32. *See also* Communism
Spanish Civil War, 144
Spengler, Oswald, 3, 12, 34
Stalin, Joseph, 62, 70
Stalinism, 70, 131
"The State of Letters in a Time of Disorder" (Lytle), 168
Steinbeck, John, 67
Steiner, George, 5
The Story of My Life (Keller), 206
The Stranger (Camus), 197
Styron, William, 128
Sullivan, Annie, 206
Sullivan, Walter, 172
Symbolist movement, 62, 63

Tarnower, Herman: murder of, 128–29, 144–51
Tate, Allen: on angelism, 228; and Catholicism, 30, 126; as clerk, 246; on clerks, 30; and Cowley, 78; on criticism, 151; on Dickinson, 118–20; generational sensibility of, 194; and Lytle, 165–66; on myth, 30; on poet's culture, 123; Simpson's relationship with, ix, 110; teaching career of, 111–12; and L. Trilling, 110–12, 118–19, 125–26; as university faculty member, 169; and Voegelin, 31, 34
—works: *The Fathers,* 111; *I'll Take My Stand,* 110; *The Man of Letters in the Modern World,* 30, 124, 125–26; "Ode to the Confederate Dead," 30; "The Profession of Letters in the South," 119; *Reactionary Essays on Poetry and Ideas,* 118–20
The Thanatos Syndrome (Percy), 192, 236, 243–46, 247
"A Theory of Language" (Percy), 201–5, 208, 211
Think Back on Us (Cowley), 57
Thomas, Norman, 62
Thomas Aquinas, 7, 2123
"Thomas Hole" (Simpson), xiii
To the Finland Station (Wilson), 68–69
Tolson, Jay, 210, 216, 219–20, 222
Tolstoy, Leo, 124
Townsend, Mary Bernice "Bunt," 228
Toynbee, Arnold, 12, 34
La trahison des clercs (Benda), x, 2–3, 6–8, 10, 26, 38n2, 51
Trilling, Diana: on anti-anti-Communism, 143–44; as anti-communist, 129–33, 143–44; on antiwar protests, 140–41; career of, as critic, 129–30, 133–52; and Communism, 71–72, 112, 129, 131–33, 144; compared with Lionel, 148; on Cowley, 71–72, 77, 112; and Harris case, 128–29, 144–51; and husband's *Matthew Arnold,* 134, 137; as Jew, 152n1; on John Kennedy's assassination, 138; on Robert Kennedy's assassination, 141–42; and liberalism, 130, 136–37, 143–44; on McCarthy, 128; on McCarthyism, 132; as *Nation* fiction critic, 133–37, 151; in *Newsweek* articles, 128–33, 146; on women's liberation, 152n3
—works: *The Beginning of the Journey,* 71–72, 128, 131–35, 137; *Claremont Essays,* 135, 137–38, 139, 148, 150; "Liberal Anti-Communism Revisited," 143–44; *Mrs. Harris: The Murder of the Scarsdale Diet Doctor,* 128–29, 144–51; "On the Steps of Low Library," 140–44; *Reviewing the Forties,* 135–37; *We Must March My Darlings,* 135, 138–44, 145, 151, 152n3
Trilling, Lionel: on Jane Austen, 124–25, 126, 127; and Communism, 71–72, 110, 111, 112, 114, 131; compared with Diana, 148; Freudianism of, 114, 126, 241–42; on

Trilling, Lionel *(continued)*
   Hemingway, 111, 112–13, 115; as Jew, 113, 114–15; as man of letters and critic, 113–27; and *Nation* position for Diana Trilling, 133–35, 151; notebooks of, 110, 112–14, 116–17, 121, 122; and Tate, 110–12, 118–19, 125–26; on Tate's *Fathers*, 111; as university faculty member, 112, 114–15, 122; and Victorians, 115–16; and vocation of writing, xiv, 112–23, 126–27
—works: "Art and Neurosis," 121; *Beyond Culture*, 110, 124; *The Liberal Imagination*, 110, 116, 118; *Matthew Arnold*, 111, 134, 137; "The Meaning of a Literary Idea," 123; *The Middle of the Journey*, 116, 118; *Mind in the Modern World*, 110; *The Opposing Self*, 110, 123, 124–26; *Sincerity and Authenticity*, 110, 123–24, 126; "Wordsworth and the Rabbis," 115
Turgot, Anne-Robert-Jacques, 18, 22
Twain, Mark, 194

Ulysses (Joyce), 31, 75, 221
Universities: Franklin on, 43; Jefferson and University of Virginia, xi, 47–51, 94; medieval universities, 41–42; and republic of letters versus democracy of letters, 51–52. *See also* specific universities
University of Chicago, 14
University of Chicago Press, 14
University of Florida, 169
University of Iowa, 169
University of Kentucky, 170
University of Minnesota, 112
University of North Carolina, 47, 190, 193, 234
University of Pennsylvania, 43
University of Texas, xv, 1–2, 77
University of the South, 169
University of Virginia, xi, 47–51, 94
University of Wisconsin, 11
Der Untergang des Abendlandes (Spengler), 3
Updike, John, 248

Utopia (More), 214

Valéry, Paul, 3–5, 10, 37, 194
Vanderbilt University, 165
The Velvet Horn (Lytle), 169
Vidal, Gore, 128
Vietnam War, 99, 139, 140–41
Vietnam War Memorial, 107n1
Virgil, 28
Virginia Document (1799), 50
Virginia Quarterly Review, 166
Voegelin, Eric: and Benda's writings, x, 2–3, 10–11; on Camus, 34; as clerk, 1, 246; on clerks, 12–27, 31–38; and Common Sense philosophy, 11; on Comte, 18–19; escape from Gestapo by, 3, 37; on historian of ideas, 14–15; on Joachim of Flora, 16, 19, 21–22; as Louisiana State University faculty, 3, 13; on Marx, 19; on *metaxy*, 22–23, 24–25; on Paul, 23, 24, 25, 26; as philosopher, 1; on polis, 19–21; on self-interpretation, 12; Simpson's article on, 1–39, 246–47; Simpson's personal recollection of, x, 1–3; in United States (1924–1926), 11–12; on Voltaire, 15–18; and Walgreen Lectures at University of Chicago, 14
—works: *Anamnesis*, 26, 31–36; "Autobiographical Memoir," 11–12; "The Cannons of Kronburg," 35–36; "The Cloud Castle," 35; "The Concrete Consciousness," 26–27; *The Ecumenic Age*, 14, 22–26, 247; "Eternal Being in Time," 31–34; *From Enlightenment to Revolution*, 13, 14–19; *Israel and History*, 247; *The New Science of Politics*, 19–22; *On the Form of the American Mind*, 11; *Order and History*, xi, 13, 14, 22, 36, 246; *The World of the Polis*, 36
Voltaire, 7, 15–18, 27–28, 42, 43, 65

A Wake for the Living (Lytle), 169
Walzer, Michael, 45
Warren, Robert Franklin, 97–98

Warren, Robert Penn: and allegorizing mind, x; burial of, 106; Dante as influence on, 88, 108n9, 108–9n18; essay on Conrad's *Nostromo* by, 89–90; generational sensibility of, 194; as LSU faculty member, xii; and Lytle, 165, 166–67; novels by, 90–91; poetry by, xiii, 98–99, 106; and Simpson, ix, x, xii–xiii; and *Southern Review*, xii, 180
—works: "Afterthought" to Being Here, 98–99; *All the King's Men*, xiii, 90, 98, 102, 108n9, 108–9n18; *At Heaven's Gate*, 90; "Bearded Oaks," 106; *Being Here*, 98–99, 100; *Brother to Dragons*, xii, xiii, 83–105; *I'll Take My Stand*, 110; *Night Rider*, 90; "Proud Flesh," 108n9; "Why Do We Read Fiction?," 81, 104; *World Enough and Time*, 90, 91
Washington, George, xii, 82, 83
Washington, D.C., xii, 81–82, 107n1
Washington Monument, 81, 107n1
The Waste Land (Eliot), 31, 75, 221, 233
We Must March My Darlings (D. Trilling), 135, 138–44, 145, 151, 152n3
Weber, Max, 12
Weil, Simone, 248
Welty, Chestina, 182
Welty, Christian, 182
Welty, Eudora: autobiographical cast to writings of, 173, 185; and being lost in the world, 172–73; birth year and place of, 172, 181; compared with Faulkner, 181–82; death of, 173; family background of, 182; generational sensibility of, 194; good and evil in works of, 168–69; home of, 172, 185; honors and awards for, 181, 185; Percy on, 185; photographs by, 182–85; and Simpson, ix, 172, 185; and WPA job, 183; writings by, 173
—works: *The Bride of the Innisfallen*, 173, 179; *The Eye of the Story*, 176–81; "Music from Spain," 173; "No Place for You, My Love," 173–79; *One Time, One Place*, 182–85; *The Optimist's Daughter*, 182, 185; "Petrified Man," 180; "Place in Fiction," 178–79; "Some Thoughts on Time in Fiction," 179–81; "Writing and Analyzing a Story," 175–78
Wheeler, Otis, xv
Whitman, Walt, 57, 58, 120, 139, 140
Who's Afraid of Virginia Woolf (Albee), 139
"Why Do We Read Fiction?" (Warren), 81, 104
Wilson, Edmund: antipathy to English departments of, 111; and Bishop, 60; and Communism, 64, 70–71; as poet-critic, 120; D. Trilling on writings by, 136, 151–52
—works: *I Thought of Daisy*, 136; *Memoirs of Hecate County*, 136, 151–52; *To the Finland Station*, 68–69
Wittgenstein, Ludwig, 195
Wolfe, Thomas, 76
Woodward, C. Vann, x
Woolf, Virginia, 194
Wordsworth, William, 120, 124
"Wordsworth and the Rabbis" (L. Trilling), 115
"The Working Novelist and the Myth Making Process" (Lytle), 168
Works Progress Administration (WPA), 183
World Enough and Time (Warren), 90, 91
The World of the Polis (Voegelin), 36
World War I, 75, 160, 161, 193–94
World War II, 194–95
WPA. See Works Progress Administration (WPA)
Wright, Richard, 56
"Writing and Analyzing a Story" (Welty), 175–78
Wythe, George, 47

Xenophanes, 36

Yaddo, 71–72
Yale University, 165
Yeats, William Butler, 34, 116, 120, 125, 194

Zeller, Edmund, 21
Zola, Emile, 6